OXFORDSHIRE SESSIONS OF THE PEACE

The Oxfordshire Record Society

OXFORDSHIRE SESSIONS OF THE PEACE IN THE REIGN OF RICHARD II

Edited by Elisabeth G. Kimball

Volume LIII

Issued for the years 1979 and 1980

1983

ISBN 0 902509 17 9

Printed in England by

CHENEY & SONS LIMITED

BANBURY

CONTENTS

FOREWORD

I am grateful to Mr James Campbell and Miss Susan Reynolds for their help with this text at various times, and particularly to Mr Christopher Day for his assistance with the volume as a whole in its final stages.

The Society acknowledges with gratitude the generosity of the Greening Lamborn Trust and of the Oxfordshire Magistrates Association in making grants towards the publication of this volume.

Christ Church, Oxford
June 1983

J. F. A. Mason
Hon. Editor, O.R.S.

LIST OF ABBREVIATIONS

C. C. R.	*Calendar of Close Rolls.*
C. F. R.	*Calendar of Fine Rolls.*
C. P. R.	*Calendar of Patent Rolls.*
K.B.	King's Bench
List of Escheators	*List of Escheators for England and Wales,* List and Index Society, 72, London, 1971.
List of Sheriffs	Public Record Office, *Lists and Indexes.* ix, *List of Sheriffs for England and Wales.* Kraus Reprint Corporation, New York, 1963.
Members of Parliament	*Returns of Members of Parliament, Accounts and Papers,* xvii, part i (1878), *Parliaments of England, 1213-1702.*
Putnam, *Proceedings*	*Proceedings Before the Justices of the Peace in the Fourteenth and Fifteenth Centuries*, ed. by B. H. Putnam (The Ames Foundation, London, 1938).
V. C. H.	*Victoria County History.*

INTRODUCTION

GENERAL BACKGROUND

The activities of the Oxfordshire justices of the peace recorded in this volume took place in the second half of the reign of Richard II. These years, 1387-1398, were the years of the Merciless Parliament and the seizure of control of the government by the Appellants, of Richard's resumption of authority in 1389, and of the events which shortly led to his overthrow and death in 1399.[1] These happenings are too familiar to require amplification here.

Although none of these events is mentioned in the indictments made before the Oxfordshire justices of the peace, discussion of the justices' activities and of the cases which came before them requires frequent reference to the contemporary scene. The more serious offences and the government's policy in respect to the appointment of justices of the peace reflect the unsettled state of the country and the concern of the king and the commons for improvement in the administration of justice. Although the success of these efforts cannot be measured by results in one county what was happening in Oxfordshire contributed to what happened in all of England.

In the parliament that met at Cambridge in September 1388, following the Merciless Parliament of the spring of the same year, the commons among other matters concerned themselves, as they had done for some years, with the disorders caused by liveried retainers.[2] Particularly they complained of the subversion of the legal process by maintenance, i.e. interference by bands of armed men with the judicial process. This concern showed itself in a petition relative to the office of justice of the peace and in legislation that incorporated some of the reforms requested in the petition.[3] For the first time the payment of wages to the justices was authorized: 4s. per day for a justice and 2s. per day for the clerk.[4] The justices were admonished to hold their sessions quarterly as required by

[1]For accounts of the period see: T. F. Tout, *Chapters in the Administrative History of Mediaeval England,* iii, iv (Manchester, 1928); May McKisack, *The Fourteenth Century* (Oxford, 1959); A. Steel, *Richard II* (Cambridge, 1941); R. H. Jones, *The Royal Policy of Richard II* (Oxford, 1968); J. A. Tuck, *Richard II and the English Nobility* (London, 1973).

[2]R. L. Storey, 'Liveries and Commissions of the Peace, 1388-90,' *The Reign of Richard II, Essays in Honour of May McKisack*, ed. by F. R. H. Du Boulay and Caroline M. Barron (London, 1971), pp. 131-152; J. A. Tuck, 'The Cambridge Parliament, 1388,' *English Historical Review*, lxxxiv (1969), 226-243.

[3]12 Richard II, st.1, c.10.

[4]*Ibid.*; see also 14 Richard II, c.11. Payments were to be made from the proceeds of sessions; Putnam, *Proceedings*, p. lxxix; see also below p. 34.

the statute of 1362 and commissions were to be reduced to six justices in addition to the justices of assize.[5] The continuing interest of the commons in the maintenance of law and order and Richard's promise when he resumed control of the government in May 1389 to promote greater tranquillity and provide more amply for justice are reflected in the policy of the government in the next few years towards the office of justice of the peace. On petition of the commons new commissions were issued for all counties in July and November 1389 and again in June and December of 1390 and changes were made in personnel designed to increase efficiency.[6] In July 1389 the number of justices on the county peace commissions was reduced in number, the majority like the commissions for Oxfordshire having eight members; no magnates were named to any commissions. After the issue of four commissions in two years new commissions were not generally issued again until 1394.[7] By the time of the next general issue of commissions in 1397 the zeal for reform had given way to the king's need for political support. Like that for Oxfordshire these commissions were larger and contained members of the nobility.[8] A more detailed study of the Oxfordshire commissions is made below.

The peace rolls always present a picture of the lawless elements of medieval society. While this is to be expected, given the nature of the responsibilities of the justices of the peace, there are in the Oxfordshire records, in addition to homicides and thefts which were endemic, two episodes of greater significance; a riot by students at Oxford University in the spring of 1389 and an insurrection centred in Bampton hundred in the spring of 1398 when the king was in the west of England after the dissolution of the Shrewsbury parliament in January 1398.[9] These two incidents were more serious and at the same time more symptomatic of the general unrest throughout the country than were the thefts of cattle and other goods found in these records as on other peace rolls.

Thus it cannot be said of the material in this volume as it can of that on some peace rolls that it is unconnected with events of general concern to the country as a whole. Both in the picture they provide of Oxfordshire at the end of the fourteenth century and by extension of England, and in their significance for developments relating to the office of justice of the peace, these records have importance beyond the details of individual offences, sessions, and justices. The information on the peace rolls relating to the sessions held by the Oxfordshire justices of the peace in the

[5]36 Edward III, st. 1, c. 12.

[6]*C. P. R.* 1388-1392, pp. 135 ff. 341 ff.; Storey, *op. cit.*, pp. 136 ff.

[7]*C. P. R.* 1391-1396, pp. 434 ff.; Storey, *op. cit.*, p. 151.

[8]*C. P. R.* 1396-1399, pp. 227 ff.; Storey, *op. cit.*, pp. 151-152.

[9]Tout, *Chapters*, iv, 33 ff.

last years of Richard II's reign has been supplemented by material from the records of the justices of gaol delivery and the exchequer. These details include dates, justices present, and most important the business done.

RECORDS OF THE OXFORDSHIRE JUSTICES OF THE PEACE

The extant records of the Oxfordshire justices of the peace during the reign of Richard II consist of two short peace rolls, one for 1387, the other chiefly for 1397-1398. To supplement these rolls there has been included in this volume a substantial block of material for the years 1389-1398 from a gaol delivery roll. This material records business done at sessions held by the Oxfordshire justices of the peace delivering Oxford Castle gaol, by justices of gaol delivery delivering the same gaol, and by justices appointed to a special commission to deal with prisoners in the gaol who were accused of serious crimes. Those tried had been indicted before the Oxfordshire justices of the peace. Thus there is provided a more adequate picture of the work of the justices of the peace than is shown on the two peace rolls alone.

The earlier peace roll, JUST. 1/717, designated Roll A, consists of two membranes. The first is written on both sides, the second only on one. The roll records work done by the justices at four sessions held in 1387. The business of the first, second and fourth sessions is recorded under appropriate session headings. The work of the third session is mentioned as a continuation of that of the second. The only recorded business of these sessions was the trial of offenders who had already been indicted before the justices of the peace, whether those currently sitting or those appointed under earlier commissions is not stated. No doubt other business such as the hearing of indictments was also done although no formal record of it remains. The roll is in generally good condition except for a few spots illegible because of damage from stain or damp and seems to have been prepared with some care. On the first membrane a space was left for completion of an unfinished entry. Also the clerk entered in appropriate places the results of subsequent action taken by the justices of the peace or the justices of gaol delivery.

Why this roll, containing records of finished business, was prepared and how it came to be preserved are questions not readily answered. It was not, like other extant peace rolls of this period, compiled in anticipation of a visit of the king's bench to the neighbourhood.[1] Although the bench sat at Reading in Michaelmas term 1387 there is no evidence that this roll came before it then or at a subsequent session. Indeed, since the business recorded on it had been completed the bench would have had no interest in it. Rather it is suggested that the peace roll was prepared to show what and how much business the justices had

[1]Putnam, *Proceedings*, pp.lxiv ff.

completed or attempted to complete in the year 1387. Fines made by trespassers were noted, and trials of felons and the outlawries of those who failed to appear for trial were recorded in full. Also the large percentage of convictions of felons, six of the seven whose trials were recorded, is unusually high for the justices of the peace, or for any court. This number would seem to indicate a devotion to duty or a desire to make a good impression. Thus it may be that these enrolments were prepared in response to the demands of the Cambridge parliament for the better administration of justice to show that the justices of the peace in Oxfordshire had been doing a responsible job.[2] An order of 20 November 1389 addressed to John Lord Lovell, and instructing him to turn over all records to Sir Robert Cherlton may have provided the immediate stimulus for the preparation of the roll.[3] Similar orders were addressed to former justices of the peace in thirty-one counties, the three ridings of Yorkshire, and the three parts of Lincolnshire.[4] There are also extant on a peace roll covering the years 1381-1396 for the parts of Lindsey in Lincolnshire records of trials and outlawries for the years 1382-1385, and similarly on two of the three extant rolls for Warwickshire for the years 1381-1385 there are records of trials conducted and outlawries reported at sessions held in 1383-1384.[5] Although the Lindsey and Warwickshire rolls also contain records of unfinished business and were before the king's bench when it came to Lincoln in Easter term 1396 and to Coventry in Trinity term 1387 respectively, there is no evidence that the bench concerned itself with those portions of the rolls which contained finished business. Probably these enrolments were in the custody of whoever was responsible for the preparation of records of unfinished business and so were presented before the bench and taken to London with its other records. The same is probably true of the two Oxfordshire rolls, the difference being that enrolments of finished business in Lincolnshire and Warwickshire were at some time combined with the records of unfinished business to form the present rolls; those for Oxfordshire remained as two rolls.[6] While evidence based on these rolls or portions of rolls is too scanty

[2]Above pp. 9-10.

[3]*C. C. R.* 1389-1392, p. 39. Cherlton was on the commission of 15 July 1389.

[4]*Ibid.*, pp. 38 ff. Storey, *op. cit.*, p. 145, suggests that this order indicates a reluctance on the part of the replaced justices to surrender their records; since justices were under no obligation to deposit their records, particularly of finished business, this may not have been so.

[5]*Some Sessions of the Peace in Lincolnshire*, 1381-1396, ed. by Elisabeth G. Kimball (Lincoln Record Society, 49, 56, 1955, 1962), ii, 115-131; *Rolls of the Warwickshire and Coventry Sessions of the Peace, 1377-1397*, ed. by Elisabeth G. Kimball (Dugdale Society, 16, 1939), pp.113-117, 170-177.

[6]The fact that the two rolls were kept separate may explain why one is classified as an Assize Roll and the other in Ancient Indictments.

to support a definitive conclusion, it does suggest that in these years enrolments of finished business were prepared for a purpose other than that of use by the king's bench.

The later peace roll, Ancient Indictments (K.B. 9) 99, designated as Roll B, also consists of two membranes, only the first of which is written on the dorse. Both membranes are damaged along the left-hand margins. As a result one of the seven sessions recorded on the roll cannot be dated and two others can be dated only tentatively. There are twelve lists each of which contains names of twelve jurors arranged in four or six columns. Some of the names in the left-hand columns on the fronts of the membranes cannot be read because of the damage. Missing words in some of the indictments can be supplied from other entries, from entries on the king's bench roll, or from the sense of the entry. The roll records no completed business but only the indictments of felons and a few trespassers, common law and economic. The roll was before the king's bench when it sat at Oxford in Easter term 1398 and the enrolment was probably made in anticipation of that visit.[7] The sessions were not enrolled in chronological order and no rearrangement of the membranes will achieve a chronological ordering. It would appear that the membranes were in their present order when they were before the bench because in the lists of felons and of trespassers summoned before the bench for trial the names are in the order in which the indictments appear on the peace roll.[8] As these lists contain a few names not found among the indictments on the peace roll there may have been a third membrane or a file which has been lost. The unchronological order of the sessions, the fact that at least one session was held in mid-April 1398, and the generally rather untidy appearance of the roll, suggest that it was prepared in some haste for the visit of the bench.[9] It was undoubtedly carried to London with the records of the bench and so preserved. Like the earlier roll it may record only a portion of the business done by the justices during the brief period it covers.[10]

The session headings on both peace rolls contain the date and the place of the sessions. Those on Roll A name as present one or more justices and add the uninformative phrase *et socij sui*.[11] The headings on Roll B

[7]The sign approximating the letter *s* at the foot of each membrane indicates that they had been dealt with in the king's bench; R. F. Hunnisett, 'The Medieval Coroners' Rolls,' *American Journal of Legal History*, iii (1959), 112-113. I am indebted to Mr. John Post for calling my attention to this reference.

[8]K. B. 27/548, Rex, m.19.

[9]Below p. 33.

[10]Below p. 33. On 15 February the Oxfordshire justices of the peace delivered Oxford Castle gaol and probably held a peace session.

[11]Below pp. 60 ff.

are more explicit listing as present two, three, or four of the local justices.[12]

The gaol delivery material, designated for convenience as Roll C, has been taken from JUST. 3/180. On this roll which contains sixty-two membranes, are recorded deliveries of gaols in the counties of the Oxford or northwestern circuit, Gloucester, Hereford, Oxford, Salop, Stafford, and Worcester, in the years 1389-1398, by especially appointed justices of gaol delivery and by justices of the peace acting as justices of gaol delivery.[13] The entries pertaining to Oxfordshire are on mm. 1-3, 5-15. Only those cases in which offenders had been indicted before Oxfordshire justices of the peace have been included. Indictments made before coroners and officials holding view of frankpledge and before Berkshire justices of the peace have been omitted.[14] The gaol delivery roll, which was probably prepared by clerks of Justice Sir John Hill, is in excellent condition; the writing is legible and the entries are generally consistent in form and wording.[15] The session headings name the date and place of the delivery as well as the gaol. When the justices of gaol delivery sat the two or three who did so were named. When the justices of the peace delivered the gaol one justice, who was in every case a justice of the central courts, was named and the others designated as *socij sui,* perhaps because the clerk was unfamiliar with the local men or did not bother to record their names. It is probable that the description of an offence on the gaol delivery roll repeated the wording of the indictment as it had been made before the justices of the peace.

In addition to the session records there were copied on to the gaol delivery roll six commissions for the delivery of Oxford Castle gaol, two peace commissions, that of 15 July 1389 and that of 24 December 1390, and the special commission to deal with prisoners in Oxford Castle gaol issued on 5 February 1395.[16]

Because Roll B and the gaol delivery records contain indictments and Roll A records of trials there is presented here a fairly comprehensive picture of certain types of business done by the Oxfordshire justice of the

[12]Below pp. 71 ff.

[13]R. B. Pugh, *Imprisonment in Medieval England* (Cambridge, 1968), p. 282; Putnam, *Proceedings*, p. 42. Berkshire was also included in this circuit, prisoners from it being gaoled in Oxford Castle (Pugh, *op. cit.*, p. 64).

[14]For a table of gaol delivery sessions see below Roll C, Appendix.

[15]Public Record Office, *Lists and Indexes, Supplementary Series, no. 1, List of Various Common-Law Records* (Reprint, New York, 1970), p. 233, n. 4. The footnote mentions Roll 179 but it is attached to Roll 180; also I have been told by Mr. C. F. A. Meekings that Roll 180 was probably the work of Hill's clerks.

[16]Below pp. 140 ff. The records of this special commission have been included because several of the men who came before it had previously been before the justices of the peace.

peace at the end of Richard II's reign. While records of indictments and trials of felons are numerous, records of the indictments and trials of trespassers are scarce. Indicted trespassers were not usually gaoled. If apprehended they were released after providing pledges for their appearance. Thus the indictment and trial of trespassers, a large part of the work of the justices of the peace, is not adequately illustrated.[17] On the other hand, the relations of the justices of the peace with other agencies of justice, particularly the justices of gaol delivery, are more fully documented than on rolls which record only indictments. Lastly, the detailed descriptions of less common offences such as the riot of the Oxford University students, the Bampton uprising, and other offences of a treasonable nature, as well as the number of articles of value which were stolen provide a relief from the assaults and the thefts of horses and oxen which are so common on many peace rolls.

[17]The definition of 14th century 'trespass' is a most complex problem. The term covers indictable crimes less serious than felonies, i.e. crimes not punishable by hanging, crimes which later became misdemeanours.

COMMISSIONS OF THE PEACE

The Commissions

In the twelve years of the reign of Richard II, 1387-1398, during which the sessions of the peace for which records are printed in this volume were held, eight commissions of the peace were issued for Oxfordshire. All but those of 13 January 1386 and 20 February 1394 were issued at the same time as commissions for all counties; on 15 July and 10 November 1389, 28 June and 24 December 1390, 18 June 1394, and 12 November 1397.[1] The sessions of 1387 recorded on the earlier peace roll were probably held under the 1386 commission; a gaol delivery held by the justices of the peace on 18 February 1390, although it follows the enrolment of the commission of 15 July 1389 on the gaol delivery roll, was presumably held under the commission of November of that year. The gaol delivery on 14 April 1393 was held under the peace commission of 24 December 1390 also enrolled on the gaol delivery roll. The gaol delivery held by the justices of the peace on 15 February 1398 and the peace sessions of 1397-1398 were probably held under the peace commission of 12 November 1397. Under which commission the undatable session recorded on the later peace roll was held cannot be determined. No peace commission is enrolled on either peace roll.

As Miss Putnam and Miss Sillem have analysed commissions of the peace in considerable detail only a summary of their contents and of the powers of the justices is given here.[2] The format of the peace commission had become fixed in the later years of the reign of Edward III, only changes in detail being made necessary by the addition of new statutes such as the statute of Cambridge of 1388, and by alterations in the powers given the justices. After the salutation, the justices named were assigned to keep the peace and enforce the statutes of Winchester, Northampton, and Westminster (1361-1362), and beginning with the commissions of June 1390, that of Cambridge. They were to inquire by sworn inquest concerning felonies and trespasses, including forestalling, regrating, violations of the labour laws and of the statutes regulating weights and measures, extortion, and livery and maintenance. The determining power, i.e. the power to try those indicted for these offences, was granted in some commissions for all offences; in others it was limited. A quorum

[1] *C. P. R.* 1385-1389, p. 82; 1388-1392, pp. 136, 139, 342, 345; 1391-1396, pp. 434, 440; 1396-1399, p. 236. The commissions of 15 July 1389 and 24 December 1390 are printed below pp. 95-8.

[2] Putnam, *Proceedings*, pp. xix ff.; Rosamond Sillem, 'Commissions of the Peace, 1380-1485,' *Bulletin of the Institute of Historical Research*, x (1932-1933), 81-104.

of two or more named justices, one of whom was to sit, was sometimes specified in the inquiry clause, sometimes in the determining clause, and sometimes in both.[3] Difficult cases such as those involving extortion were to be tried only in the presence of a justice from one or other bench or of a justice of assize. Dates and places of sessions were to be fixed by the justices and the sheriff was to be notified so that he might make the necessary arrangements including the summoning of jurors. In some commissions one justice was named to be in charge of the records.[4]

Only in respect of the power of the justices to try those indicted for felonies and common-law trespasses does this analysis need reconsideration. According to Miss Putnam and Miss Sillem the power to try such offenders was given to the justices in commissions issued between 1362 and 20 December 1382. In the commissions of that date and those of the next seven years this power was denied them.[5] This interpretation has recently been challenged by Mr. J. B. Post who argues that the omission of felonies and trespasses from the determining clause in these commissions was accidental. He points out that since the justices were empowered to try felons and trespassers indicted before their predecessors and since they were enjoined to hear and determine all offences falling under the statutes listed in the peace clause which would include felonies and common-law trespasses, it is unlikely that they were denied the power to try those whom they themselves had indicted. As further evidence he cites the trials of felons and trespassers conducted by the justices of the peace in Warwickshire in 1384 and in Lindsey in 1383 and 1384, the descriptions in the session headings on the Lindsey roll of the justices as assigned to hear and determine felonies and trespasses and similar entries on a Cambridgeshire peace roll for 1383, and notations by chancery clerks of associations of new members with commissions whose

[3]The members of the quorums of the Oxfordshire peace commissons were: 13 January 1386, Tresilian, Bealknap, R. Abberbury, Cherlton, Barentyn, Rede, Somerton, in the inquiry clause; Patent Roll, 9 Richard II, part i, m. 32d.

15 July 1389, Cherlton, Hill, in the inquiry clause; below p. 95.

10 November 1389, 28 June, 24 December 1390, Cherlton, Hill, Somerton, Rede, in the inquiry clause; Cherlton, Hill, to determine felonies; Patent Roll, 13 Richard II, part i, m. 26d.; 14 Richard II, part i, m. 34d.; below pp. 125, 126.

20 February 1394, Cherlton, Hill, Rede, J. Abberbury, in the inquiry clause; Cherlton, Hill, to determine felonies; Patent Roll, 17 Richard II, part ii, m. 21d.

18 June 1394, Cherlton, Hill, Wilicotes, Rede, to determine felonies; *ibid.*, m. 20d.

12 November 1397, Hill, Huls, Wilicotes, Rede, to determine felonies; *ibid.*, 21 Richard II, part i, m. 25d.

[4]Sir Robert Cherlton was named *custos rotulorum* in the 10 November 1389 commission, Nicholas Somerton in that of 24 December 1390; *ibid.*, 13 Richard II, part i, m. 26d.; below p. 121.

[5]Putnam, *Proceedings*, pp. xxiv-xxv, xxviii-xxix; Sillem, 'Commissions of the Peace,' *B. I. H. R.*, x, 94-95; for the commissions of 20 December 1382 see *C. P. R.* 1381-1385, pp. 251-255; Kimball, *Warws.*, pp. 152-154.

members were empowered to hear and determine felonies and trespasses. He might also have noted that the Cambridgeshire justices tried an accessory to a felony and that a similarly worded heading appears on a Gloucestershire peace roll recording a session held in 1384 under a commission of that year.[6]

Examples from Oxfordshire may be added. At the sessions of the peace held in 1387, the justices like their fellows in other counties tried and convicted felons and trespassers the exact nature of whose offences was not specified, and they secured the outlawry of others who failed to appear for trial. In the headings for these sessions the clerk described the justices as assigned *ad diuersa felonias transgressiones et alia malefacta audienda et terminanda.*[7] And a chancery clerk in a writ associating a new member with the commission of 1386 described the justices as *custodes pacis et iusticiarios ad diuersa felonias transgressiones et malefacta audienda et terminanda.*[8]

It would therefore seem that Mr. Post's interpretation of the powers granted the justices of the peace in the 20 December 1382 commissions is the interpretation put on the commissions issued-between 1382 and November 1389 by those responsible for issuing these commissions and by those who functioned under them. It seems certain that after full powers of hearing and determining felonies and trespasses were granted the justices of the peace in 1368, they were not again deprived of this authority.

Personnel—Policy

In view of the political shifts of the middle and later years of the reign of Richard II and the legislation passed by the Cambridge parliament specifying changes in the personnel of the peace commissions, it will be well to look at the composition of the Oxfordshire peace commissions to see what changes were made, whether these changes conformed to the specifications of the legislation, and whether they were in line with

[6] J. B. Post, 'The Peace Commissions of 1382,' *English Historical Review*, xci (1976), 98-101. The examples cited are found in Kimball, *Warws.*, pp. xviii, 113-117, 170-177; Kimball, *Lincs.*, i, xiv; ii, 115-131; *Some Sessions of the Peace in Cambridgeshire in the Fourteenth Century, 1340, 1380-1383*, ed. by Mary M. Taylor (Cambridge Antiquarian Society, lv, 1942), pp. lvii, lviii, 48-49. 52; *Rolls of the Gloucestershire Sessions of the Peace, 1361-1* ed. by Elisabeth G. Kimball *Transactions of the Bristol and Gloucestershire Archaeological Society*, 62 (1942), p. 100. For a clerk who used the word *audienda* without *terminanda* but headed his record of indictments *Placita* see Putnam, *Proceedings*, p. 225. My discussions of the relevant peace commissions for Warwickshire and Lindsey (*Warws.*, pp. xvi-xxii; *Lincs.*, i, xii-xv) need revision in the light of Mr. Post's conclusions. Similarly the Cambridgeshire justices cannot be accused of exceeding the authority given in their commissions; Taylor, *op. cit.*, pp. lvii-lviii.

[7] Below pp. 60, 62, 65, 67.

[8] Patent Roll, 9 Richard II, part ii, m. 29d.

changes in the peace commissions generally. It has been pointed out that the concern of the Cambridge parliament with the maintenance of law and order and the king's promise of better administration of justice led to the issuing of peace commissions for all counties in July and November 1389 and again in June and December of 1390 at the request of the Commons. Prof. R. L. Storey has analysed the composition of these peace commissions in connexion with a study of the statute against livery and maintenance of 1390. He has pointed out that prior to July 1389 the last general issue of peace commissions had been made in December 1382, although one or more new commissions, two in the case of Oxfordshire, had been issued for all but four counties in the intervening years. The commissions of July 1389 were smaller than previous ones; they contained eight justices, six representatives of the local community, two central court justices, and no magnates. These appointments were in accordance with the statute of Cambridge which specified six justices exclusive of the justices of assize. The local men were in varying degrees new appointees. A movement to return to earlier practices, such as larger commissions, was begun in some of the commissions issued in November 1389 and further changes such as the inclusion of magnates were made in many of the December 1390 and subsequent commissions.[9]

We may now consider the changes made in the personnel of the Oxfordshire peace commissions of January 1386 through November 1397 to see to what extent these changes were in accord with those made for the country as a whole. The membership of the Oxfordshire commissions for these years is shown in the accompanying table. The commission of 15 July 1389 and the next five commissions had eight members, two central court justices and six local men, as did the 15 July commissions for the rest of the country. In contrast the commission of 1386, like commissions for other counties, was larger, having thirteen members. A commission of more than eight men was not issued for Oxfordshire until 1397 when the appointment of two peers raised the membership to ten.[10] The commissions of 1386 and 1397 each contained two magnates; that of 1386 had three central court justices and six local men. Why no peers were appointed to the Oxfordshire peace commissions until 1397 although appointments from this group had been made in other counties as early as the commission of December 1390 is not clear. Perhaps no member of the nobility was anxious to re-establish his interest in the county.[11] When peers were again named one appointment went to Lord Lovell who had

[9]Storey, *op. cit.*, p. 149.

[10]The commission of 20 December 1382 had eight members; that of 24 November 1383, sixteen; *C. P. R.* 1381-1385, pp. 252, 347.

[11]It may have been because there were no peers with strong family connexions in the county; *V. C. H. Oxon.* i (London, 1939), 440 ff.

Commissions of the Peace, Oxfordshire, 1386-1397

(Numbers in parentheses indicate position on commission).

	13 January 1386	*15 July 1389*	*10 November 1389*	*28 June 1390*	*24 December 1390*	*20 February 1394*	*18 June 1394*	*12 November 1397*
Magnates	John, Lord Lovel (1)							Thomas, earl of Gloucester (1)
	Amaury, Lord St Amand (2)							Lord Lovell (2)
Justices of the Central Courts	*Sir Robert Tresilian (4)	*Cherlton (2)	†Cherlton (2)	†Cherlton (2)	†Cherlton (3)	†Cherlton (3)	†Cherlton (3)	†Hill (4)
	*Sir Robert Bealknap (5)	*Sir John Hill (5)	†Hill (3)	†Hill (3)	†Hill (4)	†Hill (4)	†Hill (4)	†Sir Hugh Huls (5)
	*Sir Robert Cherlton (9)							
Gentry; Men with Local Connexions	Sir Hugh Segrave (3)	Bardolf (1)	Bardolf (1)	Bardolf (1)	R. Abberbury (1)	R. Abberbury (1)	R. Abberbury (1)	R. Abberbury (3)
	*Sir Richard Abberbury (6)	Sir Thomas Paynell (3)	Paynell (4)	Paynell (4)	Bardolf (2)	Bardolf (2)	Bardolf (2)	†Wilicotes (6)
	Sir Robert Bardolf (7)	Sir Thomas Poure (4)	Poure (5)	Poure (5)	Poure (5)	Poure (5)	†Sir William Wilicotes (5)	Barentyn (7)
	Sir Gilbert Wace (8)	Barentyn (6)	Barentyn (6)	Barentyn (6)	Barentyn (6)	Barentyn (6)	Barentyn (6)	†Rede (8)
	*Thomas Barentyn (10)	Somerton (7)	*Somerton (7)	*Somerton (7)	*Somerton (7)	*Rede (7)	†Rede (7)	John Golafre (9)
	*John Rede (11)	Richard Overton (8)	*Rede (8)	*Rede (8)	*Rede (8)	*John Abberbury (8)	J. Abberbury (8)	John Hilton (10)
	Walter atte Halle (12)							
	*Nicholas Somerton (13)							
	Thomas del Stokes associated, 13 February 1386							
	C. P. R. 1385-1389, pp. 82, 168	*C. P. R.* 1388-1392, p. 136; below pp. 95-7	*Ibid.*, p. 139	*Ibid.*, p. 342	*Ibid.*, p. 345; below pp. 121-4	*C. P. R.* 1391-1396, p. 434	*Ibid.*, p. 440	*C. P. R.* 1396-1399, p. 236

†quorum, determining clause
*quorum, enquiry clause

been on earlier peace commissions for the county and the other to Thomas Despenser, earl of Gloucester, a royal favourite.

The changes in membership from among the justices of the central courts are easily explained. Tresilian had been executed by the Lords Appellant in 1388, Bealknap was banished in 1388, and Cherlton who had succeeded Bealknap died in 1396. Hill and Huls, both justices of the king's bench, were logical replacements.

The changes in the local men named to the commissions are of greater significance since it was appointments from this group which were to mark the government's concern for greater efficiency in the administration of justice. Six men from this category were named on the July 1389 commission, three being carried over from the 1386 commission. Sir Robert Bardolf whose name headed the list on this commission, on that of November 1389, and on that of June 1390, had first been appointed justice of the peace for Oxfordshire in 1383. He was named on all subsequent commissions until 1394, the year before his death. Continuity of membership was also provided by the appointments of Thomas Barentyn and Nicholas Somerton both of whom had also been first appointed to the peace commission in 1383. Barentyn was named on all subsequent peace commissions issued under Richard II and Somerton on all commissions through that of December 1390. New appointees to the July 1389 commission were Sir Thomas Paynell who also was reappointed in November of that year and in June 1390 but not again until the next reign; Sir Thomas Poure, reappointed through February 1394; and Richard Overton who was not reappointed for the county but was frequently named justice of the peace for the town of Oxford in the last years of Richard II's reign.

The local men appointed as replacements on the November 1389 and subsequent commissions either had been members of peace commissions prior to 1389 or were new men. The delay in reappointing two who had served earlier perhaps represents some attempt to conform to the demand for reform. Sir Richard Abberbury, appointed to the Oxfordshire peace commission in 1383 and again in 1386, was a member of the king's entourage who was retired from court in 1388. He was not reappointed justice of the peace in Oxfordshire until December 1390 when he replaced Paynell; he remained on the commission through 1397, his name preceding Bardolf's on three commissions and following those of the earl of Gloucester and Lord Lovell on that of 1397. John Rede, appointed November 1389 to replace Overton, had been a member of the 1386 commission; he remained on the commission until his death in 1404.[12]

[12] Although a lawyer, Rede was not a central court justice.

Among men not previously appointed to the Oxfordshire peace commissions were Sir William Wilicotes, named in June 1394 and subsequently, John Abberbury, named to the two 1394 commissions, and John Golafre and John Hilton named in 1397 and subsequently.[13] It may be noted that none of the local men named to the July 1389 commission or to later commissions had been on the peace commission of December 1382 although a number of them had been named to one or more of the special commissions appointed in 1381 and 1382 to deal with rebels. Of the four appointed to or associated with the 1386 commission who were not again appointed two, Sir Hugh Segrave, a member of Richard II's court with few Oxfordshire connexions, and Walter atte Halle had died before 1389; of Thomas del Stokes nothing is known; only Sir Gilbert Wace may have been a casualty of the effort at reform. Although he held numerous county offices prior to 1387, his name does not appear after that date.

Thus it would seem that in Oxfordshire a clean sweep of the local men on the peace commission had been made between 1383 and 1389, that changes had been begun as early as 1383, and that the commissions of the remaining years of Richard II's reign did contain a number of new men, some of whom replaced justices removed by death. Unfortunately too little is known of many of these men to make it possible to determine why they were or were not appointed to a given commission.

Personnel—The Justices

Magnates John Lovell, Lord Lovell of Titchmarsh and Holand (d. 1408), succeeded to the title in 1361 and was knighted by 1367. He served in Ireland, France, and Scotland. Among the first to join Bolingbroke before his accession as Henry IV, Lovell abandoned Richard in August 1399 after that king's return from Ireland. Although he was not a principal landholder in Oxfordshire he was appointed to various commissions in that county as he was in Berkshire and Wiltshire including special commissions to deal with rebels in Oxfordshire and Berkshire in 1381 and 1382. He was named first on the Oxfordshire peace commission of 1386 and second on that of 1397. The position of his name on the 1386 commission explains why the order of 20 November 1389 to transmit the records to Sir Robert Cherlton was addressed to him and why his is the one name mentioned in connexion with the peace sessions to be held in 1387.[14]

Amaury de St Amand (d. 1402) who succeeded to the barony of St Amand in 1381 was a member of the Oxfordshire peace commissions of

[13]Although a lawyer, Hilton was not a central court justice.

[14]*The Complete Peerage*, i-xii, ed. by V. Gibbs etc. (London, 1910-1956), *sub nomine; C. P. R.; C. C. R.* 1389-1392, p. 39; below pp. 60, 63, 65. These biographies are not intended to be complete but to give only enough information to show the type of man appointed justice of the peace.

1383 and 1386. He was a royal councillor under both Richard II and Henry IV and a member of various commissions including peace commissions in Bedfordshire, Berkshire, Buckinghamshire, Oxfordshire, and Wiltshire. The family held the hundred of Bloxham from 1278 to 1418.[15]

Both Lord Lovell and Lord St Amand were named as the custodians of the chattels of a felon convicted at the gaol delivery of Oxford Castle gaol on 30 April 1389. Whether they were present in person and if so, why, is not known.[16] There is no record that either sat as justice of the peace for Oxfordshire, which seems to have lacked important locally-based peers.

Thomas Despenser (b. 1373) was for his support of Richard II created earl of Gloucester in 1397. He deserted the king in 1399 and was one of those sent to inform Richard of his deposition. He was beheaded by a mob in Bristol in 1400 when he joined a conspiracy against Henry IV. He was named on the Oxfordshire peace commission of 1397 and to other commissions in the counties of the Oxford circuit.[17]

Justices of the Central Courts Sir Robert Bealknap (d. c. 1400) of Kent was pleading in the upper courts by 1362, was named king's serjeant in 1366, and in 1374 was appointed chief justice of the court of common pleas. His departure in 1387 did not save him from being appealed for high treason in the same year and banished to Ireland with the other justices in 1388. After his return in 1397 he played no further part in public affairs. Prior to 1387 he had been appointed to numerous commissions in counties of the Oxford circuit and elsewhere including the Oxfordshire peace commission of 1386 and its quorum. There is no evidence that he sat as justice of the peace for the county.[18]

Sir Robert Cherlton, or Charlton (d. 1396), of Shropshire was in 1388 appointed chief justice of the common pleas to succeed Bealknap. He was named on numerous commissions, chiefly in the counties of the Oxford circuit including the Oxfordshire peace commissions between 1383 and his death; he served as a justice of gaol delivery for Oxford Castle gaol during much of the same period, conducting most of the gaol delivery sessions and some of the peace sessions at which felons who appeared before the justices of gaol delivery were indicted. He was named *custos*

[15]*C. P.; V. C. H. Oxon.* vi (1959), 340; ix (1969), 4, 16, 46; *C. P. R.*

[16]Below p. 95, no. 6.

[17]*C. P.*; Putnam, *Proceedings,* p. 422; *C. P. R.*

[18]E. Foss, *A Biographical Dictionary of the Judges of England, 1066-1870* (London, 1870), *sub nomine*; Putnam, *Proceedings,* p. 235; Kimball, *Gloucs.*, p. 24; *C. P. R.*; see above p. 18, n. 3. For Bealknap, Tresilian and Segrave, see *D.N.B.*

rotulorum on the peace commission of 10 November 1389 and to the quorum in all commissions between 1386 and 1394.[19]

Sir John Hill, Hille, or Hull (d. c. 1407), of Devonshire was made a serjeant-at-law in 1382 and named to the court of king's bench in 1389. He was appointed to numerous commissions in counties of the Oxford circuit and elsewhere between 1388 and 1399, justice of the peace for Oxfordshire and justice of gaol delivery for Oxford Castle gaol with Cherlton in 1389 and thereafter. He was named to the quorum in the peace commissions from 1389 through 1397. He frequently delivered Oxford Castle gaol and it is thought that his clerks were responsible for the preparation of Gaol Delivery Roll 180[20].

Hugh Huls (d. 1414) of Cheshire was named a justice of the king's bench in 1389 and to numerous commissions in counties of the Oxford and northern circuits. He was appointed a justice of the peace for Oxfordshire in 1397 to succeed Cherlton and he also succeeded him as justice of gaol delivery for Oxford Castle gaol. He sat with Hill in the latter capacity in February 1397 and no doubt subsequently. He was named to the quorum in the peace commission of 1397.[21]

Sir Robert Tresilian was a Cornishman who had considerable property in Oxfordshire. A favourite of Richard II, he was appealed for high treason in 1387 and executed in 1388. He had become a serjeant-at-law in 1377, justice of the king's bench in 1378, and chief justice in 1381. He was appointed to numerous commissions including those to suppress rebels in Oxfordshire. He was a member of the 1386 Oxfordshire peace commission and of its quorum.[22]

Gentry: Men with Local Connexions Most of the remainder of those named to the Oxfordshire peace commissions between 1386 and 1397 were men with county connexions. Some of them served or had served at court; others were active locally in Oxfordshire or neighbouring counties. Some were obscure or are difficult to identify because their names were common or because the same first name belonged to several members of a family.

John Abberbury, a relative of Sir Richard Abberbury, inherited land at Adderbury from Walter atte Halle in 1389. Abberbury represented Oxfordshire in parliament in 1393-1394 and 1396-1397 and was named to

[19]Foss, *Judges, sub nomine;* Putnam, *Proceedings*, p. 401; Kimball, *Gloucs.*, p. 25; Patent Roll, 13 Richard II, part i, m. 26d.; *C. P. R.;* above p. 18, n. 3; below, index, *sub nomine.*

[20]Foss, *Judges, sub nomine;* Putnam, *Proceedings*, p. 423; Kimball, *Gloucs.*, p. 25; *Shropshire Peace Roll, 1400-1414*, ed. by Elisabeth G. Kimball (Shrewsbury, 1959), p. 21; *C. P. R.;* above p. 18, n. 3; below, index, *sub nomine.*

[21]Foss, *Judges, sub nomine;* Putnam, *Proceedings*, p. 423; Kimball, *Gloucs.*, p. 26, and *Shropshire*, p. 22; *C. P. R.;* above p. 18, n. 3; below, index, *sub nomine.*

[22]Foss, *Judges, sub nomine;* Putnam, *Proceedings*, p. 401; *C. P. R.;* above p. 18, n. 3.

the county peace commissions of 1394 and to the quorum of the February commission. He was appointed tax collector in 1401 and 1404. He sat as justice of the peace for ten days between 1393 and 1397.[23]

Sir Richard Abberbury (d. by 1401) served the Black Prince and Prince Richard: he was a chamber knight after Richard became king, the king's secretary in 1382, and the queen's chamberlain in 1383. He was expelled from court by the Merciless Parliament in 1388. The family took its name from Adderbury in Oxfordshire and had land in that county at Steeple Aston. It also had considerable property in Berkshire where in 1386 Sir Richard was licensed by the king to rebuild Donnington Castle; in 1393 he founded Donnington Hospital. His wife was the daughter of Chief Justice Sir William Shareshull. Sir Richard represented Oxfordshire in parliament in 1373 and 1386. He was named to the Oxfordshire commissions to suppress rebels in 1381 and 1382 and appointed justice of the peace for the county in 1383 and 1386, being named to the quorum of the latter commission. He was omitted from the two commissions of 1389 and that of June 1390 but was reappointed in December 1390, in 1394, and in 1397, although he had been exempted from further office holding in 1390. He was also appointed justice of the peace in Berkshire and Wiltshire. He was named first on the Oxfordshire commissions of December 1390 and 1394 and immediately after the magnates on that of 1397. He is listed as presiding at three sessions in 1387 and at many of those mentioned in the gaol delivery records. In 1391 he accounted at the exchequer for the fines from sessions held in 1386-1388. Whether he sat after his reappointment is not certain.[24]

Sir Robert Bardolf (d. 1395) of Mapledurham was squire to Edward III and knight of the royal chamber under Richard II. He had land at Headington and elsewhere in Bullingdon hundred and was related to Lord Bardolf of Wormegay in Norfolk. He was named to the 1382 commissions to suppress rebels in Oxfordshire and to the commissions of the peace for the county between 1383 and 1394, being named first on the commissions of 1389 and June 1390 and immediately after Sir Richard Abberbury on the next three. According to entries on the gaol delivery roll he presided at some peace sessions.[25]

[23]*V. C. H., Oxon.* ix, 21; W. R. Williams, *The Parliamentary History of the County of Oxford . . . 1213-1899* (Brecknock, 1899), p. 28; *Members of Parliament;* Pipe Rolls, 17 and 19 Richard II, Berks., Nova Oblata; *C. P. R.; C. C. R.; C. F. R.;* above p. 18, n. 3.

[24]C. C. Brookes, *A History of Steeple Aston and Middle Aston* (Shipston-on-Stour, 1929), *sub nomine;* Tout, *Chapters,* iv, *sub nomine;* B. H. Putnam, *The Place in Legal History of Sir William Shareshull* (Cambridge Studies in English Legal History, Cambridge, 1950), p. 12; *V. C. H. Berkshire,* ii (London, 1907), 93; *V. C. H. Oxon.* v (1957), 193; vi. 304; ix. 115; Williams, pp. 24, 27; *Members of Parliament;* Pipe Roll, 15 Richard II, Berks., Nova Oblata; *C. P. R.; C. C. R.;* above p. 18, n. 3; below, index, *sub nomine.*

[25]Tout, *Chapters,* iv. 344; *V. C. H. Oxon.* v. 171; vi. 74, 316; *C. P. R.; C. C. R.*; below, index, *sub nomine.* Bardolf and Golafre were retained by Richard II for life.

Thomas Barentyn, or Barantyn (d. 1399), of Chinnor, Little Haseley, and Chalgrove in Ewelme hundred was one of those who bore much of the burden of local government in Oxfordshire. He frequently served as knight of the shire from 1387 until his death, was named sheriff of Oxfordshire and Berkshire four times, in 1378, 1382, 1386, and 1394, escheator in 1388 and 1392, and to various commissions of array and inquiry for the county. He was appointed to all the Oxfordshire peace commissions from 1383 until his death, to the quorum of the 1386 commission, and to the special commissions to suppress rebels in 1382. He sat as justice of the peace in 1387, for thirteen days between March 1393 and October 1396, and in 1397 and 1398. He accounted at the exchequer for the receipts from fines for sessions in 1389.[26]

John Golafre (d. 1442) is not to be confused with his cousin, also John, who died in 1396. The family had land at Beckley and Fifield in Oxfordshire and also in Berkshire. Golafre was a member of the committee of the Shrewsbury parliament of 1398 appointed to handle petitions and the dispute between the dukes of Hereford and Norfolk. He was sheriff of Oxfordshire and Berkshire in 1397-1398 and again in the fifteenth century, escheator in 1409, and knight of the shire for Oxfordshire in 1397 and for Berkshire in the reign of Henry IV. He was named to the Oxfordshire peace commissions of 1397 and 1399 and later to peace commissions in Berkshire. He sat at least twice for Oxfordshire in 1397-1398.[27]

Walter atte Halle (d. by 1389) had land at Adderbury in Oxfordshire which, as has been said, was inherited by John Abberbury. Halle was appointed to the Oxfordshire peace commission of 1383 and to that of 1386, and was named on two of the special commissions of 1382 to suppress rebels. Otherwise nothing is known of him.[28]

John Hilton, or Hulton (d. after 1412), who became prothonotary or chief clerk of the king's bench in 1388, was a landholder in Oxfordshire and had other local connections. He was named justice of the peace for Oxfordshire in 1397 and under Henry IV. He sat at least four times under the 1397 commission.[29]

Richard Overton (d. c. 1409) had land in Oxfordshire, Berkshire, and Buckinghamshire and was steward of the manor of Cookham in

[26] *V. C. H. Oxon.* viii (1964), 61, 62, 152; Williams, pp. 27-28; *Members of Parliament; List of Sheriffs; List of Escheators;* Pipe Rolls, 14, 17, 18 and 19 Richard II, Berks., Nova Oblata; *C. P. R.; C. C. R.;* above p. 18, n. 3; below, index, *sub nomine.*

[27] Tout, *Chapters,* iv, 38; *V. C. H. Oxon.* v. 62; Williams, p. 28; *Members of Parliament; List of Sheriffs; List of Escheators; C. P. R.; C. C. R.; C. F. R.;* below, index, *sub nomine.*

[28] *V. C. H. Oxon.* ix, 21; *C. P. R.; C. C. R.*

[29] J. B. Post, 'King's Bench Clerks in the Reign of Richard II', *B.I.H.R.* xlvii, 159-60. (I am grateful to Mr. Post for letting me see this article in manuscript); *C. P. R.; C. C. R.; C.F. R.;* below, index, *sub nomine.*

Berkshire. He was named justice of the peace for Berkshire in 1385, for Buckinghamshire in 1389, 1394, 1395, and 1397, and for Oxfordshire in the commission of 15 July 1389. He was also named on various peace commissions for the town of Oxford and on numerous other commissions for both town and county including that of 16 July 1392 to deliver Oxford Castle gaol.[30]

Sir Thomas Paynell (d. by 1410) who held land at Ufton in Berkshire is not known to have had any landed interest in Oxfordshire. He was named to the commissions to deal with rebels in Oxfordshire in 1382 although he protested that he did not receive that of 8 March, and justice of the peace for the shire twice in 1389 and on the commission of June 1390; he was not reappointed until 1399. He was knight of the shire for Oxfordshire in 1392-1393 and he was also named to various other commissions. According to the gaol delivery records he presided at some Oxfordshire peace sessions.[31]

Sir Thomas Poure, or Power (d. 1398), had land at Black Bourton and Wendlebury in Oxfordshire. He was named justice of the peace for the county in 1389, 1390, and 1394 and sat five days between March 1393 and March 1394 and probably earlier as he accounted at the exchequer for fines collected at sessions held between 1390 and 1393 and was named in the gaol delivery records.[32]

John Rede (d. 1404) was a lawyer whose wife held land at Checkendon and Stoke Marmion in Oxfordshire. He had represented Oxfordshire in parliament in 1388 and 1391 and was made a serjeant-at-law in 1396. He was appointed justice of the peace for Oxfordshire in 1386, omitted from the commission of July 1389 but reappointed in November of that year and thereafter until his death. He was a member of the quorum of some of these commissions and sat in 1387, for nineteen days between March 1393 and October 1396, and in 1397-1398. He was also appointed justice of the peace in Buckinghamshire and for the town of Oxford, on commissions to deliver Oxford Castle gaol in 1392 and 1394, and on the special commission of 1395 to deal with prisoners in the gaol. He sat at the single recorded session of that commission. His legal training no doubt accounted for some of these appointments.[33]

Sir Hugh Segrave (d. 1386 or 1387) was a person of considerable prominence having been comptroller of the wardrobe 1360-1368, steward

[30]*C. P. R.; C. C. R.; C. F. R.*

[31]*V. C. H. Berks,* iii (1903), 441; Williams, p. 28; *Members of Parliament; C. P. R.; C. C. R.; C. F. R.;* below, index, *sub nomine.*

[32]*V. C. H. Oxon.* vi, 82, 340; Pipe Rolls, 15, 16 and 17 Richard II, Berks, Nova Oblata; *C. P. R.; C. C. R.; C. F. R.;* below, index, *sub nomine.*

[33]*Boarstall Cartulary*, ed. by H. E. Salter (Oxford Historical Society, lxxxviii, 1930), pp. vii-viii; *V. C. H. Oxon.* viii (1964), 9, 153; Williams, pp. 27, 28; *Members of Parliament;* Pipe Rolls 17, 18 and 19 Richard II, Berks, Nova Oblata; *C. P. R.; C. C. R.;* above p. 18, n. 3; below, index, *sub nomine.*

of the household of the Black Prince and of Richard II until 1381, one of the negotiators of Richard's marriage with Anne of Bohemia, treasurer of England 1381-1386, and temporarily keeper of the great seal in 1381. He was named to numerous commissions including the Oxfordshire peace commission of 1386 and the commissions to suppress rebels in 1381 and 1382. These appointments were no doubt due to his position at court, although his family had land in Oxfordshire.[34]

Nicholas Somerton had land at Deddington in Oxfordshire. He was named justice of the peace for the county in 1377 and 1378 and again from 1383 to 1390, being on the quorum of various commissions and *custos rotulorum* on the commission of December 1390. He was also a member of the commissions to suppress rebels in Oxfordshire in 1382. He sat at sessions of the peace held in 1387. He appears to have been still alive in 1401 but nothing is known of his activities in his later years.[35]

Thomas del Stokes who had land at Shelswell was associated with the 1386 Oxfordshire peace commission but seems not to have been named to serve the county or elsewhere in any other capacity. Since his name was a common one identification is uncertain.[36]

Sir Gilbert Wace (d. by 1409) of Ewelme served Oxfordshire in numerous capacities until 1387. After that date his name does not appear although it was not until 1398 that he was reported too sick and old to serve. Previously he had been knight of the shire for Oxfordshire nine times between 1372 and 1386, sheriff of Oxfordshire and Berkshire four times between 1371 and 1387, and also coroner, escheator, tax collector, and a member of numerous commissions. He was named justice of the peace for Oxfordshire in 1377, 1378, 1383, and 1386 and on the commissions of 1381 and 1382 to suppress rebels. He sat as justice of the peace in 1387 and according to the gaol delivery records presided at some peace sessions.[37]

Sir William Wilicotes, Wilcotes, Wilecotes, or Wylicotes (d. c. 1412), had land at Woodperry, Headington, and North Leigh in Oxfordshire, at Willicote and elsewhere in Gloucestershire, and in Worcestershire. In 1407 he was appointed custodian of the royal park at Cornbury in Oxfordshire. He served as knight of the shire for Oxfordshire eight times between 1385 and 1410, was sheriff of Oxfordshire and Berkshire in 1392 and 1399, and was appointed justice of the peace for Oxfordshire almost continuously from June 1394 until his death. He was also named to the special commission of 5 February 1395 to try prisoners in Oxford Castle gaol. He was on the quorum of the June 1394 and the 1397 peace

[34]Kimball, *Warws.*, pp. xxxix-xl; *C. P. R.; V. C. H. Oxon.* x (1972), 177, 213.

[35]*C. P. R.; C. C. R.;* above p. 18, n. 3; below pp. 62, 65, 67.

[36]*V. C. H. Oxon.* vi, 286; *C. P. R.; C. C. R.*

[37]*V. C. H. Oxon.* vii (1962), 60; Williams, pp. 23 ff.; *Members of Parliament; Lists of Sheriffs; List of Escheators; C. P. R.; C. C. R.;* below, index, *sub nomine.*

commissions; he sat nine days between December 1394 and October 1396, at sessions held in 1397-1398, and probably at other times, according to the gaol delivery records. He accounted at the exchequer for fines collected at sessions in the later years of Richard II's reign.[38]

The Justices of Gaol Delivery

Brief mention may be made of the men appointed justices of gaol delivery and members of the special commission of 1395 who were not also named as justices of the peace.

Twelve commissions for the delivery of Oxford Castle gaol were issued between 1389 and 1398 to two, three, or in one instance five men. These commissions contained one justice from one of the central courts and frequently, two. These men, Cherlton, Hill, and Huls, were at the same time members of the county peace commission. Two other men occasionally sent to deliver Oxford Castle gaol were probably lawyers although their identification is not certain. Henry Brown, a clerk in the court of common pleas, was named as the third member on five commissions; he sat once with Cherlton and Hill and once with Woderove. That he was a lawyer is suggested by these appointments and by the fact that a Henry Brown was appointed justice of assize for the counties of the Oxford circuit and to commissions in the counties of that circuit. His name is too common to permit precise identification.[39] John Woderove was appointed to deliver Oxford Castle gaol in 1396 and sat at least once. That there was more than one man of this name is suggested by the designations, of Oxfordshire and of Yorkshire. A John Woderove was pleading in the upper courts by 1388-1389, was named justice of assize for the counties of the Oxford and midland circuits, and justice of the peace in several jurisdictions including the East and West Ridings of Yorkshire. How many bore this name is not known.[40]

Among the local men occasionally named to gaol delivery commissions were John Rede and Richard Overton who were also justices of the peace for Oxfordshire, and Lawrence Dru of Berkshire, chief clerk of the court of common pleas, who was a justice of the peace for that county.[41]

Four of the five members of the special commission of February 1395 were also justices of the peace for Oxfordshire, Cherlton, Hill, Rede, and

[38]F. N. Macnamara, 'The Wilcotes Family,' *Berks., Bucks.,* and *Oxon. Archaeological Journal*, iii (1897-1898), 97-107; *V. C. H. Oxon.* v. 161, 286; Williams, pp. 27 ff.; *Members of Parliament; List of Sheriffs;* Pipe Rolls, 19 and 21 Richard II, Berks., Nova Oblata; *C. P. R.; C. C. R.;* above, p. 18, n. 3; below, index, *sub nomine.*

[39]P.R.O., *Lists and Indexes, Supplementary Series*, no. I, Gaol Delivery Rolls and Files, Index of Justices, *sub nomine; C. P. R.;* below pp. 155, 156.

[40]Putnam, *Proceedings,* p. 464; P. R. O., *Lists and Indexes, Supplementary Series,* no. I, Gaol Delivery Rolls and Files, Index of Justices, *sub nomine;* below pp. 156.

[41] *Members of Parliament; C. P. R.;* below pp. 155, 156.

Wilicotes. The fifth member was John Cassy (d. by 1400) of Deerhurst in Gloucestershire. He had been made chief baron of the exchequer and justice for South Wales in 1389 and was named on numerous commissions. He sat with John Rede at the one recorded session of the special commission.[42]

[42]Putnam, *Proceedings*, p. 422; Kimball, *Gloucs.*, p. 24; P. R. O. *Lists and Indexes, Supplementary Series*, no. I, Gaol Delivery Rolls and Files, Index of Justices, *sub nomine; C. P. R.*; below p. 139.

THE SESSIONS OF THE PEACE

The records printed in this volume contain uneven information about the dates and places at which sessions of the peace were held in Oxfordshire in the last ten years of the reign of Richard II and about the justices present at these sessions. About the work of the justices there is more information. Additional details are provided by entries on the Pipe Rolls and other Exchequer records.

The Dates, Places, and Justices Present

No table of sessions of the peace held in the years 1387-1398 can be drawn up. Only for one year, 1387, is there full information about four general sessions. For some of the sessions held in 1397 and 1398 full information is lacking because the manuscripts have been damaged. For sessions in the years between details are mostly wanting, although there is considerable evidence that sessions were held in these years. About the justices who sat the information varies. If the clerk listed several justices by name in the session heading, they probably sat. If he listed one name followed by *socij sui,* that justice if a local man may have sat. If he was the man named first on the commission, he may or may not have done so.

By a statute of 1362 the justices of the peace were required to sit four times a year, during the week of 6-13 January, during the second week of Lent, between Whitsunday and 24 June, and during the week of 29 September – 6 October. These sessions were presumably general sessions at which the justices did such business as trying offenders.[1] Only for 1387 is it known that four sessions of this type were held by the Oxfordshire justices of the peace.

Dates		*Place*	*Justices Present*	*Reference*
Statutory	Actual			
6-13 January	24 January	Burford	Sir Richard Abberbury; *socij sui*	Below p. 60
27 February-6 March	26 March	Banbury	Sir Richard Abberbury; Nicholas Somerton; *socij sui*	Below p. 62
26 May-24 June	29 July	Burford	?Lord John Lovell; *socij sui*	Below p. 63
29 September-6 October	19 September	Oxford	Sir Richard Abberbury; Sir Gilbert Wace; Thomas Barentyn; John Rede; Nicholas Somerton; *socij sui*	Below p. 65

There is no formal enrolment of the business done at the 29 July session,

[1] 36 Edward III, st.1, c. 12; Putnam, *Proceedings*, p. xcvi.

reference to it having been made in the reports of the proceedings which appear in connexion with the completion of business begun at the session of 26 March. It seems unlikely that Lord Lovell sat; he was probably named because his name led the list in the commission. While none of these sessions was held within a statutory period, the dates would suggest an intention to hold four sessions annually at regular intervals.

In 1397-1398 sessions at which the justices heard presentments and tried trespassers were held as follows:[2]

	Date	*Place*	*Justices Present*
1397	15 January		Sir William Wilicotes; John Rede; John Abberbury
	17 January		The same justices
	26 March		Sir William Wilicotes; Thomas Barentyn; John Rede
	2 May		Sir William Wilicotes; Thomas Barentyn; John Rede; John Abberbury
	3 May		Sir William Wilicotes; John Rede; John Abberbury
	Friday (Easter term) [torn]		Sir William Wilicotes; Thomas Barentyn; John Rede
	Wednesday (Trinity term) [torn]		Sir William Wilicotes; John Rede
	10 December	Oxford	Sir William Wilicotes; John Rede
	22 December	Witney	Sir William Wilicotes; John Hilton
1398	9 January		The same justices
	?15 February	Oxford	Sir William Wilicotes; Thomas Barentyn John Rede; John Hilton
	11 March	Henley	Thomas Barentyn; John Rede
	?9 April	Woodstock	Sir William Wilicotes; John Golafre; John Hilton
	15 April	Thame	Aforenamed justices: Thomas Barentyn; John Rede

The dates of two of these sessions, 15 February and 9 April are questioned because words are missing in the session headings due to damage to the roll. If the suggested date of 15 February for the session at Oxford is correct, it coincided with the delivery of Oxford Castle gaol on that date by the justices of the peace, Sir John Hill and fellows. If so it was probably part of a general session at which separate groups of justices

[2]The main source for this table is E101/582/45, a single membrane in the class entitled Sheriffs' Administrative Accounts. It contains an accounting by the sheriff, John Golafre, for 20-21 Richard II (1397-1398) preparatory to paying the wages of the Oxfordshire justices of the peace for ten sessions held in 1397 and January 1398. After the sum available, presumably from fines, is noted the sessions with the justices sitting at each are listed by law terms, three sessions in Hilary, Easter, and Michaelmas, and one in Trinity. It is assumed that at some if not all of these sessions the justices tried and convicted trespassers. The sessions held in January and May may have been general sessions. The two December sessions also appear on Roll B; that other sessions do not also appear there may be because no unfinished business remained from them or because a membrane once part of Roll B has been lost.

conducted different types of business. The gaol was delivered on Friday the morrow of the feast of St Valentine, 15 February.[3] The peace session was held on the Friday *proximo* . . . the feast of St Peter *ex cathedra,* 22 February, which in 1398 fell on a Friday. If the missing word after *proximo* is *ante,* the peace session was held on 15 February, the same day as the delivery of the gaol; if the word is *post,* on 1 March. Inasmuch as one of the offenders tried by the justices delivering the gaol was indicted at the peace session, the later cannot postdate the former and must have coincided with it. The session held at Woodstock has been dated, 9 April, because the missing word is assumed to be *pasche,* there not being space in the manuscript for a longer designation such as a saint's day. As the latest offence presented at the session was committed on 6 April and the roll was before the king's bench sitting at Oxford in Easter term 9 April is a reasonable date, the more so because at it were presented offenders accused of the riot at Bampton on 31 March.

That the Oxfordshire justices of the peace were busy during the years between 1387 and 1397 is amply attested although but two sessions can be dated. On 18 February 1390 and 14 April 1393 the justices of the peace sat at Oxford to deliver the castle gaol.[4] The presiding justice at one session was Sir Robert Cherlton; at the other he was Sir John Hill; associates were not named. Thomas Barentyn and John Rede sat at Oxford to hear indictments in February of a year that cannot be determined because of damage to the roll.[5] That Sir Richard Abberbury, Sir Robert Bardolf, Cherlton, Sir Thomas Paynell, Sir Thomas Poure, Sir Gilbert Wace, and Sir William Wilicotes probably presided at sessions at which presentments were made is indicated in the reports of indictments made to the justices of gaol delivery.[6] The name of one justice was given but no date or place of session. Those at which Cherlton presided may have been held in Oxford when he was there to deliver the castle gaol.

Entries on the Pipe Rolls show that during these years the Oxfordshire justices of the peace tried trespassers. Between 1386 and 1397 Sir Richard Abberbury, Barentyn, Poure, Rede, and Wilicotes accounted for approximately £200 in fines. The sum for 1386-1387 probably included the profits of the 1387 sessions at which fines are known to have been made by eight trespassers. As one half of the total amount was collected in the year 1389-1390, it may not represent all of the fines for these years.[7] Fines were also collected at some or all of the sessions held in 1397 and January 1398.

[3]Below pp. 152 ff.

[4]Below pp. 97, 124.

[5]Below p. 78.

[6]Below, index, *sub nomine.*

[7]Pipe Rolls, 14-19 and 21 Richard II, Berks, Nova Oblata; below p. 49.

Further and more specific evidence about the justices who sat during these years is available for two periods. The statute of Cambridge of 1388 provided that the justices of the peace should be paid 4*s*. a day for their service and their clerk, 2*s*.[8] Between 18 March 1393 and 31 March 1394 payment was made to four Oxfordshire justices for a total of twenty-one days: Poure for five, Barentyn for six, Rede for nine, and John Abberbury for one. The clerk, William Felmersham, was paid for nine days. The justices had sat at diverse places in the county.[9] During twenty-two months, 11 December 1394 through 3 October 1396, four justices were paid for a total of thirty-one days and the clerk for eleven. The justices were Wilicotes, nine days. Barentyn, seven, Rede, ten, and John Abberbury, five.[10] Whether the clerk attended all sessions so that in the first period nine were held and in the second, eleven, is not certain. From this evidence it would appear that the pattern of more than four sessions a year held in different towns in the county which is exhibited on the later peace roll and in the sheriff's accounting was one commonly followed by the Oxfordshire justices of the peace.

While this information is sketchy, if put together with what is certainly known, it shows that the Oxfordshire justices of the peace at the end of the fourteenth century were sitting fairly regularly at different places throughout the county to hear indictments and try offenders and that the work was done by the local men with some assistance from the justices of the central courts who were members of the commission. In the early years Sir Richard Abberbury seems to have been the responsible justice, Sir Thomas Poure in the middle years, and Sir William Wilicotes at the end of the period. The records do not show that Nicholas Somerton, named *custos rotulorum* in the 24 December 1390 commission, either presided at sessions or accounted for fines at the exchequer.

The Work of the Sessions

The major business undertaken by the justices of the peace at their sessions throughout the fourteenth century as later was the hearing of presentments of offenders made by local juries. That the Oxfordshire justices of the peace were actively engaged in this task is fully illustrated in the records in this volume. The entries on the later roll consist entirely of undetermined indictments. Those offenders tried before the justices of the peace in 1387 and by the justices of gaol delivery between 1389 and 1398 had been indicted before the justices of the peace.[11]

[8] 12 Richard II, c. 10.

[9] Pipe Roll, 17 Richard II, Berks, Nova Oblata.

[10] *Ibid.*, 19 Richard II, Berks, Nova Oblata. Indentures for these payments are in E101/582/44, mm. 1, 2

[11] Below Roll A., *passim;* Roll C, *passim.*

Another task performed by the justices was the trial of indicted offenders. This function is illustrated in detail on the earlier peace roll,[12] which because it was prepared with care also provides an excellent picture for the year covered of how the justices went about trying offenders and of how they worked with the sheriff and the justices of gaol delivery.

At the first session of the year, held on 24 January at Burford, twenty indicted felons were to be produced for trial by the sheriff, Thomas Barentyn, who was in this year a justice of the peace.[13] Barentyn reported that six of those summoned were in Oxford Castle gaol and that the remainder could not be found. He was ordered to produce the missing offenders at the next session to be held at Banbury on 26 March. It was noted that the justices of gaol delivery had acquitted four of the six in custody and sentenced the other two to be hanged. Barentyn was also ordered to produce eleven men indicted for unspecified trespasses; seven of these came and made fines; the remaining four were to appear at Banbury on 26 March.

At that session the four trespassers did not appear, nor did five others summoned because they had been indicted for violations of the labour legislation. A sixth so indicted came and made a fine. The sheriff was ordered to produce the nine delinquents but as the entry breaks off at this point whether he did is not known. Eleven of the fourteen felons who had not appeared at the January session again failed to come and the sheriff was instructed to investigate whether they possessed any chattels and to start outlawry proceedings in the county court against all except one who was reported to be in Oxford Castle gaol. They were, in any case, summoned to appear before the justices of the peace at their next session at Burford on 29 July. It was noted that at this session the sheriff reported that the outlawry of the nine men and the waiver of the one woman had been completed at the required five county courts held one in April, two in May, and one each in June and July. The eleventh offender, John Grenelef, who appeared and indicated he was ready to stand trial, was sent to prison in the custody of the sheriff. The coroners were notified of the outlawries and inquiry concerning chattels was continued. At this same 26 March session six other indicted felons were summoned; four failed to come and were ordered to appear at Burford on 29 July; the other two were reported to be in the castle gaol. Of the four who failed to come nothing further was recorded ; presumably if they did not appear they were outlawed. The two in gaol were probably tried by the justices of gaol delivery.

At the 19 September session at Oxford seven felons were tried.

[12]Above p. 12.

[13]Below Roll A, *passim*. Sheriffs were usually named in November and so served for most of the calendar year following that in which they were appointed.

Grenelef who had been imprisoned was brought before the justices. He pled not guilty but was convicted and sentenced to be hanged; he had no chattels. In view of his willingness to stand trial perhaps he expected acquittal. Six other felons indicted chiefly for theft and robbery one of whom had been reported as outlawed at the July session, were tried. They all pled not guilty but with one exception were convicted and sentenced to be hanged; none had any possessions. No other business was recorded for any of these sessions, perhaps because the roll for whatever reason it was prepared, was intended to be complete in itself so that no currently received indictments were entered on it. In any case at the four sessions of a single year the justices of the peace in Oxfordshire attempted to secure the appearance for trial of twenty-six felons of whom they tried and convicted six. They received fines from eight trespassers and tried to secure the appearance of nine others. Although their commission did not give them the power to try felons and common-law trespassers the justices made no effort to conceal the fact that they had done so with some success.

Other evidence that the justices tried offenders is provided by the fines they accounted for at the exchequer and by an occasional reference to trials. Some of those accused of involvement in the disorders at Oxford in 1389 were outlawed for failure to appear for trial before the justices of the peace.[14] Also, as has been noted, on 18 February 1390, 14 April 1393, and 15 February 1398, they acted as justices of gaol delivery and tried prisoners in Oxford Castle gaol.[15]

One other function of the justices of the peace is recorded on the gaol delivery roll.[16] It was their responsibility to hold inquests on those arrested on suspicion in accordance with a provision in the statute of Winchester. At such an inquest any one having evidence relating to the accusation was invited to appear and present it. If no one came and the justices had no other information they declared the suspect to be of good repute. This fact was reported to the justices of gaol delivery who then released him.

Juries

Only for juries that made presentments at the sessions held in 1397-1398 were the names of the jurors recorded. At these sessions twelve juries each composed of twelve men made presentments. The lists are so damaged and contain so few place designations that identification of juries with hundreds or villages cannot be made. What little duplication of personnel there was suggests that each jury represented a

[14]Below p. 111, no. 20.
[15]Below p. 97.
[16]Below p. 95.

local jurisdiction, either a hundred or a village. At a given session no jury made more than four recorded presentments; most of them made one or two. The jurors in one panel were not listed by name but only identified as the jurors from Wootton.[17] In the margin beside the names of jurors presenting at Henley, 11 March 1398, are the words *Oxon' xij*^{cim}[18]. Although this notation may indicate a grand jury representing the county, the lack of place name identifications for the jurors and the local character of the offences presented suggests otherwise. If similar notations were made beside the names of other juries they have been lost because of damage to the margins of the membranes. That a jury did not confine itself to the presentment of offences committed within the limits of the jurisdiction it represented is suggested by the fact that juries cannot be identified with jurisdictions by means of the places named in the cases they presented. At the session held at Thame on 15 April 1398 the single recorded presentment was made by the constable who presented a man for assaulting him and resisting arrest.[19]

The names of the jury presenting before the justices investigating felons and traitors in Oxford Castle gaol under the special commission of 5 February 1395 are listed. The fact that three of its members also presented at a peace session held at Oxford suggests the possibility that this jury may have been chosen from the county at large.[20]

Trial juries were used by the justices of the peace in 1387 and by the justices of gaol delivery but no names were enrolled. For gaol deliveries and the session of the special commission of 1395 the sheriff was instructed to summon twenty-four knights or freemen from the hundreds, boroughs, or towns from which the prisoners came.[21] The parties to the appeal before the justices of gaol delivery in 1394 approved the jurors selected to try the appeal as did offenders tried before the justices of the peace in 1387.[22]

The Clerk of the Peace

The clerk of the peace for Oxfordshire during part of the period covered by the peace records was William Felmersham who served the county from 1393-1407. His name does not appear on the later peace roll but since he was paid for serving twenty days between March 1393 and October 1396 he probably served at later sessions also.[23]

[17]Below p. 74.
[18]Below p. 76.
[19]Below p. 77, no. 15.
[20]Below p. 140, no. 53; John Archere, John Comptone, William atte Mulle.
[21]Below p. 140.
[22]Below pp. 65-70, nos. 6-10; p. 133, no. 47.
[23]Pipe Rolls, 17 and 19 Richard II, Berks, Nova Oblata; E. Stephens, *The Clerks of the Counties, 1360-1960* (1961), p. 145.

OFFENCES

The offences described in the records printed in this volume will be discussed under three headings: treason and quasi-treasonable offences, felonies, and trespasses. The first category includes crimes which were certainly treason and were so classified and others the classification of which is doubtful in spite of the use of the term *proditorie* in the indictment or their similarity to offences which were treasonable. It has already been pointed out that because the majority of the offenders in these records were tried before the justices of gaol delivery, the offences for which they had been indicted were felonies or treasons, not trespasses, so that few of the latter category appear.

Also it may be noted that because of the nature of some of the records and of some offences it is difficult to arrive at meaningful figures for the number of offences or for the number of indictments and to relate these figures to the number of offenders. Some of the previously indicted offenders who were summoned before the justices of the peace for trial were designated only as felons or trespassers, no description of their offences being given. Many of those tried had been indicted for several offences which were not always of the same kind. If several men were indicted for one offence, some of them might also be charged with other and different kinds of crimes. Lastly, for some of the serious crimes such as insurrections, the named offenders were said to have been joined by unspecified numbers of others or the distinction between principal and accessory was not clear. Thus one set of figures can be obtained for named offenders, another for offences, and a third for indictments, some of these being only approximations. An offence such as riot was serious because of its nature and the numbers involved, not because of frequency. Therefore, offences will be described and some indication given of how often they occurred, but totals will not in all cases be given; only for those summoned for or brought to trial are there meaningful figures.

Treason, quasi-treasonable offences, insurrection

There are in the records printed in this volume ten offences which were described as committed treasonably *proditorie* which resembled those described as treasonable, or which are generally recognized as such. These offences were counterfeiting the coinage, insurrection, arson, not at this date considered treason, and the murder of a husband by his wife which was a form of petty treason. Some of these indictments are not specific as to the nature of the offence. The justices of the peace or their clerk may have been uncertain of the exact nature of the offence and left final determination to the justices of gaol delivery or the king's bench. Although it is questionable whether at this date the justices of the peace had the power to handle any crime more serious than petty treason, they certainly did so.[1] While these cases are too few to permit definite conclusions on the subject of treason they do provide illustrations of what were considered treasonable offences and of the unrest prevalent at the end of the fourteenth century.

According to the statute of treasons of 1352 treason consisted in compassing the death of the king, his consort, or his eldest son; violating his consort, or eldest unmarried daughter, or the wife of his eldest son; levying war against the king in his realm, or adhering to his enemies in his realm, giving them aid and comfort in the realm or elsewhere; forging the great seal or the coinage, and knowingly importing or uttering false coin; slaying the treasurer, chancellor, or judges while sitting in court.[2] Distinct from these offences which were considered to constitute high treason was what came to be known as petty treason: the slaying of a master by his servant, a husband by his wife, and a prelate by a lesser cleric.[3] The scope of treason was extended in a statute passed in 1381 after the Peasants' Revolt by a provision that any one making riot or rumor was to be treated as a traitor to the king and his realm. Presumably it was this provision which was referred to in some indictments by the phrase, *insurgendo de nouo.*[4] The penalty for treason was drawing to the place of execution, hanging, forfeiture of goods to the king, and disinheritance of heirs. A woman guilty of petty treason was sentenced to be burned.[5]

Holdsworth citing Hale and Coke has said that any indictment for treason contained the words *proditorie* and *contra ligeantiae suae debitum.*[6] That this rule was not strictly followed at the end of the fourteenth century is shown in the three cases of counterfeiting the coinage. Only in one indictment was the phrase used. Yet this offender and one other were punished for treason, being sentenced to drawing and hanging. The use of the term *proditorie* in indictments for offences such as arson which were probably not treasonable may reflect a fear of violence due to the unsettled state of the country. Only if an offender was

[1]Putnam, *Proceedings,* p. cxiv; see also J. G. Bellamy, *The Law of Treason in England in the Later Middle Ages* (Cambridge Studies in English Legal History, Cambridge, 1970), p. 138.

[2]25 Edward III, st. 5; see also Bellamy, *passim;* Putnam, *Proceedings,* pp. cl ff.

[3]25 Edward III, st. 5; Bellamy, pp. 225 ff.

[4]5 Richard II, st. 1, c. 6; Bellamy, pp. 105-106; below pp. 73-4, 76, nos. 4, 6, 11; pp. 83-4, 86. nos. 1, 6, 11, 12; p. 124, no. 32. The statute of 1397, 21 Richard II, c. 3, which further defined treason appears to have been directed against the baronage; Bellamy, p. 208.

[5]*Ibid.*, p. 226; below pp. 71, 152.

[6]W. S. Holdsworth, *A History of English Law,* iii (5th edition, London, 1942), pp. 287-293.

found guilty and sentenced to drawing as well as hanging is there a clue to the thinking of the justices and so certainty as to whether the crime was treason or only felony.

Counterfeiting the coinage. Although the justices of the peace were not given the power to inquire into cases of counterfeiting until the reign of Henry IV, there are three indictments for this offence in the records printed below.[7] In one case the offence was described as feloniously and treasonably making false money, namely farthings of copper to look like gold, groats of pewter to look like silver to the amount of £40. The offender was said to be a common thief and guilty of felony; he was sentenced to be drawn and hanged (Roll C, no. 1). Six men were indicted because *felonice et proditorie ut proditores et felones domini regis contra ligeanciam suam controfecerunt cuneam domini regis.* They had used pewter mixed with lead and alchemy to make groats, pennies, halfpennies, and farthings, and passed them off as true money.[8] One of these men was judged guilty of treason and sentenced to be drawn and hanged (Roll C, no. 53). In the third case the offence was making groats of alchemy and other metals feloniously and traitorously and the offender was called a common counterfeitor. He was acquitted of treason and felony by the king's bench (Roll B, no. 16).[9]

Petty treason. There are in these records two instances of what was probably petty treason although in one the facts are somewhat confused because in two separate indictments the responsibility for the murder was allotted differently. A man was indicted before the justices of the peace for homicide, the wife of the victim being named as an accessory (Roll B, no. 1). The justices of gaol delivery sentenced him to be hanged (Roll C, no. 73); the king's bench delivering Oxford Castle gaol sentenced her to be burned. She was also presented before the king's bench by the hundred juries as a principal in the murder of the husband and she was summoned for trial and waived for non-appearance before the bench whether as a principal or an accessory is not clear. In the second instance the man was indicted before the justices of the peace and tried before the king's bench which sentenced him to be hanged (Roll B, no. 3). The wife of the victim who was not mentioned in the indictment of the man was separately indicted for killing her husband with the aid of the man; she

[7] Putnam, *Proceedings,* pp. 415, 416; Sillem, 'Commissions of the Peace', *B.I.H.R.,* x. 93, n. 3, 95; Bellamy, p. 208.

[8] *Alchemy* was a white alloy, based on copper and containing tin and significant amounts of arsenic, too brittle to be shaped except by casting. It was used for spoons, buttons, and the like, and for counterfeiting silver coins. I am indebted to Professor C. S. Smith of the Massachusetts Institute of Technology for this information.

[9] For classification of counterfeiting as felony see Bellamy, pp. 85, 93; Putnam, *Proceedings*, pp. cli, 416 ff.

was sentenced by the justices of gaol delivery to be burned (Roll C, no. 72). No mention was made in the records of the special character of these offences but the penalty imposed on the women was the penalty for petty treason.

Arson. Although as has been said arson was not at this date a treasonable offence it has been included in this category because in an indictment the accused was said to have feloniously and treasonably set fire to a house and feloniously and treasonably burned forty-nine sheep and feloniously stolen 271 others. In spite of the wording of the indictment the justices of gaol delivery did not consider the offence treason and sentenced the accused to hang as a felon (Roll C, no. 50). The use of the adverb *proditorie* in the indictment is interesting in view of the request made by the commons in 1429 that arson be considered a form of treason.[10] In another case in which arson followed homicide no mention was made of treason and the penalty was again hanging (Roll C, no. 23).

Insurrection. The four instances of insurrection, although they differed in their seriousness, may be considered together if only to emphasize that the line between what constituted treason and what did not was a fine one. Of the four, one was considered treasonable, two felonious, and one a trespass.

The insurrection that without question was treasonable was the work of men from several towns, chiefly in Bampton and Wootton hundreds in the western part of Oxfordshire, who converged on the village of Bampton on the night of Palm Sunday, 31 March 1398. Because the rising seems to have been serious and because it is well documented, it will be considered in some detail. Three presentments of men involved were made before the justices of the peace for Oxfordshire at a session held at Woodstock probably on 9 April 1398.[11] Presentments were also made before the king's bench sitting at Oxford in Easter term 1398 by a grand jury for the county and by juries from Bampton, Wootton, and Chadlington hundreds, and a jury from the village of Witney. Trials of some of those accused were held before the bench at this and subsequent sessions. Thus accounts of the rising appear on the later peace roll, in the file of presentments made before the bench, and on the bench rolls. These accounts vary as to detail and in the men named as responsible. In the three indictments before the justices of the peace ten, nine, and six men were listed by name. Additional names provided by other presentments and by the list of those summoned before the king's bench bring the total to thirty.[12] The number of unknown men from various

[10] *Ibid.*, p. cli; Bellamy, p. 131.

[11] Below Roll B, nos. 4, 6, 11, Appendix; Bellamy, pp. 106-107. In n. 5, p. 208, he wrongly identifies Ropere as Pope.

[12] K. B. 27/548, Rex, m. 19.

towns who were reported as participating was given as approximately sixty, one hundred, and two hundred. In the indictments before the justices of the peace no one was singled out as leader. In the grand jury presentment and in some of the trial accounts Henry Ropere was so named ; in other accounts, Gilbert Vaughan, Thomas Gildesowe, John Milford, and John Bedemansone.

In the indictments before the justices of the peace the insurgents were accused of having banded together in warlike array to choose leaders and of having risen, *insurgendo nouo proditorie,* against the king and his peace thus violating their allegiance; they had also sought to kill certain men who refused to join them, shouting; *aryseth aryseth alle men et goth wyth us et ho so wilnot gou wiht us he schal be ded.* One of the men mentioned by name as threatened by the rioters was a constable who was perhaps trying to keep the peace. The account in the grand jury presentment which is repeated in the record of the trial of John Milford adds further details. The insurgents were said to have feloniously, treasonably, and against their allegiance conspired to kill the king and destroy the law and the magnates. About two hundred men, in addition to six named in the indictment had assembled at Cokethorpe near Cogges in Bampton hundred. They had chosen Gilbert Vaughan as leader and given him a pair of gold spurs as a symbol of authority. He had led the group to Yelford, Aston, and finally to Bampton. There Henry Ropere of Bampton, holding in one hand lighted candles and in the other a battle-axe, had led the insurgents through the town shouting their slogan and threatening those who would not join them. By common consent Ropere had been chosen to seek out the king and the government at Bristol and Gloucester and on the Monday and Tuesday following Palm Sunday he had gone to Burford and elsewhere to seek support. The other accounts add little except the names of other leaders, approximate numbers of men from various localities, and the mention of Ducklington Wood and unidentified towns in Berkshire as places involved in the uprising. Piecing together the information from these accounts it would appear that bands of men from various towns under their own leaders converged on Bampton on the night of Palm Sunday 1398 and that Henry Ropere either assumed or was chosen leader. Whether the insurgents did anything more than shout their slogan and molest those who would not join them is not apparent. The king was in Gloucestershire following the dissolution of the parliament at Shrewsbury but it seems unlikely that Ropere went there as he was in Oxford Castle gaol when the king's bench arrived in Oxford in late April or early May.[13]

In none of the accounts were any reasons for the uprising given. None of the insurgents appears to have been prominent in either the county or

[13]Below p. 84.

his community, although some of them had property that was forfeited to the king because of their treason.[14] A few were identified in the presentments by occupation: weaver, slater, souter, charcoal maker; in other words, they were small village craftsmen. One was a bailiff of an estate; the clerks named in the indictment made by the Bampton hundred jury may have been followers of Wycliff or men who shared or supported whatever grievances their fellow townsmen had.

What immediate measures were taken, if any, beyond the imprisonment of Ropere and a few others, is not known. It would appear that the rising did not receive sufficient support to make necessary action other than that taken in the courts. That the king's bench visited Oxford during Easter term may have been a consequence of the rising. On the other hand, the grant of the forfeited goods of seven of the men involved which was made on 12 April 1398 would indicate prompt action by some jurisdiction which is not named. As to what happened to the men named in the indictments positive information is scanty. Ropere, after being acquitted at the delivery of Oxford Castle gaol by the bench was sentenced in the same term to be drawn, hanged, decapitated, and quartered, and instructions were given to send the parts to Reading, Colchester, Norwich, Northampton, and Coventry as an example to other traitors.[15] At the same session John Redeman was acquitted and at a later one, Philip Webbe was sentenced to be drawn and hanged. At least six others appeared before the bench for trial at subsequent sessions. Three of these produced pardons; what happened to the other three is not known. Others who had been indicted were pardoned. As has been said seven, including two later pardoned, had their property forfeited; another escaped from gaol. Presumably the remainder or at least those who failed to answer the summons for appearance were outlawed.[16]

A serious insurrection whose instigators were described as acting feloniously, not treasonably, took place in the town of Oxford on Thursday, Friday, and Saturday in the fourth week of Lent, 25-27 March 1389. It was an episode in the running feud between Northerners and Southerners which disturbed the university during much of the medieval period.[17] The attack was made on Welshmen, who with Irishmen were

[14] *C. P. R.* 1396-1399, p. 382.

[15] K. B. 27/548, Rex, mm. 9, 22d.

[16] For a summary of the process on those indicted see below Roll B, Appendix II.

[17] A. B. Emden, 'Northerners and Southerners in the Organization of the University to 1509,' in *Oxford Studies presented to Daniel Callus*, ed. by R. W. Southern (O.H.S., n. s., xvi, 1964), pp. 1-30, esp. pp. 1-16; R. W. Hays, 'Welsh Students at Oxford and Cambridge in the Middle Ages', *Welsh History Review*, iv (1968-9), esp. pp. 334-5 and Appendix (a list of Welsh Students at Oxford). Beginning in 1364 and continuing through the fifteenth century, justices of the peace were appointed for the town of Oxford as well as for the county. The chancellor of the university was named to the town commission; in some fourteenth-century commissions he was ordered not to sit when felons were to be indicted or tried; in all commissions the privileges of the university were to be respected. From

considered Southerners, by various men known and unknown. Having chosen leaders they ran armed through the streets shooting arrows and shouting: *ware ware ware sle sle sle the Walshe dogges and al here helpes and ho so lokes out of his hous he sal be ded.* Welshmen were forced to the town gates where they were subjected to various indignities; several halls and inns were entered, and weapons, clothes, and books were taken from a principal and at least eight scholars. Four men were killed, one a Welshman, another by a Welshman.[18]

In all seventeen men were in Oxford Castle gaol having been indicted before the justices of the peace as principals and accessories and thirty-three others were reported to have been outlawed for failure to appear before the justices of the peace. Trials of the seventeen were held, on 18 February 1390 before Sir John Hill and associate justices of the peace delivering the gaol (Roll C, no. 7), and on 15 July 1390 (Roll C, no. 14) and 20 February 1391 (Roll C, no. 20) before Sir Robert Cherlton and Hill, justices of gaol delivery. The ten who had been indicted as principals were acquitted and so perforce were the seven accessories. Two of those outlawed were later pardoned, one for diverse insurrections, felonies, and trespasses committed during this riot.[19] It is clear that some of those indicted for participation in the riot were not members of the Northern faction. As has been noted one charged with homicide was a Welshman. Among the accessories was Adam Usk, a well known Welshman. Among the thirty-three outlawed was one identified as a Welshman and three Irishmen; others have names that may have been Welsh. Some may have been townsmen.[20] It is probable that the authorities in putting down the riot gathered in both Northerners and those who were resisting attack. Others beside Usk came to hold important positions. Robert Alynton became chancellor of the university in 1393 and John Alkebarwe, bursar of University College.[21]

December 1381, when outstanding commissions for urban jurisdictions were suspended, until September 1390, the town of Oxford was without its own peace commission. Consequently cases involving both the town and the university came before the county justices. The chancellor's court received jurisdiction over felonies in 1406; Kimball, *Warws.*, pp. lxxxvi, xxvi ff.; W. A. Pantin, *Oxford Life in Oxford Archives* (Oxford, 1972), chapters v, vi, esp. pp. 59, 72. For the Oxford town peace commission of 15 March 1391 see *Mediaeval Archives of the University of Oxford*, ii, ed. by H. E. Salter (O. H. S., lxxiii, 1921), 16-19.

[18] *Records of Mediaeval Oxford, Coroners' Inquests, etc.*, ed. by H. E. Salter (Oxford, 1912), p. 48.

[19] Below Roll C, no. 20.

[20] Below Roll C, no. 7. William Gymel may have been the same William Gymel who acted as a pledge before the justices of the peace for the town of Oxford: *Mediaeval Archives of the University of Oxford*, ii. 5.

[21] A. B. Emden, *A Biographical Register of the University of Oxford to A. D. 1500,* 3 vols. (Oxford, 1957-1959), *sub nomine*.

A third case of insurrection seems to have been considered by the justices of the peace who received the indictment and by the justices of gaol delivery who tried the offenders as a trespass, not a felony (Roll C, no. 29). Two men assembled approximately two hundred others from Warwickshire, not feloniously but against the king's peace. After announcing that no one might withdraw from the group under threat of a fine and mutilation, they had with the cattle of the village of Showell trampled the fields and herbage of a resident and burned his fuel; they had also sought to kill his servants; and they had harrassed the countryside and supported false claims. The offence sounds more like a private feud than an insurrection in spite of the size of the force assembled. As the accused were acquitted no penalty was imposed.[22]

It is the classification of the fourth case of possible insurrection that presents problems. Three men with others unknown were indicted because they had banded together and being armed risen, *de nouo insurrerunt,* not against the king but to kill the abbot of Rewley who only escaped by fleeing to one of his manors. They broke into the abbot's close *contra inhibicionem domini regis. Arraiati de nouo insurgente*, they assaulted a servant of the abbot, beat him, and stole a horse; they were reported to be common insurgents against the peace (Roll C, no. 32). The offence sounds like an example of maintenance, perhaps made felonious by the theft of the horse.[23] The significance of the royal prohibition is not clear unless it had to do with the position of the abbey as a royal foundation. Use of the phrases referring to the new treason suggests that the justices of the peace who heard the indictment considered the offence to be treason according to the statute of 1381. The justices of gaol delivery, led by Sir Robert Cherlton, seem not to have accepted this classification and the accused were acquitted of felony.

From the evidence of these four cases, admittedly too few to be conclusive, it would seem that even after the added definition of treason in 1381, there was considerable uncertainty as to what constituted treason. Men had not necessarily committed treason because they were armed and operated as a group.

Breach of prison At this point it may be well to consider an indictment for breach of prison (Roll C, no. 54).[24] The penalty for this offence was the penalty for the offence for which an accused was imprisoned, in this

[22]Miss Susan Reynolds has suggested that this disturbance may have been an anti-enclosure riot as Showell became a depopulated village between 1334 and 1377 (K. J. Allison, M. W. Beresford, J. G. Hurst *et al., The Deserted Villages of Oxon*. (Leicester, 1965), pp. 44, 1-29, esp. 7).

[23]P. H. Wingfield, *The History of Conspiracy and Abuse of Legal Procedure* (C.S.E.L.H., Cambridge, 1921), *passim*.

[24]See Pugh, *op. cit.*, chapter x.

instance treason and felony. The case is a complicated one. Three men involved in the attempted escape from Oxford Castle gaol included two of five who had been returned to prison pending release to the bishop of Lincoln as convicted clerks. The five with a sixth, a layman and one of the three to break prison, were indicted for counterfeiting before the special commission appointed to deal with felons and traitors in the castle gaol. Some of the men had one or more aliases and one of them the same name as another man involved in the break. The case is of interest in that the terms, *burgaria* and *burgare,* were used not to describe a breaking in to steal goods but a breaking out of one part of the castle, the gaol, into another. The circumstances of the break were these. The three men forced four other prisoners to flee from the gaol to the castle chapel, presumably to seek sanctuary though the term was not used. Three of the latter returned to the prison voluntarily leaving four men in the chapel. Two of these left to relieve themselves and were taken by officials and returned to the gaol. Thereupon certain men unknown to the jurors broke into the chapel and released the two still there. Upon the hue and cry being raised the two were brought back to prison; the unknowns escaped. A trial of the original six for counterfeiting and breach of prison resulted in the conviction of one man for counterfeiting and breach of prison, *burgaria,* and of two others for breach of prison only. The three not involved in the prison break were acquitted of counterfeiting, e. g. of treason. The counterfeitor was sentenced to drawing and hanging; the other five were returned to prison because the justices of the special commission wished more information. Thus no penalty was imposed on those guilty only of gaol break. Presumably they eventually were released to the bishop.

Felonies

The remaining offences of a serious nature were without doubt felonious and may be considered under the common categories within that general classification. The greater number of felonies were thefts or robberies.

Homicide. Excluding the four deaths reported in connexion with the Oxford University riot for which there were no separate indictments and the two instances of petty treason, nine men were indicted for seven killings at the peace sessions reported in this volume. Five of the killings were described as homicides by the phrase *felonice interfecit* (Roll C, nos. 23, 40, 55, 76). The others including the instances of petty treason as murder, *felonice interfecit et murdrauit* or *interfecit et murdrauit* (Roll B, nos. 1, 3, 7, 18). These latter indictments were received at the 1397-1398 sessions of the peace which were held during the period when the verb *murdrare* was used in indictments as a result of the statute of 1390 which attempted to limit the king's power to grant pardons for the more heinous forms of culpable homicide.[25]

Rape. Five indictments for rape involved seven offenders who were accused of raping or attempting to rape six women. Two of the women were also abducted, one with goods valued at 40*s*.

Larceny. The indictments for grand larceny included over fifty different thefts. A number of these were preceded by entry, usually forcible, *felonice fregit,* of a house, a chamber, a church, a close, a mill, a sheepfold. The theft was described by the phrase *felonice furatus fuit:* as has been said the verb *burgare* was not used.

There was one instance of petty larceny, the theft of goods valued at less than 12*d.* for which the penalty was a fine instead of hanging. In this instance forcible entry was followed by the theft of four bushels of peas valued at 10*d.*

Robbery. Robbery as distinct from larceny involved some form of bodily injury inflicted on the victim in addition to the theft of his goods. The offence was described by the phrase *felonice depredauit* or *felonice despoliauit* and the attack if specified as an assault. The nature of the injury was usually not mentioned, the emphasis being on what was taken, not how it was taken.

Numerous offenders whether or not their offence was larceny or robbery were described as common thieves.

Accessories. As accessory to a felony was one who had aided and abetted in the commission of a crime or had knowingly received a principal after he had committed a crime. In two instances accessories were indicted independently of the principals. In one, two men were accused of receiving the son of one and his companion who had already been tried and sentenced to be hanged for a series of thefts (Roll C, no. 4). In the second, the accessory was accused of aiding a felon who had broken out of the Bocardo, the Oxford town gaol (Roll C, no. 57). Other accessories were accused of assisting thieves to gain entry to a house, of receiving felons and stolen goods, and of aiding in the Oxford University riot. An accessory could not be tried until the principal had been tried; he was released if the principal was acquitted or outlawed.

[25] J. M. Kaye, 'The Early History of Murder and Manslaughter,' part 1, *Law Quarterly Review*, lxxxiii (1967), pp. 365-395.

Trespasses

The trespasses described in these records were few in number, there being none described on the 1387 peace roll and but one on the gaol delivery roll, already discussed as an insurrection. The indictments of ten men for trespasses were recorded at the 1397-1398 sessions; only two of them for common-law trespasses. One man was accused of assault followed by resistance to arrest by a constable who himself made the presentment (Roll B, no. 15); another was indicted for general lawlessness, night-walking, and disturbing the peace (Roll B, no. 8). The remainder were charged with violations of the labour laws or other economic regulations. Because the roll is either illegible or damaged, details are lacking. Four men who operated barges on the Thames at Henley were indicted for overcharging, having taken 14*d.*, an excess of 8*d.* per barrel (Roll B, nos. 13, 14). Three men who sold defective tiles may also have overcharged for the tiles (Roll B, no. 12). One man had hunted without having the required 40*s.* property qualification and had kept hunting dogs contrary to the statute (Roll B, no 10).[26]

[26]13 Richard II, st. 1, c. 13.

THE RELATIONSHIPS AMONG JURISDICTIONS AND THE PUNISHMENT OF OFFENDERS

In England at the end of the fourteenth century the punishment of criminals was primarily the responsibility of three agencies, the court of king's bench, the justices of gaol delivery, and the justices of the peace. The work of two of these, the justices of the peace and the justices of gaol delivery, is directly shown in the records in this volume. Also shown is how the justices of the peace worked in conjunction with both the justices of gaol delivery and the king's bench.

When the king's bench came into a county, as it came to Oxfordshire during Easter term 1398, lesser jurisdictions including the justices of the peace ceased to function.[1] The bench while at Oxford heard presentments of offenders made by juries from hundreds and villages and a grand jury of the county and it summoned for trial those offenders and others previously indicted before the justices of the peace and other local courts.[2] In subsequent terms it continued to summon those who had not appeared and try those who did.[3] It also when in Oxford delivered the castle gaol.[4] Thus it was that the king's bench had before it the later Oxfordshire peace roll which as has been suggested was probably prepared for this visit.

The relationship between the justices of the peace and the justices of gaol delivery was somewhat different in that the two groups worked together closely and continuously. There was an overlapping of personnel as the justices of the central courts appointed to the gaol delivery commissions were also justices of the peace and local men were named to both commissions. The justices of gaol delivery came to the county fairly regularly and their visits did not interrupt the work of the justices of the peace. Also the latter sometimes delivered the gaol, the records of these sessions being included in the gaol delivery roll probably because the presiding justice was one of the regularly assigned justices of gaol delivery. Examples of co-operation between the two sets of justices are numerous. The justices of the peace at their 1387 sessions were informed that some offenders they had summoned for trial had already been tried by the justices of gaol delivery or were in gaol awaiting trial.[5] Many of those in gaol had been indicted before the justices of the peace,

[1]Putnam, *Proceedings,* pp. lxiv ff.

[2]K. B. 27/548, Rex, *passim;* K. B. 9/100, *passim.*

[3]E. g., K. B. 27/550, Rex, m. 23; 551, Rex, mm. 1d., 5; 556, Rex, m. 7d.

[4]K. B. 27/548, Rex, m. 9.

[5]Below p. 60. On gaol delivery in the 14th century see Pugh, *op. cit.*, pp. 278-94, 304-313.

some having been committed to gaol by these justices.[6] Indictments of gaoled offenders were sent to the justices of gaol delivery by the justices of the peace and if further information was needed offenders were returned to prison pending consultation with the justices of the peace.[7]

Unlike the justices delivering a gaol who dealt with offenders already awaiting trial, the justices of the peace and the king's bench had the difficult task of securing the appearance those accused who were still at large. This these courts attempted to do by the process of outlawry which was proclaimed in the county court. An offender who failed to answer the summons to appear at five successive county courts was declared an outlaw, or, if a woman, was waived. Since many offenders did not appear for trial and were outlawed or presumably outlawed, the effectiveness of the process as a means of compelling court appearance may be questioned. On the other hand, the fact that some went to the trouble of having outlawry reversed or declared erroneous suggests there may have been some force in the penalty, although it is doubtful that many left the country.[8]

The key man in the relationship among the courts was the sheriff. Five times during the sessions of the peace and of gaol delivery held between 1387 and 1398 the sheriff of Oxfordshire and Berkshire was also named justice of the peace for Oxfordshire : Thomas Barentyn appointed sheriff in 1386 and 1394, Sir Gilbert Wace in 1387, Sir William Wilicotes in 1392, and John Golafre in 1397.[9] It was the sheriff who was responsible for summoning offenders for trial, for presenting those who did appear, for investigating whether those convicted had any possessions and if so what these were worth; and for initiating outlawries in the county court and reporting the results to the justices of the peace. He was also charged by the crown with the responsibility for scheduling sessions of the peace and deliveries of the gaol on days set by the justices. It was his duty to summon juries. He was also in charge of the castle gaol and of the prisoners there and he was fined for their escape as was Thomas Barentyn in 1395.[10] Although some of this work was delegated, the responsibility remained with the sheriff.

There is considerable information about the adjudged guilt or innocence of offenders indicted before the Oxfordshire justices of the peace who were tried or summoned for trial by all three of these jurisdictions. Since the information is not available for periods of comparable length or for equal numbers of accused, a comparative study

6Below p. 141. no. 54.

7*Ibid*.

8K. B. 27/551, Rex, m. 5. On outlawry see R. F. Hunnissett, *The Medieval Coroner* (C.S.E.L.H., Cambridge, 1961), pp. 61 ff.

9Above pp. 27, 29.

10*C. P. R.* 1391-1396, p. 565.

of the effectiveness of the three jurisdictions in punishing criminals is not possible. Rather it seems more useful to summarize the results of trials before each court and to make such comments as seem relevant.

As has been pointed out for the years covered by the recorded indictments there are few indictments for trespass compared with those for felony and treason. The only two trespassers who appeared before the justices of gaol delivery for trial were acquitted. Of the seventeen summoned before the justices of the peace at their 1387 sessions, eight made fines. The other nine were presumably outlawed if they failed to answer further summons.[11] Nine of the eleven trespassers indicted at the 1397-1398 sessions made fines before the king's bench at Oxford in Easter term 1398 or subsequently. One was presumably outlawed for failure to appear and one was not summoned. Thus of thirty trespassers, two were acquitted and seventeen made fines ; about the others there is no certain information.

In all thirty-two felons were tried by the justices of the peace, seven at the session held on 19 September 1387 and twenty-five at the three sessions at which the justices of the peace delivered Oxford Castle gaol. Six of the seven were convicted; the other, acquitted. Acting as justices of gaol delivery the justices of the peace acquitted twenty and convicted five. Of these latter one was a woman sentenced to be burned for the killing of her husband. Forty-three others were reported as outlawed or, in the case of a woman, waived for failure to appear before the justices of the peace for trial.[12] Of five others who did not appear on the first summons, one secured a pardon; for the others no further process was reported.

The king's bench when it sat at Oxford in 1398 attempted to deal with forty-three persons who had been indicted for felony before the Oxfordshire justices of the peace or in the case of the Bampton rioters for treason. It acquitted one man of the charge of counterfeiting and another of larceny; it sentenced two men indicted for murder and a woman indicted for killing her husband.[13] The trial of another man was unfinished because the sheriff failed to produce the proper writ. Of eleven others whose outlawry the sheriff was instructed to begin in the county court, two were pardoned and the others presumably outlawed. Two accessories were repeatedly summoned and postponed pending the trial of the principals. Of the twenty-five rioters indicted before the

[11]The enrolment breaks off at this point. One of the trespassers, John Loveney, who was also listed among the indicted felons has been counted as a trespasser as his name was dropped from the list of felons with no indication that he had been acquitted or sentenced.

[12]This figure includes thirty-three reported as outlawed for failure to appear for trial before the justices of the peace in connexion with the Oxford University riot; two were subsequently pardoned.

[13]The woman was also summoned as an accessory.

justices of the peace and summoned before the bench, one was acquitted when the bench delivered the castle gaol. Ropere, also acquitted at this delivery, was convicted as has been noted. The remaining twenty-three were ordered outlawed for non-appearance. Of these five eventually appeared ; two were released on producing pardons as was another whose outlawry was pronounced erroneous. For two others no final trial record has been found. The rest were presumably outlawed including one who escaped from prison.

As has been said the justices of gaol delivery did not have to summon accused for trial. They had only to order the sheriff to bring the offender from the gaol. At the eleven recorded gaol delivery sessions held between 1389 and 1398 sixty-five accused were tried, the enrolment of the record of the trial of one other having been unfinished. Of these, forty-one were acquitted and fifteen convicted. Four convicted as criminous clerks were ordered turned over to the bishop of Lincoln. Five other men who had proved their clergy were returned to gaol pending further information on their offences. During these years twenty men who had been imprisoned on suspicion of larceny or unspecified felony having been found by the justices of the peace to be of good repute were released at the gaol delivery sessions. Four other men were reported to the justices of the peace to have been acquitted by the justices of gaol delivery and two convicted.

The special commission appointed to deal with traitors and felons in Oxford Castle gaol sitting on 19 February 1395 received indictments on six men, five of them being the convicted clerks returned to gaol by the justices of gaol delivery. They were again returned to gaol and the sixth man, a layman, was convicted.

In considering these figures it should be remembered that the trials before the justices of gaol delivery and the justices of the peace acting in that capacity were held over a period of nine years, whereas the recorded trials before the justices of the peace as justices of the peace were held at one session. Similarly the king's bench was dealing with offenders summoned before it in a single term, although a few offenders appeared at later sessions. That the justices of the peace at that one session convicted six and acquitted but one is an interesting figure since it is unusual for convictions to exceed acquittals. The fact that overall convictions were approximately half as numerous as acquittals may be due to the fact that the majority of those tried were in gaol. Certainly the figures are higher than those often found. The number on whom outlawry was pronounced or ordered is large because of the thirty-three reported at one of the trials of the Oxford University rioters.

The matter of conviction may also be considered from the point of view of the seriousness of the crime. Of those accused of treason in the

Bampton riot only two, Henry Ropere and Philip Webbe, who was not indicted before the justices of the peace, are known to have been sentenced to a traitor's death. Two of the men accused of counterfeiting were similarly sentenced. The two men and the two women convicted of what seems on the women's part to have been petty treason were sentenced to hanging and burning respectively. One man accused of homicide, two of homicide and arson, one of theft and arson, and another of theft and threats to kill were all convicted. The remaining seventeen who were found guilty had committed thefts or robberies, some of which followed forcible entry. In some, although by no means all, of the cases the goods taken were of considerable value. Conclusions from this information are dangerous since the reasons for a jury's decision are not given and modern ideas of serious crime may differ from those of the middle ages. It does, however, seem reasonable to say that at least the majority of those convicted had committed serious crimes. Whether some of those acquitted had also done so is another matter.[14]

A number of those involved in felonies were considered accessories, not principals. There seems to have been a certain amount of confusion among and within jurisdictions about the status of offenders if principal and accessory were not tried at the same time. The king's bench continued to summon as a principal a woman who had been convicted as a principal in the death of her husband. In another case it summoned an accessory after one principal had been acquitted and another pardoned. Similarly accessories continued to be summoned although principals had not been tried. In other instances communication was better. The justices of gaol delivery acquitted two men charged as accessories after receiving information about the conviction of the principals. In one of the trials of those accused in the Oxford University riot a principal and seven accessories were tried together, and on the acquittal of the principal the accessories were immediately released.

Something may be said of the convicted clerks.[15] In all nine men sought benefit of clergy. Four of these entered such a plea at the beginning of their trials, at which point the ordinary of the bishop of Lincoln was summoned and the accused required to prove his clergy. On the plea

[14]Mr. T. A Green has analysed convictions for murder and acquittals for simple homicide as evidence of societal attitudes which were at variance with the law, there being no legal distinction between murder and manslaughter until the sixteenth century; T. A. Green, 'Societal Concepts of Criminal Liability for Homicide in Mediaeval England,' *Speculum*, xlvii (1972), 669-694. Although the verb *murdrare* was not used in all the indictments before the Oxfordshire justices of the peace in which the accused was convicted, those who were judged guilty had committed such serious crimes as petty treason and homicide followed by arson.

[15]On benefit of clergy see Leona Gabel, *Benefit of Clergy in England in the Later Middle Ages.* (Smith College Studies in History, xiv, nos 1–4, 1928–9), esp. chapter ii.

being successful but before the offender was released to the bishop's official, the court requested the jury to give an opinion on the man's guilt or innocence. All four were judged to be guilty and were turned over to the ordinary as convicted clerks for imprisonment in the bishop's gaol at Banbury. The other five did not plead clergy until after they had been convicted of the thefts for which they had been appealed. They were judged to be clerks but instead of being released to the bishop's official were returned to prison. In their indictment and trial for another offence before the special commission no mention was made of their status as convicted clerks. In the initial indictments none of the men who pled clergy immediately, and but one of those who pled it after conviction, was designated by a clerical title. Other men so described did not seek benefit of clergy and were in all cases acquitted. Similarly only one of those accused in the Oxford University riot was described in the indictment as a clerk; none of the accused pled clergy and all were acquitted.

The chattels of convicted felons were forfeited to the crown so it was the responsibility of the sheriff to secure information of this sort. Most of those convicted were reported to be without property but six laymen did have goods ranging in value from 3*s.* 4*d.* to 56*s.*, the joint worth of two men. Three of the convicted clerks had possessions valued from 12*d.* to two marks.

Among the felons there were only a few cases of men accused of at least one subsequent offence. Two men who in February 1391 were acquitted of breaking into and robbing the church of St Mary in Oxford were again in April 1393 acquitted of stealing from a man in the church at Chipping Norton (Roll C, nos. 28, 39). Although the two offences were committed within three days of each other, the men seem to have been gaoled a second time for the later one. Another man acquitted of robbery by the justices of the peace in September 1387 was convicted for another offence (Roll A, no. 8). A third man either led a charmed life or his name is too common to make identification certain. One John Brown of Ireland was in 1387 sentenced by the justices of the peace to be hanged for a series of thefts committed with another man. A John Brown of Ireland was sentenced to be hanged by the justices of gaol delivery for a series of similar offences and in November 1399 John Brown, alias John Brown of Ireland, received a pardon.[16] Two men who were in July 1390 acquitted by the justices of gaol delivery for a theft committed at Shirburn in August 1390 were in February 1391 sentenced by the same justices for another theft at Shirburn in May 1390 and a planned homicide in Buckinghamshire (Roll C, nos. 12, 16).

[16]Below, index, *sub nomine*.

ECONOMIC AND SOCIAL MATERIAL IN THE INDICTMENTS BEFORE THE JUSTICES OF THE PEACE

Fourteenth-century Oxfordshire, like most of medieval England, was predominantly agricultural. It had, however, the distinction of having in its county town one of England's two universities. Because of the nature of the material on the peace and gaol delivery rolls, the information about the social and economic life of the county and the town is scanty and uneven. The town of Oxford had its own gaol, the Bocardo prison, and after 1390 its own justices of the peace, so that townsmen and members of the university did not appear in any numbers before the county justices of the peace or the justices delivering the castle gaol during much of the period covered by their records. Because trespass cases involving violations of the legislation regulating prices, wages, and conditions of labour are few, evidence about economic conditions in the county is scarce. The detailed indictments of those accused in the riot of 1389 give some information about the university, and the thefts and robberies which list and value stolen goods provide some figures indicative of the economic status of some of the rural population, although such figures must be used with comparable figures from other sources for the county and for the whole country. The scanty evidence of labour unrest and charges of excessive prices and payment of excess wages does not indicate that there was little unrest or overcharging. The rolls of labour cases before the town justices of the peace in 1390-1394 provide plenty of evidence of such conditions.[1] What will be given here is an indication of the type of information the records in this volume contain. No attempt is made to analyse it or relate it to information from other sources.

In the accounts of the university riot and elsewhere there are references to features of the town of Oxford: High Street, East Gate, South Gate, and North Gate, Penchirch Lane, the parishes of All Saints, St Giles, and St Ebbe, the churches of St Aldate, St Mary, St Mary Magdalen, and St Michael at the Northgate, Bocardo prison, and the castle. The buildings of the university entered by the rioters were Deep Hall, Hampton Hall, Mildred Hall, Oven Hall, Pyry Hall, St Agate Hall, St Lawrence Hall. Bastaple's Entry, Neville's Entry, and Charlton Inn. Terry's Inn, a hospice at the South Gate has not been identified either as an inn for travellers or students. The suburb of Grandpont is mentioned as are the church of Holywell outside the walls and the religious houses of St Frideswide in the town, St John's Hospital outside the East Gate, and Rewley Abbey nearby.

[1]Salter, *Mediaeval Archives of the University of Oxford,* ii. 1-127.

Aside from the riot the offence which seems particularly related to the town was the counterfeiting of money, which was twice committed by men making Oxford their headquarters. No doubt it was easier and more profitable to pass false coins in a town than in rural districts.

There is no comprehensive picture of the classes of society in the county. The gentry are represented by the justices of the peace and by victims of crimes and perhaps by perpetrators of crimes. Of officials in addition to the sheriff mention is made of two coroners and two constables. For the rest of the population information is equally scanty. Identification of an individual by his occupation was not yet required as it was in the fifteenth century and when made was probably done to distinguish two men of the same name. Rural occupations such as hayward (Roll B, no. 7), shepherd (Roll C, no. 51), huntsman (Roll B, no. 10), were noted as were those more likely to be associated with a town, ironmonger (Roll C, no. 57), dealer in lead or feather (Roll C, no. 43), laundress (Roll C, no. 53), and pouch or patten maker (Roll B, no. 18). Others who might have worked anywhere were a weaver (Roll C, no. 45), fisherman (Roll C, no. 48), porter (Roll C, no. 49), gardener (Roll C, no. 14), saddler (Roll C, no 30), carpenter (Roll A. nos. 3, 9), mason (Roll A, no. 3), and slater (Roll C, no. 15).[2] The occupations of some men can be inferred from the offences they committed or those of which they were victims. Men who overcharged for hauling barrels in their barges on the Thames were probably bargemen (Roll B, nos. 13, 14); men who sold poor quality tiles, one of whom bore the surname Tyler, probably tilers. The man who was robbed of furs and furred garments belonging to himself and to others was presumably a furrier (Roll C, no. 47). Those who had occupational surnames may or may not have been currently engaged in that occupation. Some of the few servants who were accused of offences against their masters may have been agricultural labourers.

The members of the clergy appear frequently on these rolls; the upper clergy as the victims of offences, the lower as victims and offenders. Various others as ordinaries of the bishop of Lincoln appeared in court to verify claims of clergy; the abbot of Rewley was threatened with death (Roll C, no. 32), the prior of Cold Norton, the prior and convent of St Frideswide, and the master of St John's Hospital were victims of theft (Roll C, nos. 21, 33, 74). The abbot of Bicester and the prior of St John's Hospital were given charge of goods forfeited by felons (Roll C, nos. 5, 6). Several lesser clergy were robbed (Roll C, nos. 10, 12, 37, 47). Clerical offenders were usually described as clerks or chaplains although, as has been noted, those who pled clergy were not generally so identified in

[2]Occupation designations for some of the Bampton rioters are contained in the indictments before the king's bench; below pp. 82-6. For occupations see index.

indictments. Similarly the scholars, manciples, and the principal of Deep Hall were not designated as clergy although they were presumably in orders. Mention has been made of Adam Usk, one of those accused in the university riot, who later was prominent in the government, and of Robert Alynton who became chancellor of the university in 1393 and as such was appointed justice of the peace for the town in 1395.[3] Others named in connexion with the riot later held university posts and were named to benefices.

In addition to the Welshmen and Irishmen at the university, others not necessarily scholars were identified as from those parts (Roll C, nos. 37, 48). Mathew de Almayne may have been a German (Roll B, no. 18).

The goods stolen were varied both in kind and in value. Many of the valuations were large and give the impression of a fairly prosperous society. This can, however, be only an impression since a variety of goods were often listed together with a single valuation. Farm implements, horses, oxen, draught animals, sheep, pigs, household goods, particularly sheets and coverlets, and wearing apparel were commonly taken. The theft of furs and fur-lined and fur-trimmed garments, the total valued at £10 11*s*. 4*d*., from a single individual who was probably a furrier has been mentioned. Church fittings and liturgical books including missals valued at £10 and 100*s*. and other goods, were taken from Holywell church and other less valuable objects from other churches. The theft of a bull sealed in the Roman fashion belonging to the abbot of Biddlesden is curious as no explanation for the theft or for the abbot's possession of the bull is given. Weapons, swords, bows and arrows, a musical instrument, clothing, and books were taken from students' rooms. Although the articles were not valued individually it would seem that not every student, like Chaucer's poor clerk, spent all his money on books. There are no titles given for the latter; they are described as grammatical and dialectical. The student who had a copy of *liber ciuilis* must have been studying Roman law.

That there was unrest in Oxfordshire at the end of the fourteenth century is fully illustrated in the records in this volume. The Bampton insurrection and the university riot involved comparatively large numbers. There were also breaches of the peace against individuals such as the attempt to kill the abbot of Rewley and the destruction of property by two hundred men from Warwickshire as well as rapes, homicides, and thefts. Unfortunately the specific reasons for the more serious disturbances were not given in the indictments. That many of those indicted for these breaches of the peace were acquitted does not mean that these or similar disturbances had not taken place. The appointment

[3] *C. P. R.* 1391-1396, p. 588.

of the special commission of 5 February 1395 to deal with traitors and felons in Oxford Castle gaol suggests a fairly large prison population, whether or not individuals were found guilty of the offences for which they had been apprehended. That some grievances were economic is shown by the men punished for violations of the labour laws after indictment before the county justices of the peace and by the numerous presentments before the town justices.

As has been said only a very incomplete picture of life in Oxfordshire at the end of the fourteenth century is to be found in the records in this volume. They do, however, provide examples and some figures that can be useful for a detailed study of the county and for comparisons among counties.

RULES FOR TRANSCRIPTION

1. The cases on each roll have been numbered for ease of reference; cases omitted from the Gaol Delivery Roll are not noted.

2. Punctuation has been introduced into the text only as necessary for clarity.

3. *I* has been used in preference to *J* and *i* rather than *j* except in the case of *ij*. Initial *v* has been used; otherwise *u*.

4. In dates the abbreviation *pr*' or its equivalent has been extended *proximo* in Rolls A and C and *proxima* in Roll B in accordance with the apparent intention of the clerks.

5. Place and personal names have been extended only when the extension is certain; abbreviations are indicated by '.

6. Round brackets with a superscript i $(\quad)^{i}$ have been used to indicate interlineations; with a superscript c $(\quad)^{c}$, cancellations. Square brackets have been used for additions to the legible text.

SESSIONS OF THE PEACE

1387

ROLL A

ASSIZE ROLL 717

[*m.1*]

Placita corone coram Ricardo Abberbury et socijs (suis)[i] custodibus pacis domini regis in comitatu Oxon' necnon iusticiarijs ipsius regis ad diversa felonias transgressiones et alia malefacta in comitatu predicto perpetrata audienda et terminanda assignatis apud Boreford' die Iouis proximo ante festum conuercionis sancti Pauli anno regni regis Ricardi secundi post conquestum decimo [24 January 1387].

1. *Marg:* Oxon', Preceptum fuit vicecomiti quod non omitteret propter aliquam libertatem etc. quin caperet Iohannem filium Ade Taillour de Hempton' Willelmum Sadelere Ricardum Bocher de Chadlyngton' Thomam atte Hole et Beatricem vxorem eius Iohannem Grenelef Iohannem Carkwelle de Chadlyngton' Henricum Scot Iohannem Muluard seruientem Iohannis Faytour Iohannem Louenye Iohannem Burden Iohannem Tresshere de Ascote Robertum Reynold de Radeford Robertum Perat quondam de Hogenorton' nunc manens apud Brayles Walterum Beamond de Faulore Iohannem Tredewell' capellanum Iohannem Peyntour de Combe Ricardum Whitemor Iohannem Tresshere de Ascote Doyly et Ricardum Homet iuniorem capellanum si etc. et saluo etc. ita quod haberet corpora eorum coram Iohanne Louell' et socijs suis iusticiarijs etc. apud Boreford' die Iouis proximo ante festum conuercionis sancti Pauli [24 January 1387] ad respondendum domino regi de diuersis felonijs vnde indictati sunt: Ad quos diem et locum vicecomes videlicet Thomas Barentyn retornit quod predicti Iohannes filius Ade Taillour Willelmus Sadeler Ricardus Bocher Iohannes Carkwell' Iohannes Burdon et Iohannes Tresshere de Ascote capti sunt quorum corpora remanent in prisona domini regis gaole castri Oxon' quousque de felonijs predictis secundum legem et consuetudinem Anglie deliberentur: Et quod predicti Thomas atte Hole et ceteri in dicto precepto nominati non fuerunt inuenti in balliua sua etc. Ideo sicut prius preceptum est vicecomiti quod non omitteret etc. quin capiat predictos Thomam atte Hole et Beatricem Iohannem Grenelef Iohannem

Muluard' Iohannem Loueneye Robertum Reynald' Robertum Perat Walterum Beamond' Iohannem Tredewell' et Iohannem Peyntour si etc. et saluo etc. ita quod habeat corpora eorum coram prefatis iusticiarijs apud Bannebury die Martis proximo post festum anunciacionis beate Marie [26 March 1387] ad respondendum domino regi de felonijs predictis. Et quod diligenter inquirat (que bona et catalla)[i] quilibet predictorum Thome atte Hole et aliorum subscriptorum habet in balliua sua et ea in manus domini regis seisiri facit. Ita etc. et qualiter etc. Et postea coram Dauid Hannemere et socijs suis iusticiarijs ad gaolam predictam deliberandam assignatis predicti Iohannes filius Ade Willelmus Sadeler Iohannes Burden et Iohannes Tresshere de Ascot alias dictus Iohannes Tresshere de Ascote Doyly acquietati fuerunt. Et predicti Ricardus Bocher Iohannes Carkwelle suspensi fuerunt.

The sheriff was ordered to produce John son of Adam Taillour of Hempton, William Sadelere, Richard Bocher of Chadlington, Thomas atte Hole and his wife Beatrice, John Grenelef, John Carkwelle of Chadlington, Henry Scot, John Muluard servant of John Faytour, John Lovenye, John Burden, John Tresshere of Ascot, Robert Reynold of Radford, Robert Perat once of Hook Norton now of Brailes [Warws.], Walter Beamond of Fawler, John Tredewell chaplain, John Peyntour of Combe, Richard Whitemor, John Tresshere of Ascot d'Oyley, and Richard Homet, jr., chaplain, indicted for felony. The sheriff Thomas Barentyn reported that John son of Adam Taillour, William Sadeler, Richard Bocher, John Carkwell, John Burdon, and John Tresshere of Ascote were in Oxford Castle gaol, and that Thomas atte Hole and the rest could not be found. He was ordered to produce Thomas and Beatrice atte Hole, John Grenelef, John Muluard, John Loveneye, Robert Reynald, Robert Perat, Walter Beamond, John Tredewell, and John Peyntour before the justices at Banbury 26 March 1387 and to inquire what chattels they have and take such in the name of the king. Later, before David Hannemere and his companion justices of gaol delivery John son of Adam, William Sadeler, John Burden, and John Tresshere of Ascot also called John Tresshere of Ascot d'Oyley were acquitted; Richard Bocher and John Carkwelle were hanged.

[*For further process see below no. 4; for trials of Grenelef and Peyntour see below nos. 6, 8; for a pardon for Scot, 20 July 1386, see C. P. R. 1385-1389, p.195*].

2. *Marg:* Oxon' Preceptum fuit eciam vicecomiti quod non omitteret etc. quin venire faceret coram prefatis iusticiarijs ad prefatos diem et locum Willelmum Bordew de Kelmescot Iohannem Loueneye Ricardum seruientem vicarij de Norton' Bruyn Isabellam vxorem dicti Ricardi seruientis dicti vicarij Iohannem seruientem dicti vicarij Iohannem Symmes et Iohannam vxorem eius Willelmum Gabber de Gadelyngwell'

Robertum Clifford de Newenton' Robertum Clifford de Tywe Magna et Iohannem Clerk firmarium rectorie de Wotton' ad respondendum domino regi de diuersis articulis super ipsos presentatos. Ad quos diem et locum coram prefatis iusticiarijs venerunt predicti Willelmus Bordew Ricardus Isabella Iohannes Iohannes Iohanna et Iohannes et fecerunt finem etc. Et de predictis Willelmo Gabber (Iohanne Loueneye)[i] Roberto et Roberto vicecomes retornat quod ipsi nichil habent etc. per quod etc. Ideo preceptum est vicecomiti quod capiat eos si etc. et saluo etc. ita quod habeat corpora eorum coram dictis iusticiarijs apud Bannebury die Martis proximo post festum anunciacionis beate Marie [26 March 1387] ad respondendum domino regi de articulis predictis etc.

The sheriff was ordered to produce William Bordew of Kelmscott, John Loveneye, Richard servant of the vicar of Brize Norton and his wife Isabel, John servant of the said vicar, John Symmes and his wife Johanna, William Gabber of Gagingwell, Robert Clifford of Newington, Robert Clifford of Great Tew, and John Clerk farmer of the rector of Wootton to reply concerning various articles for violation of which they have been presented. William Bordew, Richard, Isabel, John, John, Johanna, and John came and made fines. William Gabber, John Loueneye, Robert, and Robert are reported by the sheriff to have nothing; he is to produce them at Banbury, 26 March 1387.

[*For further process see below no. 3.*]

Placita corone apud Bannebury coram Ricardo Abberbury Nicholao Somerton' et socijs suis custodibus pacis etc. necnon iusticiarijs etc. ad diuersa felonias transgressiones et alia malefacta in comitatu Oxon' perpetrata audienda et terminanda assignatis die Martis proximo post festum anunciacionis beate Marie anno regni regis Ricardi secundi decimo [26 March 1387].

3. *Marg:* Oxon' Preceptum fuit vicecomiti quod non omitteret etc. quin caperet Iohannem Loueney Willelmum Gabber de Gadelyngwell' Robertum Clifford' de Newenton' et Robertum Clifford de Magna Tywe si etc. et saluo etc. ita quod haberet corpora eorum prefatis iusticiarijs ad prefatos diem et locum ad respondendum domino regi de diuersis transgressionibus vnde indictati sunt. Preceptum fuit eciam vicecomiti quod non omitteret etc. quin venire faciat coram prefatis iusticiarijs ad prefatos diem et locum Nicholaum Bercarium de Hethrop' Iohannem Prentys de Cherlebury Iohannem Hokclyue carpenterium Iohannem Crabbe carpenterium Willelmum Haddon' carpentarium et Iohannem Ramesden cementarium ad respondendum domino regi de diuersis excessibus vnde indictati sunt. Ad quos diem et locum coram prefatis iusticiarijs venit predictus Iohannes Hokclyue et fecit finem et alij non venerunt. Et vicecomes retornat quod ipsi non sunt inuenti nec aliquid

habent etc. per quod etc. Ideo preceptum est vicecomiti quod non omitteret etc. quin caperet tam predictos Iohannem Loueneye Willelmum Gabber Robertum et Robertum quam predictos Nicholaum Iohannem Prentys Iohannem Crabbe Willelmum Haddon' et Iohannem Ramesden' si etc. et saluo etc. ita quod habeat corpora eorum coram prefatis iusticiarijs apud[1]

The sheriff was ordered to produce John Loveney, William Gabber of Gagingwell, Robert Clifford of Newington, and Robert Clifford of Great Tew indicted for trespass; he was also to produce Nicholas Bercarius of Heythrop, John Prentys of Charlbury, John Hokclyue carpenter, John Crabbe carpenter, William Haddon carpenter, and John Ramesden mason indicted for excess charges. John Hokclyue came and made a fine; the others did not come. The sheriff was to produce John Loveneye, William Gabber, Robert, and Robert and Nicholas, John Prentys, John Crabbe, William Haddon, and John Ramesden

4. *Marg:* Oxon' Preceptum fuit eciam vicecomiti (sicut prius)[i] quod non omitteret etc. quin caperet Thomam atte Hole et Beatricem vxorem eius Iohannem Grenelef Iohannem Mulward seruientem Iohannis Faitour [Ricardum] Homet iuniorem capellanum [Robertum] Reynald de Radeford' Robertum Perat quon[dam] de Hogenorton' nunc m[anetem a]pud Brayles Walterum Baumond de F[aulore] Iohannem Tredewell' capellanum [Iohannem] Peyntour de Combe et Ricardum Whitem[or si] etc. et saluo etc. ita quod haberet corpora eorum coram prefatis custodibus predictos diem et locum ad respondendum domino regi de diuersis felonijs vnde indictati sunt. Et [interim] diligenter inquireret de catallis suis etc. Et ipsi non venerunt et vicecomes retornat quod predictus Iohannes Grenelef captus est cuius corpus in prisona domini regis gaole castri Oxon' in custodia sua [?remanet]. Et ceteri supra nominati in dicto precepto non fuerunt inuenti in balliua sua etc. et quod *[illegible]* domino rege seisiri possunt etc. Ideo preceptum est vicecomiti quod exigi faciat eos de comitatu in comitatum quousque etc. Predicti Thomas Iohannes Mulward' Ricardus Robertus Robertus Walterus Iohannes Tredewell' Iohannes Peyntour et Ricardus vtlagentur et predicta Beatrix wayuiatur si non etc. Et similiter tunc eos caperet et saluo etc. ita quod habeat corpora eorum coram Iohanne Louell' et socijs suis custodibus pacis etc. apud[2] Boreford die Lune proximo post festum sancti Iacobi apostoli [29 July 1387] ad respondendum domino regi de quibusdem felonijs vnde coram prefatis iusticiarijs indictati sunt. Ad quos diem et locum coram prefatis iusticiarijs Thomas Barentyn vicecomes retornat quod ad comitatum Oxon' tentum apud Oxon' die

[1]The entry breaks off at this point.
[2]The entry continues in a different hand; see previous entry.

Iouis quarto die Aprilis anno regni regis Ricardi secundi post conquestum Anglie decimo predicti Thomas et Beatrix Iohannes Mulward' Ricardus Robertus Robertus Walterus Iohannes Tredewell (Iohannes Peyntour de Combe)[i] et Ricardus primo exacti fuerunt et non comparuerunt ad comitatum Oxon' tentum apud Oxon' die Iouis secundo die May anno supradicto predicti Thomas et Beatrix Iohannes et alij secundo exacti fuerunt et non comparuerunt ad comitatum Oxon' tentum apud Oxon' die Iouis xxx^mo^ die Maij anno supradicto predicti Thomas et Beatrix et alij tercio exacti fuerunt et non comparuerunt ad comitatum Oxon' tentum apud Oxon' die Iouis xxvij° die [*m. 1d.*] Iunij anno regni regis Ricardi secundi post conquestum Anglie vndecimo predicti Thomas et Beatrix et alij quarto exacti fuerunt et non comparuerunt set quidam Thomas Doo venit et manucepit de habendo corpora eorum ad proximum comitatum ad standum recto etc. Et ad comitatum Oxon' tentum apud Oxon' die Iouis xxv^to^ die Iulij anno regni regis Ricardi secundi post conquestum vndecimo predicti Thomas et Beatrix et alij quinto exacti fuerunt. Et predictus Iohannes Peyntour comparuit et eum cepit cuius corpus coram prefatis iusticiarijs ad prefatos diem et locum paratos habebit et omnes alij non comparuerunt. Ideo ad iudicium per Iohannem Harpour et Thomam Frytewell' coronatores comitati predicti predicta Beatrix wayuiata est et predicti Thomas atte Hole et omnes alij vtlagati sunt. Per quod inquiratur de terris suis etc. Et predictus Iohannes Peyntour remittitur prisone in custodia prefati vicecomitis vsque diem Iouis proximo post festum exaltacionis sancte crucis etc. [19 September 1387].

The sheriff was ordered to produce Thomas and Beatrice atte Hole, John Grenelef, John Mulward servant of John Faitour, Richard Homet, jr., chaplain, Robert Reynald of Radford, Robert Perat once of Hook Norton now of Brailes [*Warws.*], *Walter Baumond of Fawler, John Tredewell chaplain, John Peyntour of Combe, and Richard Whitemor indicted for felony and to inquire concerning their chattels. They did not appear; the sheriff reported that John Grenelef was in Oxford Castle gaol. Thomas, John Mulward, Richard, Robert, Robert, Walter, John Tredewell, John Peyntour, and Richard were to be outlawed; Beatrice to be waived. The sheriff was ordered to produce them at Burford, 29 July 1387. At that session the sheriff Thomas Barentyn reported that having been exacted and failed to appear at five county courts outlawry and waiver were proclaimed through the coroners, John Harpour and Thomas Frytewell: John Peyntour came and was remitted to prison to appear on 19 September 1387.*

[*For trials of Grenelef and Peyntour see below nos. 6, 8*].

5: *Marg:* Oxon' Preceptum fuit eciam vicecomiti quod non omitteret etc. quin caperet Ricardum Taillour quondam firmarium Walteri Clement in Cornwell' Iohannem Wyccheford' de Chepyngnorton' Willelmum rectorem ecclesie de Cornwell' Thomam Burlee filium eiusdem rectoris

Walterum Cabbe et fratrem eiusdem Iohannis si etc. et saluo etc. ita quod haberet corpora eorum coram prefatis iusticiarijs ad prefatos diem et locum ad respondendum domino regi de diuersis felonijs vnde indictati sunt. Et ipsi non veniunt set vicecomes retornat quod predicti Willelmus et Thomas capti sunt quorum corpora in prisona domini regis gaole castri Oxon' remanent quousque et quod ceteri etc. non sunt inuenti etc. Ideo sicut prius preceptum est vicecomiti quod non omitteret etc. quin capiat eos si etc. et saluo etc. ita quod habeat corpora eorum coram Iohanne Louell' et socijs suis custodibus pacis etc. apud Boreford' die Lune proximo post festum sancti Iacobi apostoli etc. [29 July 1387]. Et interim inquirat de bonis et catallis suis etc. Ad quos diem et locum coram prefatis iusticiarijs vicecomes non misit inde preceptum ideo sicut plures preceptum est vicecomiti quod non omitteret etc. quin capiat eos si etc. et saluo etc.

The sheriff was ordered to produce Richard Taillour once farmer of Walter Clement in Cornwell, John Wyccheford of Chipping Norton, William rector of Cornwell, Thomas Burlee his son, Walter Cabbe, and his brother John indicted for felony. They did not appear; the sheriff reported that William and Thomas were in Oxford Castle gaol. The sheriff was to produce the others at Burford on 29 July 1387 and inquire concerning their chattels.

Placita corone apud Oxon' coram Ricardo Abberbury Gilberto Wace Thoma Barantyn Iohanne Rede et Nicholao Somerton' et socijs suis custodibus pacis necnon iusticiarijs regis ad diuersa felonias et transgressiones et alia malefacta in comitatu Oxon' perpetrata audienda et terminanda assignatis die Iouis proximo post festum exaltacionis sancte crucis anno regni regis Ricardi secundi post conquestum vndecimo [19 September 1387].

6. *Marg:* Oxon' Iohannes Grenlef captus eo quod indictatus coram prefatis iusticiarijs de eo quod ipse die Lune proximo post festum exaltacionis sancte crucis anno regni regis Ricardi secundi nono felonice furatus fuit tres boues Ricardi atte Selere de Oxon' precij quadraginta solidorum apud Northam in dominico de Hedyngdon'; et de eo quod ipse felonice furatus fuit duos boues videlicet vnum bouem precij decem solidorum Willelmi Louelot de Wodestoke et vnam bouem precij decem solidorum Iohannis Fisshere de Gadelyngeswelle apud Nethercudyngton' die Dominica proximo ante festum sancti Clementi anno regni regis Ricardi secundi nono; et modo coram prefatis iusticiarijs venit predictus Iohannes Grenlef in propria persona sua per vicecomitem ductus et instanter allocutus est qualiter de felonijs predictis se velit acquietare qui dicit quod ipse in nullo est inde culpabilis et inde de bono et malo ponit se super patriam etc. Ideo venit inde iurata etc. Iuratores

venerunt qui ex assensu predicti Iohannis Grenlef ad hoc electi triati et iurati dicunt super sacramentum suum quod predictus Iohannes Grenlef culpabilis est de felonijs predictis. Ideo ipse suspendatur. Et nulla habet terras nec tenementa bona seu catalla etc. *Marg:* Suspendatur catalla nulla nec tenementa.

John Grenelef indicted before the justices of the peace for feloniously stealing on 18 September 1385 3 oxen, price 40s.,from Richard atte Selere of Oxford at Norham in Headington demesne, and on 19 November 1385 1 ox, price 10s., from William Lovelot of Woodstock, and 1 ox, price 10s., from John Fisshere of Gagingwell at Kiddington, pled not guilty, was tried, found guilty, and sentenced to be hanged; no chattels.

[*See above nos. 1, 4.*]

7. Willelmus Blokkele de Bannebury captus eo quod indictatus coram prefatis iusticiarijs de eo quod ipse die Sabati proximo ante festum apostolorum Simonis et Iude anno regni regis Ricardi secundi decimo vnum iumenteum Ricardi Arkel de Broughton' precij sex solidorum et octo denariorum et vnum pullanum Walteri Selyman de Broughton' precij decem solidorum apud le Cruche in campis de Bannebury felonice furatus fuit; et de eo quod ipse die Mercurij proximo ante festum omnium sanctorum anno decimo furatus fuit felonice vnum iumentum precij quinque solidos in Cruga quale [*illegible*] Ricardi Arkel de Broughton iuxta Bannebury; et est communis latro; et modo coram prefatis iusticiarijs venit predictus Willelmus Blokfeid in propria persona sua per vicecomitem ductus et instanter allocutus est qualiter de felonijs predictis se velit acquietare qui dicit quod ipse in nullo est inde culpabilis et inde de bono et malo ponit se super patriam etc. Ideo venit inde iurata etc. Iuratores venerunt qui ex assensu predicti Willelmi Blokkele ad hoc electi triati et iurati dicunt super sacramentum suum quod predictus Willelmus Blokfeld culpabilis est de felonijs predictis. Ideo ipse suspendatur. Et nulla habet terras nec tenementa bona seu catalla etc. *Marg:* Suspendatur catalla nulla nec tenementa

William Blokkele of Banbury indicted before the justices of the peace for feloniously stealing on 27 October 1386 a draught animal, price 6s. 8d., from Richard Arkel of Broughton, and a colt, price 10s., from Walter Selyman of Broughton at Crouch in Banbury fields, and on 31 October 1386 another draught animal, price 5s., from Richard Arkel in the same place, being a common thief, pled not guilty, was tried, found guilty, and sentenced to be hanged; no chattels.

8. Iohannes Peyntour de Combe captus eo quod indictatus coram prefatis iusticiarijs de eo quod ipse felonice depredatus fuit Willelmum atte Halle de Chylston' de duabus patenis et alijs vasis suis precij viginti solidorum apud Chylston' ix° die Ianuarij anno regni regis Ricardi secundi octauo; et

modo coram prefatis iusticiarijs venit predictus Iohannes Peyntour in propria persona sua per vicecomitem ductus et instanter allocutus est qualiter de felonijs predictis se velit acquietare qui dicit quod ipse in nullo est inde culpabilis et inde de bono et malo ponit se super patriam etc. Ideo venit inde iurata etc. Iuratores venerunt qui ex assensu predicti Iohannis Peyntour ad hoc electi triati et iurati dicunt super sacramentum suum quod predictus Iohannes Peyntour est in nullo inde culpabilis nec vmquam ea occasione se retraxit. Ideo ipse eat inde quietus etc. *Marg:* Quietus

John Peyntour of Combe indicted before the justices of the peace for on 9 January 1385 feloniously robbing William atte Halle of Chilson of 2 pans and other vessels, price 20s., at Chilson, pled not guilty, was tried, and acquitted.

[*See above nos. 1, 4,: Peyntour was tried before the justices delivering Oxford Castle gaol, 17 July 1391 for another offence on indictment before the seneschal of Wootton hundred, found guilty, and sentenced to be hanged; G.D.R. 180, m.6*].

[*Endorsed in another hand*] Placita corone in comitatu Oxon' annis x° & xj° Ricardi secundi

[*m. 2*]

Ad huc de placitis corone apud Oxon' coram Ricardo Abberbury Gilberto Wace Thomas Barantyn Iohanne Rede et Nicholao Somerton' et socijs suis custodibus pacis necnon iusticiarijs regis ad diuersa felonias transgessiones et alia malefacta in comitatu Oxon' perpetrata audienda et terminanda assignatis die Iouis proximo post festum exaltacionis sancte crucis anno regni regis Ricardi secundi post conquestum vndecimo [19 September 1387].

9. *Marg:* Oxon' Iohannes Whytyng' carpentarius de Bladon' et Thomas Prior carpentarius capti eo quod indictati coram prefatis iusticiarijs de eo quod predictus Iohannes similiter cum alijs latronibus die Veneris proximo ante festum sancti Mathei apostoli et ewangelice anno predicti domini regis nono noctanter felonice fregit domum Thome Donsen' de Bladen' et ibidem felonice asportauit vnam ollam eneam et alia bona et catalla ad valenciam sex solidorum et octo denariorum; et de eo quod idem Iohannes Whytyng die Mercurij proximo ante festum purificacionis beate Marie anno supradicto noctanter felonice fregit molendinum domini regis de Bladon' et ibidem felonice asportauit grana et alia bona et catalla ad valenciam decem solidorum; et de eo quod idem Iohannes Whytyng die et anno supradictis noctanter felonice fregit domum Alicie Pynot de Bladen' et ibidem felonice asportauit bona et catalla ad valenciam sex solidorum et octo denariorum; et de eo quod

idem Iohannes Whytyng die et anno supradictis felonice fregit domum Willelmi Loueney de Bladon' et ibidem felonice asportauit bona et catalla ad valenciam vj s. et viij d.; et de eo quod idem Iohannes et predictus Thomas Prior die Martis proximo post festum sancti Michelis archangeli anno regni regis nunc nono noctanter felonice depredauerunt et dispoliauerunt Robertum seruientem rectoris de Bladon' in le groue iuxta Wodestock' et felonice ibidem ab eo asportauerunt quinque solidos et quatuor denarios; et de eo quod ijdem Thomas Prior et Iohannes Whytyng die Lune proximo post festum sancti Michelis archangeli anno predicti domini regis sexto in aurora felonice fregerunt domum Willelmi Aylon' de Cudlyngton' prepositi redditus Philipi de la Wiche chiualeris et dominum ibidem et bona et catalla videlicet aurum et argentum asportauerunt felonice ad valenciam x librorum et xiiij paria linthiaminium dicti Willelmi et alia bona et catalla ad valenciam xl s. et dicti latrones Margaretam vxorem dicti Willelmi Aylon' sedere fecerunt super tripidem et ardebant cubum eius ad narrandum vbi erat aurum et argentum dicti Philipi; et de eo quod ijdem Thomas Prior et Iohannes Whytyng' die Lune proximo post festum omnium sanctorum anno predicti domini regis sexto noctanter felonice fregerunt molendinum de Carsyngton' et ibidem felonice asportauerunt grana et alia bona et catalla ad valenciam xiij s. et iiij d. Et modo coram prefatis iusticiarijs venerunt predicti Thomas Prior et Iohannes Whytyng' in propriis personis suis per vicecomitem ducti et instanter allocuti sunt (seperatim)[i] qualiter de felonijs predictis se velint acquietari qui dicunt (seperatim)[i] quod ipsi in nullo sunt inde culpabiles et inde de bono et malo ponunt se super patriam etc. Ideo venit inde iurata etc. Iuratores veniunt qui ex assensu predictorum Thome Prior et Iohannis Whytyng' ad hoc electi triati et iurati dicunt super sacramentum suum quod predicti Thomas Prior et Iohannes Whytyng' culpabiles sunt de felonijs predictis. Ideo ipsi suspendantur. Et nulla habent terras nec tenementa bona seu catalla etc. *Marg:* Suspendatur Suspendatur catalla nulla nec tenementa

John Whytyng of Bladon and Thomas Prior, carpenters, indicted before the justices of the peace for the following: John with other thieves at night on 15 September 1385 feloniously broke into the house of Thomas Donsen of Bladon and feloniously took a copper pot and other goods valued at 6s. 8d.; at night on 31 January 1386 he broke into a mill belonging to the king at Bladon and feloniously took grain and other goods valued at 10s.; on the same night he feloniously broke into the house of Alice Pynot of Bladon and feloniously took goods valued at 6s. 8d.; on the same day he feloniously broke into the house of William Loveney of Bladon and feloniously took goods valued at 6s. 8d.: John and Thomas at night on 3 October 1385 feloniously robbed Robert servant of the rector of Bladon of

5s. 4d. in the grove near Woodstock on 6 October 1386 they broke into the house of William Aylon of Kidlington, rent officer of Sir Philip de la Wiche, and feloniously took gold and silver worth £10 and 14 pairs of sheets and other goods valued at 40s., forcing Margaret, wife of William Aylon, to tell them where Sir Philip's gold was by burning her hand; on 3 November 1382 they feloniously broke into a mill at Cassington and feloniously took grain and other goods valued at 13s. 4d.; they pled not guilty, were tried, found guilty, and sentenced to be hanged; no chattels.

10. Iohannes Broun de Hibernia et Iohannes Brasyer de Baldyndon' iunior capti eo quod indictati coram prefatis iusticiarijs de eo quod ipsi similiter cum alijs die Mercurij in prima septimana quadragesime anno regni regis Ricardi secundi post conquestum decimo venerunt ad domum Ricardi Bayly de Newenham et ibidem j coopertorium precij xij d. j quadrantem de auro et quinque solidos argenti in pecunia numerata eiusdem Ricardi noctanter felonice furati fuerunt; et de eo quod predicti Iohannes Bron' et Iohannes Brasyer die et anno supradictis domum eiusdem Ricardi Baylly apud Newenham noctanter felonice fregerunt et ibidem duas mappas mensales precij iiij s. j tunicam precij ij s. et alia bona et catalla ad valenciam xiij s. iiij d. felonice furati fuerunt et asportauerunt; et de eo quod predicti Iohannes Bron' et Iohannes Brasyer venerunt super Haryndon' inter villam de Hasele et villam de Ruycot die Sabati in vigiliam pasche anno supradicto et ibidem Hugonem Cormongere de j equo precij ij s. j sacco precij xij d. et xij d. obulus in pecunia numerata eiusdem Hugonis felonice depredauerunt; et de eo quod predicti Iohannes Bron' et Iohannes Brasyer in vigiliam pasche venerunt apud Combe et ibidem iumentum precij v s. j couerlyt precij xij d. j canauas precij viij d. de Thoma Cameys noctanter felonice furati fuerunt; et de eo quod predicti Iohannes Bron' et Iohannes Brasyere venerunt ad domum Willelmi Bruxby apud Waterstoke et ibidem duas sellas duo frena precij x s. ij chargeos xiiij discos de pewtre precij v s. et chaffour et j vrcielum precij xl d. noctanter felonice furati fuerunt; et quod sunt communes latrones. Et modo coram prefatis iusticiarijs venerunt predicti Iohannes Bron' et Iohannes Brasyere in proprijs personis suis per vicecomitem ducti et instanter allocuti sunt seperatim qualiter de felonijs predictis se velint acquietare qui dicunt seperatim quod ipsi in nullo sunt inde culpabiles et inde de bono et malo ponunt se super patriam etc. Ideo venit inde iurata. Iuratores veniunt qui ex assensu predictorum Iohannis Bron' et Iohannis Brasyere ad hoc electi triati et iurati dicunt super sacramentum suum quod predicti Iohannes Bron' et Iohannes Brasyere culpabiles sunt de felonijs predictis. Ideo ipsi suspendantur. Et nulla habent terras nec tenementa bona seu catalla etc. *Marg:* Suspendatur Suspendatur catalla nulla nec tenementa

John Broun of Ireland and John Brasyer, jr., of Toot Baldon indicted before the justices of the peace for the following: they with others at night on 27 February 1387 feloniously stole a coverlet, price 12d., a gold farthing, and 5 silver shillings from the house of Richard Bayly of Newnham Murren; on the same night they feloniously broke into the house of Richard Baylly at Newnham Murren and feloniously stole 2 table cloths, price 4s., a coat, price 2s., and other goods valued at 13s. 4d.; at Haryndon between Hasely and Rycote on 6 April 1387 they feloniously robbed Hugh Cormongere of a horse, price 2s., a sack, price 12d., and 12d. halfpenny in cash; at Combe on the same night they feloniously stole a draught animal, price 5s., a coverlet, price 12d., and a piece of canvas, price 8d., from Thomas Cameys; from the house of William Bruxby at Waterstock they feloniously stole at night 2 saddles with bridles, price 10s., 2 large dishes, 14 pewter dishes, price 5s., and a chafing dish and a pitcher, price 40d.; they are common thieves; they were tried, found guilty, and sentenced to be hanged; no chattels.

[*For another offence committed by John Broun of Ireland see below Roll C, no. 24; for a pardon for John Broun of Ireland, 24 November 1399, see Pardon Roll 32, m. 23; for the acquittal before the justices of gaol delivery, 30 April 1389, of two men indicted as accessories to some of these thefts see below Roll C, no. 4.*]

SESSIONS OF THE PEACE

1397-1398

ROLL B

Ancient Indictments 99

[*m. 1 The left-hand margin of this membrane is damaged.*]
[Inquisicio capta] coram Willelmo Wilicotes Thoma Barentyn Iohanne Rede et Iohanne Hilton' custodibus pacis domini regis et iusticiarijs [eiusdem regis] ad diuersa felonias transgressiones et malefacta in comitatu Oxon' audienda et terminanda assignatis apud Oxon' die Veneris proxima [?ante festum sancti Petri] in cathedra anno regni regis Ricardi secundi post conquestum vicesimo primo [?15 February 1398][1].

[*torn*], [*torn*]; Iohannes Houchyn, Iohannes Colman; Robertus Rose, Iohannes Dod; Willelmus Andrew, Henricus Rose, Simon Taillour de Chalgraue, Iohannes Smyth' de Ouerton'; Thomas Bryd', Willelmus Bedell'; *iuratores*[2]

1. [Qui dicunt super] sacramentum suum quod Iohannes Adam [Suspensus][i] de Chalgraue die Martis proxima ante festum decollacionis sancti Iohannis baptiste anno regni regis Ricardi secundi vicesimo primo [post conquestum] apud Rytherfeld Pippard quemdam Iohannem Bokynden' de Chalgraue felonice interfecit et murdrauit ac [*torn*] quod Ebota vxor dicti Iohannis Bokynden' fuit illum die (et)[i] anno predictis concenciens et auxilians morti dicti Iohannis viri sui.

John Adam (sentenced to be hanged) of Chalgrove at Rotherfield Peppard on 28 August 1397 feloniously killed and murdered John Bokynden of Chalgrove; Ebota wife of John Bokynden consented to and aided in the death of her husband.

[*Adam was tried before the justices delivering Oxford Castle gaol, 15 February 1398; sentenced to be hanged; below Roll C, no. 73. Ebota tried as an accessory before the king's bench delivering Oxford Castle gaol, Easter 1398; sentenced to be burned; K.B. 27/548, Rex, m. 9d.; she was also presented as a second principal by the Bullingdon hundred jury before*

[1]Above p. 33.

[2]Semi-colons (;) indicate columns in MS. Cf. above, p. 37.

the king's bench, Easter 1398, and subsequently summoned for trial; K.B. 9/100, m. 4; 27/551, Rex, m. 16d.; 554, Rex, m. 2; 555, Rex,m. 2.]

2. [Qui] dicunt quod Thomas Taillour de parochia de Brythwell' die Lune proxima ante festum sancti Luce euuagelisti anno regni regis Ricardi [secundi post co]nquestum xxj° apud Ouerton' in parochia de Bryghtwell' vnum bidentem precij xx d. de Iohanne Haley felonice furatus [fuit et est] communis latro.

Thomas Taillour of parish of Brightwell Baldwin at Uppertown in said parish on 15 October 1397 feloniously stole 1 sheep, price 20d., from John Haley; he is a common thief.

[*Taillour was tried before the king's bench, Easter 1398, on indictment before the justices of the peace; acquitted; K.B. 27/548, Rex, m. 4d.*]

[*torn*], [*torn*]gour; Iohannes Scot, Iohannes Lyngere; Thomas Huntyndon', Willelmus atte Hall' de Lydstan'; Iohannes Guy, Thomas Freman; Robertus atte Well', Willelmus Warde; Willelmus Tayllour de Tywe, Iohannes Bocher de eadem; *iuratores*

3. [Qui dicunt super] sacramentum suum quod Thomas Rydere de Magna Tywe die Dominica proxima ante festum sancti Iohannis baptiste anno regni regis Ricardi [secundi post c]onquestum decimo nono noctanter Iohannem Boden apud Magnam Tywe cum vno mattok interfecit et murdrauit.

Thomas Rydere of Great Tew at night on 18 June 1396 killed and murdered John Boden at Great Tew with a mattock.

[*Rydere was tried before the king's bench delivering Oxford Castle gaol, Easter 1398, on indictment before the justices of the peace; sentenced to be hanged; K.B. 27/548, Rex, m. 9d.; see also below Roll C, no. 72.*]

[Inquisicio capta apud] Wodestoke coram Willelmo Wilicotes Iohanne Golafre et Iohanne Hilton' custodibus pacis domini regis et iusticiarijs eiusdem [regis ad diuersa] felonias transgressiones et malefacta in comitatu Oxon' audienda et terminanda assignatis apud Wodestoke die Martis proxima post [?pasche anno] regni regis Ricardi secundi post conquestum vicesimo primo [? 9 April 1398].[1]

[*torn*]dell', [*torn*]aulore, Thomas Spycere; Ricardus Eyre, Simon Walkere, Edwardus Dyere; Willelmus Leggere de Burforde, Thomas Eyre de eadem, Iohannes Brasyere de eadem; Robertus Besely, Nicholas Dunyng', Nigellus Cotyngham; *iuratores*

[1]Above p. 33.

4. [Qui] dicunt super sacramentum suum quod Henricus Barriour Iohannes Milleford webbe Thomas Gildesowe de Wytteney Willelmus Hanney Gilbertus [Vau]ham Iohannes Kirkeby de Bampton Thomas Bocher de eadem Iohannes Coupere de eadem Willelmus Wawe Henricus Ropere et plures alij [malefactor]es et felones ignoti eis iurati et aligati modo guerrino arraiati apud Bampton' die Dominica in ramis palmarum anno regni regis Ricardi secundi [post conquestum vicesimo primo noctanter] ordinauerunt inter eos certos homines capitanios et gubernatores in surgendo de nouo proditorie contra pacem domini regis et quesiuerunt [certos homines] interficiendos et dixerunt clamando ante se aryseth' aryseth' alle men et goth' wyth' vs et ho so wilnot gou wiht' vs [he schal be ded] et sic vt proditores et contra ligeanceam suam insurrexerunt apud Bampton' die et anno supradictis et Iohannem Netilcombe constabularium [ville predicte] et Willelmum Barbour ac alios verberauerunt wlnerauerunt quia cum eos surgere noluerunt.

Henry Barriour, John Milleford weaver, Thomas Gildesowe of Witney, William Hanney, Gilbert Vauham, John Kirkeby of Bampton, Thomas Bocher of Bampton, Iohn Coupere of Bampton, William Wawe, Henry Ropere and other unknown evildoers and felons leagued together and armed on the night of Palm Sunday, 31 March 1398 at Bampton chose leaders and rose in new insurrection; they sought certain men to kill them shouting arise arise all men and go with us and who will not go with us shall be dead; thus treasonably and contrary to their allegiance they were insurgents; they beat and wounded John Netilcombe constable, William Barbour, and others because they refused to join the uprising.

[*For process see below Appendix II. Missing words supplied from no. 6 below*].

5. [Iuratores] dicunt super sacramentum suum quod Nicholaus Brugge clericus Iohannam vxorem Nicholai Bailly de Bampton' apud Bampton' die [Dominica proxima] post festum natalis domini anno regni regis Ricardi secundi vicesimo primo felonice rapuit.

Nicholas Brugge clerk feloniously raped Johanna wife of Nicholas Bailly of Bampton at Bampton on 30 December 1397.

[*Brugge was in exigend in the king's bench, Easter 1398; K. B. 27/548, Rex, m. 19; appeared before the king's bench, Michaelmas 1398; sheriff failed to send writ; entry unfinished; ibid., 550, Rex, m. 1d. Missing date supplied from the king's bench roll.*]

[*torn*]xforde, [*torn*]nes, [*torn*]one; Iohannes Bray, Robertus Mundy, Henricus Megre; Iohannes Northbrok, Willelmus Mason', Henricus Sauage; Iohannes Nowell, Richardus Austeyn, Iohannes Halewey;

6. [Qui dicunt] super sacramentum suum quod Iohannes Paradys de Cogg' Iohannes Leche Willelmus Makerel de Eynesham Iohannes

Donnyng de eadem Iohannes [Smyth' de] eadem Iohannes seruiens Iohannis Yerby de eadem Willelmus Shoppe de eadem Edwardus Vnderhorn de eadem Iohannes Cadewell' de [eadem et plures] alij malefactores et felones ignoti eis iurati confederati et alligati modo guerrino arraiati apud Bampton' die Dominica in [ramis palmarum] anno regni regis Ricardi secundi post conquestum vicesimo primo noctanter ordinauerunt inter eos certos homines capitanios et gubernatores in [surgendo] de nouo proditorie contra pacem domini regis et certos homines quesiuerunt interficiendos et quosdam verberauerunt wlnerauerunt et male tractauerunt clamando ante se aryseth' asyseth' alle men et goth' wt vs ho so wilnot he schal be ded et sic vt proditores et contra ligeanciam suam proditorie insurrexerunt die loco et anno supradictis.

John Paradys of Cogges, John Leche, William Makerel of Eynsham, John Donnyng of Eynsham, John Smyth of Eynsham, John servant of John Yerby of Eynsham, William Shoppe of Eynsham, Edward Underhorn of Eynsham, John Cadewell of Eynsham and other unknown evildoers and felons leagued together and armed at Bampton on the night of Palm Sunday, 31 March 1398, chose leaders rising in the new treason; they sought to kill certain men whom they beat, wounded, and maltreated, crying arise arise all men and go with us and he who will not shall be dead; they are traitors who treasonably rose against their allegiance.

[*For process see below Appendix II. Missing words supplied from no. 4 above.*]

7. Item iuratores de Wotton' dicunt super sacramentum suum quod Iohannes Coteswold hayward de Watereton' et Robertus Planke de eadem apud Frek in comitatu Oxon' die Sabbati in festo epiphanie domini anno regni regis Ricardi secundi post conquestum vicesimo primo et ibidem vnam mulierem extraneam cuius nomen est ignotum felonice interfecerunt et murdrauerunt.

John Coteswold hayward and Robert Planke both of Water Eaton in January 1398 at Frieze in Oxfordshire feloniously killed and murdered a woman, a stranger whose name was not known.
[*Both Coteswold andPlanke were in exigend in the king's bench, Easter 1398; K. B. 27/548, Rex, m. 19; also presented by jury from Wootton hundred before the bench, which added the information that she was buried before the coroner viewed the body; K. B. 9/100, m. 9. Epiphany was on a Sunday not a Saturday in 1398, 21 Richard II.*]

8. Item iuratores dicunt quod Hugo Lodere de Eynesham est communis noctiuagus et pacis perturbator apud Eynesham die Martis proxima post

festum purificacionis beate [Marie][1] anno regni regis Ricardi secundi vicesimo primo et continue aliis diebus.

Hugh Lodere of Eynsham is a common night wanderer and disturber of the peace in Eynsham on 5 February 1398 and continuously.

[*Lodere was in exigend in the king's bench, Easter 1398; K. B. 27/548 Rex, m. 19.*]

[*torn*]e, [*torn*], [*torn*]; Ricardus Whitefeld, Willelmus Eydmershe, Elias atte Bolde; Iohannes atte Hille, Thomas Murye, Willelmus atte Corn; Iohannes (Haceth')[e] Hacket, Willelmus atte Hall' de Lydhan', Willelmus atte Mulle de Clyiele; *iuratores*

9. [Dicunt] super sacramentum suum quod (Ricardus)[i] Bolde de Asterleye nene die Sabbati in vigilia pasche anno regni regis Ricardi secundi post conquestum vicesimo primo venit in [*illegible*] sclattere de Clyiele et ibidem domum suam fregit et felonice vnum equum nigris coloris precij xiij s. iiij d. felonice furatus fuit ac est communis latro.

Richard Bolde of Asterleigh broke into the house of . . . slater of Cleveley on 6 April 1398 and feloniously stole a black horse, price 13s. 4d.; he is a common thief.

10. Dicunt quod Walterus Conbryghe est communis venator et non habet quadraginta solidos redditum et tenet leporios contra formam ordinacionum statutorum [apud] Chadlyngton' die Lune proxima post festum purificacionis beate Marie anno regni regis Ricardi secundi vicesimo primo.

Walter Conbryghe commonly hunts but does not have the 40s. property qualification; he keeps greyhounds in violation of the law at Chadlington on 4 February 1398.

[*Conbryghe was to be produced before the king's bench, Easter 1398; K.B. 27/548, Rex, m. 19; made a fine for 2s. before the king's bench, Trinity 1398: ibid., 549, Fines, m. 1*].

[*Margin; illegible*]
Willelmus Hunte, [*illegible*] Smyth', [*illegible*] Cartere; Ricardus Cussyn, Thomas Strete, Thomas Isaak; Thomas Hoppedmerye, Iohannes Wytynton', Willelmus Taillour; Thomas Buntreton, Iohannes Berles, Iohannes Hood; *iuratores*

11. Qui dicunt super sacramentum suum (quod)[i] Simon Taillour de Wytteney Iohannes Warner Iohannes Bellebroughton' Phillipus Welynton' Iohannes Redeman iunior Willelmus atte Nashe de Ascote et

[1]Supplied.

plures alij malefactores et felones ignoti eis iurati confederati et alligati modo guerrino arraiati apud Bampton die Dominica in ramis palmarum anno regni regis Ricardi secundi secundi post conquestum vicesimo primo noctanter ordinauerunt inter eos certos homines capitanios et gubernatores insurgendo de nouo proditorie contra pacem domini (regis)[i] et diuersos homines quesiuerunt interficiendos et quosdam verberauerunt wlnerauerunt et male tractauerunt clamando ante se aryseth' alle men et goth' wt vs wo so wilnot he schal be ded et sic vt proditores et felones domini regis contra ligeanciam suam et contra regem et populum suum prodictorie insurrexerunt.

Simon Taillour of Witney, John Warner, John Bellebroughton, Philip Welynton, John Redeman, jr,, William atte Nashe of Ascot, and many other unknown evildoers and felons leagued together and armed at Bampton on the night of Palm Sunday, 31 March 1398, chose leaders to rise in the new treason; they sought to kill various men whom they beat, wounded, and maltreated, crying arise all men and go with us and he who will not shall be dead; as traitors and felons they rose against their allegiance and treasonably rose against the king and the people.

[*For process see below Appendix II*].

primus

[*m. 1d. The right-hand margin of this membrane is damaged.*]

Inquisicio capta apud Henle coram Thoma Barentyn et Iohanne Rede custodibus pacis domini regis et [iusticiarijs eiusdem regis] ad diuersa felonias transgressiones et malefacta in comitatu Oxon' audienda et terminanda assignatis [die] Lune proxima ante festum sancti Gregorij pape anno regni regis Ricardi secundi post conquestum vicesimo [primo][1] [11 March 1398],
Marg: Oxon' xij^{cim}
Georgius Ronden, Robertus Derham, Nicholaus Payable; Nicholaus atte Helde, Iohannes atte Haw, Willelmus Padenhale; Iohannes Catermayn, Walterus Sekyn, Iohannes Goldsmyth'; Walterus Wycher, Iohannes Barry, Iohannes Randd; [*iuratores*]

12. Qui dicunt super sacramentum suum quod Iohannes Tyler Thomas Egham (fecit finem)[i] et Iohannes Bokkyng sunt [*torn*] videlicet le mille pro dimidij marca et interdum pro v s. apud Netelbed die Veneris (et alijs diebus)[i] proxima post festum purificacionis [beate Marie anno regni regis Ricardi] secundi vicesimo primo et quod predicte tegule non sunt bene anelete ad gaue dampnum [torn], *Marg:* transgressio

[1] *Primo* is assumed on the basis of the dates of the offences presented and the appearance of offenders before the bench, Easter 1398.

John Tyler, Thomas Egham (made a fine), and John Bokkyng [?sold 1000 tiles] on 8 February 1398 and at various other times for ½ mark and later for 5s., the said tiles not being well annealed, to the damage of. . .

[Tyler and Bokkyng made fine for 2s. each before the king's bench, Easter 1398; K. B. 27/548, Fines, m. 1; Egham was to be produced before the king's bench, Easter 1398; ibid., Rex, m. 19; made fine for 40d. before the king's bench, Michaelmas 1398; ibid., 550, Fines, m. 1.]

13. Item dicunt quod Iohannes Slaple habet vnum showte et cepit de Simone Whelere pro ca[riagio] xxviij s, videlicet pro cariagio vnius barelli xiiij d. apud Henle die Veneris proxima post festum [*torn* anno regni regis] Ricardi secundi xxj^{o} et sic excessiue in vno barello xiij d. et sic cepit de pluribus alijs. *Marg:* transgressio

John Slaple has a barge and at Henley during 1397-1398 took from Simon Whelere 28s. for carrying . . . , viz, 14d. per barrel which is 8d. in excess; he also overcharged many others.

[Slaple was to be produced before the king's bench, Easter 1398; K. B. 27/548, Rex, m. 19; made a fine for 2s. before the king's bench, Michaelmas 1398; ibid., 550, Fines, m. 1.]

14. Item dicunt quod Simon Mulward de Henle Iohannes Penle Henricus Yeuele [fecit finem][i] Henricus Am[orys] habentur showtes et capiunt excessiue apud Henle vt predictus Iohannes Slaple (cepit)[i] de Nicholao P[*torn* die] (supradicto)[c] et loco supradictis. *Marg:* transgressio

Simon Mulward of Henley, John Penle, Henry Yevele (made a fine), and Henry Amorys have barges and like the aforesaid John Slaple they overcharged Nicholas P . . . , during 1397-1398.

[Mulward made a fine for ½ mark before the king's bench, Easter 1398; K.B. 27/548, Fines, m. 1; the others to be produced before the king's bench, Easter 1398; ibid., Rex, m. 19; Penle, Yevele made fines for ½ mark each before the king's bench, Trinity 1398; ibid., 549, Fines, m. 1; Amorys made a fine for 40d. before the king's bench, Michaelmas 1398; ibid., 550, Fines, m. 1. Missing name supplied from the king's bench roll.]

Inquisicio capta apud Thame die Lune proxima post clausum pasche anno supradicto et coram prefatis [iusticiarijs] [15 April 1398].

15. Willelmus Iurdon' constabularius ville presentat quod die Mercurij in septimana pasche anno regni regis Ricardi secundi [*torn* apud Waturpirye venit Lambartus Fost' et insultum fecit contra pacem domini regis et diuersos homines verberauerunt cum vno baculo et super hoc venit predictus constabularius et arestauit predictum Lambertum (et eum requisiuit)[i] ad inuenendum [?pacem] domino regi et populum suum et

predictus Lambartus hoc facere recusauit et noluit set minauit predictum [constabularium] ... et dampnum de corpore suo inponere contra pacem domini regis. *Marg:* transgressio

William Jurdon constable presents that when during Easter week he tried to arrest Lambert Foster who has beaten various men with a stick, Lambert resisted arrest and threatened the constable with bodily injury.

[*m. 2 The left-hand margin of this membrane is damaged.*]

[Inquisicio capta apud] Oxon' coram Thoma Barentyn et Iohanne Rede custodibus pacis domini regis et iusticiarijs eiusdem domini regis ad diuersa felonias transgressiones [et malefacta in comitatu] Oxon' audienda et terminanda assignatis apud Oxon' die Lune proxima post festum sancti Petri in cathedra anno regni regis Ricardi [*torn*]todecimo.

[*torn*]est, [*torn*], [*torn*] Hilton'; Iohannes Notebem, Iohannes Leche, Nicholaus Dykere; Willelmus atte Mulle, Willelmus Hert', Iohannes Hykkes; Ricardus Bygge, Iohannes Compton', Iohannes Archere; *iuratores*

16. [Qui dicunt] super sacramentum suum quod Iohannes Dyne (ponit se)[i] de Oxon' sadelere die Lune proxima post festum epiphanie domini anno regni regis Ricardi secundi [post con]questum vndecimo in suburbio Oxon' extra portam australem eiusdem ville in quodam hospicio vocato Terrysyn felonice et [proditorie] controfecit monetam domini regis vocatam grotes de alkonemye et alijs falsis metallis cum punchonnes et malliolis et alijs diuersis [instrumentis] et grotas predictas Willelmo Rose et diuersis hominibus ville Oxon' ac comitatus Oxon' pro quatuor denarijs exponi fecit felonice [et proditorie] et quod est communis controfactor monete domini regis Anglie.

John Dyne, saddler, [*appeared*] *of Oxford in the suburb of Oxford outside the South Gate in a hospice called Terrysyn on 13 January 1388 feloniously and treasonably counterfeited the coinage, making groats of alchemy and other false metals with punches, hammers, and other tools, and making William Rose and others pay 4d. for them; he commonly counterfeits money.*

[*Dyne was tried before the king's bench, on indictment before the justices of the peace, Easter 1398; acquitted; K. B. 27/548, Rex, m. 2d. Missing words supplied from king's bench roll*].

[*torn*]ron' de Enstan', [*torn*] Tackle, [*torn*] atte Hall' de Lydstan'; Willelmus Gorgh', Ricardus Whitefeld, Iohannes Sampson'; Iohannes Stowe, Ricardus Megre, Iohannes atte Well'; Walterus Rompney, Ricardus Bloxham, Willelmus Chilton; *iuratores*

17. [Qui dicunt] super sacramentum suum quod Ricardus Clerk de Chippenham die Lune proxima post festum omnium sanctorum anno

regni regis Ricardi [secundi post] conquestum decimo venit apud villam de Cogg' et ibidem felonice furatus fuit duas equas Iohannis Sheperde precij decem [s. et eas] duxit apud Burforde et ibidem veniebat Ricardus Donyngton' et receptauit dictum Ricardum apud Burforde die [Lune] post festum omnium sanctorum anno regni regis Ricardi secundi post conquestum decimo scienter predictum Ricardum fecisse feloniam predictam [et est] communis receptator latronum.

Richard Clerk of Chippenham [Gloucs. or Wilts] in Cogges on 5 Nov. 1386 feloniously stole 2 mares, price 10s., from John Sheperde; he took them to Burford where Richard Donyngton bought the mares and received Clerk; Donyngton commonly receives thieves.

[*Clerk was in exigend in the king's bench, Easter 1398; K. B. 27/548, Rex, m. 19; Donyngton, as accessory, to appear before the king's bench, Trinity 1398 and subsequently; ibid., 548, Rex, m. 9d.; 550, Rex, m. 25; in exigend, Hilary 1399; ibid., 551, Rex, m. 16d.; see also ibid., 554, Rex, m. 1d. Missing words supplied from king's bench roll,*]

[Inquisicio capta apu]d Oxon' coram Willelmo Wilicotes et Iohanne Rede custodibus pacis domini regis et iusticiarijs eiusdem domini regis [ad diuersa] felonias transgressiones et malefacta in comitatu Oxon' audienda et terminanda assignatis apud Oxon' die Lune proxima post [festum con-] cepcionis Marie anno regni regis Ricardi secundi post conquestum vicesimo primo [10 December 1397].

[*torn*], [*torn*]hell', [*torn*]son'; Thomas Ranes, Iohannes Runoy, Iohannes Northbrok; Iohannes Freman, Iohannes Lokere, Thomas Aleyn; Iohannes Mayken, Iohannes Nowell', Willelmus Reynold; *iuratores*

18. [Qui dicunt] super sacramentum suum quod Matheus de Almayne pouchemakere alias dictus patynmaker Franciscus de Rokesbarre et [*torn* (]rard)[c] Gerardus Fon de Fouter die Martis ad noctem proxima ante festum assumpcionis beate Marie virginis anno regni regis Ricardi secundi post conquestum vicesimo primo Matheum Taillour de Oxon' apud Oxon' felonice interfecerunt et murdrauerunt.

Mathew de Almayne pouchmaker, alias patten maker, Franciscus de Rokesbarre and Gerard Fon of Fouter at night at Oxford on 14 August 1397 feloniously killed and murdered Mathew Taillour of Oxford.

[*Fon was in exigend in the king's bench, Easter 1398; K. B. 27/548, Rex, m, 19.*]

19. [Item] dicunt quod Nicholaus Vpton' de Wodestok et Agnes vxor eius octauo die Nouembris anno regni regis Ricardi secundi [post conquestum] vicesimo primo fregerunt clausum Iohannis Canon' apud

Wodestok et ibidem felonice furati fuerunt boscum dicti [Iohannis precij] vj s. viij d. et dictum boscum asportauerunt contra pacem domini regis et quod minas predicto Iohanni inponunt eum.

Nicholas Upton and Agnes his wife broke into the close of John Canon at Woodstock on 8 November 1397 and feloniously took wood, price 6s. 8d., threatening John they arrested him.

[*Both Uptons were in exigend in the king's bench, Easter 1398; K. B. 27/548, Rex, m. 19.*]

[Inquisicio capta apud] Witteney coram Willelmo Wilicotes et Iohanne Hilton' custodibus pacis domini regis et iusticiarijs eiusdem [domini regis] ad diuersa felonias transgressiones et malefacta in comitatu Oxon' audienda et terminanda assignatis apud [Witteney] die Sabbati proxima post festum sancti Thome apostoli anno regni regis Ricardi secundi vicesimo primo [22 December 1397].

[*torn*]ll', [*torn*], [*torn*]; Ricardus Borewell', Willelmus Leche, Thomas Bernard; Nicholaus Donnyng, Simon Notebem, Iohannis Wylond; Iohannes Geuerner, Thomas Prodfot, Iohannes Stretende; *iuratores*

20. [Qui dicunt] super sacramentum suum quod Robertus Carlet et Iohannes Carlet filius eius die Martis proxima ante festum natiuitatis [beate Marie] virginis anno regni regis Ricardi secundi post conquestum vicesimo primo vnum bouem Willelmi Taillour precij decem solidorum apud [Filk]ynge felonice furati fuerunt et quod Thomas Tuffyn receptauit dictos Robertum et Iohannem scienter eos feloniam predictam fecisse et quod est communis latro et de assensu et consensu eorum die anno et loco supradictis.

Robert Carlet and his son John at Filkins on 4 September 1397 feloniously stole an ox, price 10s., from William Taillour; Thomas Tuffyn received them knowing of the felony; this he commonly does.

[*Robert and John Carlet were in exigend in the king's bench, Easter 1398; K. B. 27/548, Rex, m. 19; John was tried before the justices delivering Oxford Castle gaol, 15 February 1398; acquitted; below Roll C, no. 75; both pardoned, 9 June 1399; C.P.R. 1396-1399, p. 563. Thomas Tuffyn as accessory was in exigend in the king's bench, Hilary 1399; K. B. 27/551, Rex, m. 16d.; see also ibid., 554, Rex, m. 2; 555, Rex, m. 2d. Missing name supplied from gaol delivery roll.*]

Marg: Oxon' Thomas Cogyn, Iohannes Welwe senior, Ricardus Tefhomice; Iohannes Welwe iunior, Thomas Bountyng, Willelmus Bountyng; Simon Smyth', Iohannes Wyttynton', Willelmus Synthyn; Willelmus Walteres, Willelmus Dyere, Ricardus Lylywyth'; *iuratores*

21. Qui dicunt super sacramentum suum quod Gilbertus Waughwan Iohannes Pacy et Iohannes Plym venerunt die Dominica proxima post festum sancti Petri quod dicitur aduincula anno regni regis Ricardi secundi vicesimo primo in domum Willelmi Hickens in manerio infra dominium de Wytteney et ibidem Isabellam vxorem dicti Willelmi cum bonis et catallis dicti Willelmi ad valenciam quadraginta solidorum ibidem inuenta noctanter felonice ceperunt et dictam Isabellam rapuerunt et abduxerunt.
Marg: ?Wytteney

Gilbert Waughwan, John Pacy and John Plym at Witney on 5 August 1397 entered the house of William Hickens, raped and abducted his wife, Isabel, and carried away goods valued at 40s.

[*All three were in exigend in the king's bench, Easter 1398; K. B. 27/548, Rex, m. 19.*]

APPENDIX TO ROLL B

The Bampton Uprising of 1398

I Accounts of the Bampton Uprising, Palm Sunday 1398

Accounts of this uprising are found in three indictments on Roll B (nos. 4, 6, and 11), in presentments made by jurors before the king's bench sitting at Oxford in Easter term 1398 (K. B. 9/100), and in records of trials before the king's bench in this term and subsequently (K. B. 27/548 ff.). The accounts from the presentments and the trials are given here to supplement the accounts on the peace roll printed above and thus to provide as much information about the uprising as is available. The account contained in the record of the trial of John Milford is printed in Latin and summarized in English because it contains the most detail. The presentment by the Wootton jury is also given in full with an English summary. Other accounts are noted or summarized in English. The jury presentment files are so damaged that some details and names cannot be read. Names in square brackets have been supplied from the list of those in exigend for failure to appear before the bench for trial (K. B. 27/548, Rex, m. 19; see below p. 88, n. 7).

Records of Trials

1. Record of trial of John Milford, weaver of Cogges, Michaelmas 1398 (K. B. 27/550, Rex, m. 23).

Marg: Oxon' Iuratores diuersorum hundredorum comitatus predicti alias scilicet termino pasche anno regni regis nunc vicesimo primo coram domino rege apud Oxon' presentauerunt quod Iohannes Milford webbe de Cogges et alij vt primi et principales insurreccores et capitales ductores et abbettatores quorumdam rebellium ad quandam insurreccionem contra dominum nostrum regem et ligeanciam suam in comitatu Oxon' nuper subortam faciendam insimul iurati et interligati fuerunt mortem ipsius domini nostri regis legisque et magnatum regni sui Anglie destruccionem felonice et proditorie contra ligeanciam suam ymaginando proponendo et conspirando adunata sibi et aggregata quam magna potencia et multitudine diuersorum hominum de eorum assensu et falsa interligancia et couina videlicet Iohannis Bedemansone de Wytteney et aliorum simul cum quam pluribus proditoribus et felonibus ignotis ad numerum cc hominum die Dominica ad noctem in ramis palmarum anno regni regis Ricardi secundi vicesimo primo apud Cokthrop' in comitatu Oxon' felonice et proditorie contra dominum regem et ligeanciam suam de nouo insurrexerunt et ibidem hostiliter mustrauerunt et ibidem inter eos ordinauerunt quendam Gilbertum Vaughan fore capetaneum et dominum suum et ipsum nominauerunt lesour soueraigne et ad dignitatem suam predictam inter eos manutenendam ordinauerunt eidem Gilberto vnum par calcarium deauratorum et omnes homines eiusdem ville tunc ibidem cum eis ire coegerunt vsque villam de Eleford et sic ab inde vsque villam de Aston' semper homines villatarum predictarum secum trahendo adunando vsque villam de Bampton' et ibidem nocte eiusdem diei Dominice omnes homines ville predicte quesiuerunt in domibus suis; et quod Henricus Ropere de Bampton' vt primus et principalis proditor et insurrector eadem nocte tenuit in manu sua plures candelas accensas et in alia manu quoddam arma vocata axe querendo circumquaque homines in domibus suis dicendo et clamando arysith' alle men et goyth' with' vs other elles trewly and by god ye shullen be ded et pro eo quod Willelmus Barbour et quam plures alij prodicionibus suis consentire noluerunt omnes proditores prenominati in ipsos tunc ibidem insultum fecerunt et ipsos verberauerunt vulnerauerunt et male et enormiter tractauerunt et interfecisse voluerunt; et quod predictus Henricus Ropere vt principalis proditor de communi consilio et assensu predictorum proditorum tunc ibidem factus fuit communis nuncius ad explorandum de statu domini nostri regis et gubernacionem dum idem rex in partibus Bristoll' et Glouc' tunc ad libitum suum fuit quiquidam Henricus die Lune et die Martis tunc proximis sequentibus ad implendum prodicionem et feloniam predictam equitauit apud Burford et alibi in comitatu Oxon' versus partes predictas adintencionem ipsum dominum nostrum regem si de eorum iniquo et proditorie consilio et proponito citius impediti non fuissent per gentiles comitatus predicti Oxon' destruendos et omnes pares et magnates regni sui Anglie ac leges regni sui Anglie subuertendas et adnullandas in destruccionem regni Anglie. . . .

Juries of various hundreds in the county of Oxford presented in Easter 1398 before the king's bench at Oxford that John Milford weaver of Cogges and others as the principal insurgents and chief leaders and abettors of rebels rose against the king and their allegiance feloniously and treasonably plotting the death of the king and the destruction of the magnates; collecting about two hundred others including John Bedemansone of Witney, on the night of Palm Sunday 1398 they rose in the new treason and at Cokethorpe chose as their leader Gilbert Vaughan to whom as a symbol of authority they gave a pair of gold spurs; they marched to Yelford and Aston, collecting others as they went, and finally to Bampton where they sought more supporters. Henry Ropere of Bampton, chief traitor and insurgent, holding in one hand lighted candles and in the other a battle-axe, sought to recruit the men of the town crying, arise all men and go with us or else truly and by god ye shall be dead. William Barbour and others who were unwilling to be traitors were assaulted beaten, badly wounded, and threatened with death. Ropere was by common consent chosen messenger to seek the king and his government in Bristol and Gloucester; he set out on the following Monday and Tuesday for Burford to destroy the king, the peers and magnates, and the laws of the kingdom. . .

[*Both Milford and Bedemansone pled not guilty; Milford was pardoned; Bedemansone mainperned.*]

2. Record of the trial of Henry Ropere on indictment before the justices of the peace, Easter 1398; acquitted; K. B. 27/548, Rex, m. 9; for the indictment see above Roll B, no. 4.

3. Record of the trial of John Redeman, jr., on indictment before the justices of the peace, Easter 1398; acquitted; K. B. 27/548, Rex, m. 9; for the indictment see above Roll B, no. 11.

4. Record of the trial of Henry Ropere, Easter 1398 (K. B. 27/548, Rex, m. 22d.). Juries of various hundreds presented that Thomas Geldesowe of Witney, John Milford weaver of Cogges, Gilbert Vaughan, William Haney of Brize Norton, and William Makerell of Eynsham as the principal insurgents rose in rebellion against the king and their allegiance and plotted the death of the king and the magnates; Henry Ropere as the chief traitor at Cokethorpe was chosen to seek the king and his government at Bristol and Gloucester and he set out for Burford to accomplish this mission; Ropere was tried, found guilty, and sentenced to be drawn, hanged, decapitated, and quartered. His head was to be sent to Reading, and the parts to Colchester, Norwich, Northampton, and Coventry as an example to other traitors.

5. Record of the trial of John Warner, Hilary 1399 (K. B. 27/551, Rex, m.5). Juries of various hundreds presented before the king's bench, Easter 1398, that John Warner and others (wording the same as Roll B, no. 11); mainperned for future appearance; see below p. 89, n. 16.

6. Record of trial of Thomas Bocher and William Wawe both of Bampton, Hilary 1399 (K. B. 27/551, Rex, m. 1d.). Juries of various hundreds presented before the king's bench, Easter 1398, that Thomas Bocher and William Wawe both of Bampton with one hundred others rose feloniously and traitorously at Bampton in the new insurrection against the crown and their allegiance to destroy the king and the magnates; William Barbour and Ralph Trompur were among those they sought to kill for refusing to join them. (Bocher and Wawe mainperned for future appearance; for their indictment before the justices of the peace see above Roll B, no. 4.)

7. Record of the trial of John Smyth of Eynsham on indictment before the justices of the peace, Easter 1400; pardoned; K. B. 27/556, Rex, m. 7d. for the indictment see above Roll B, no. 6; for the pardon, Pardon Roll 32 m. 22.

Jury Presentments

8. Wootton Hundred, Easter 1398 (K. B. 9/100, m. 9).

Hundredum de Wotton'

Iuratores presentant quod Willelmus Makerell' de Eynesham sclater Iohannes Smyth' de eadem Iohannes Donnyng de [eadem Willelmus] Shoppe souter Iohannes seruiens Iohannis Ireby de Eynesham Iohannes Milford de Cogges (Iohannes Parys de eadem)[i] et Thomas G[ildesowe] de Wytteney felonice et proditorie machinantes dominum nostrum regem et regnum suum Anglie destruere et exheredare et quamplures [*torn*] eiusdem regni interficere ac omnes et singulas leges et consuetudines regni sui Anglie subuertere et ad[nullare *torn*] dominos secundum illorum ordinacionem et propositum facere et ordinare contra coronam et dignitatem ac [*torn*] et ligeanciam suam die Dominica in ramis palmarum anno regni regis Ricardi secundi vicesimo primo apud [*torn*] aggregando sibi quampluribus alijs proditoribus ignotis ad numerum vj[xx] personarum et abinde vsque villam [*torn*] -res ibidem sibi aggregando et colligendo; et ad illorum feloniam prodiccionem et imaginacionem in forma [*torn*] dictum Thomam Geldesowe capitaneum omnium nominandum ipsum Thomam iuuenem comitis Arun[del *torn*] Eynesham et alias villas infra comitatum Berk' ad premuniendos et imparandos omnes homines in dictis [*torn*] existentibus sub pena decollacionis quod ipsi ad certos diem et locum per dictum Thomam et socios suos [*torn*] ad exequendos illorum feloniam prodiccionem et imaginacionem predictas etc. *Marg:* prodicio

Item presentant quod Iohannes Malmesbury seruiens persone ecclesie de Kydyngton' die anno et loco predictis fuit [*torn*] ad prodiccionem predictam in forma predicta faciendam. *Marg:* accessorius

Jurors of Wootton hundred present that William Makerell slater, John Smyth, John Donnyng, all of Eynsham, William Shoppe souter, John servant of John Ireby of Eynsham, John Milford, John Parys both of Cogges, and Thomas Gildesowe of Witney feloniously and traitorously plotting to destroy the king and the kingdom and to subvert the laws in violation of their allegiance, on Palm Sunday 1398 collected about 120 men from Eynsham and villages in Berkshire; Gildesowe was chosen captain and called himself the young earl of Arundel. [*The text is too badly damaged to read more details.*] *John Malmesbury servant of the parson of Kiddington was an accessory.*

9. Witney Vill, Easter 1398 (K. B. 9/100, m. 3)

John Redeman, Henry Barriour, Philip Welyngton, [John Milford,

Thomas Geldesowe, John Warner, John] Bellebroughton, and William Hannay of Brize Norton and others rising at Bampton treasonably chose leaders and shouted their slogan through the streets.

10. Bampton Hundred, Easter 1398 (K. B. 9/100, m. 5)
William Hannay [Gilbert] Waughan, John Kirkeby, Thomas Bocher, William Wawe (note of insufficient evidence against Bocher and Wawe; below p. 89 n. 11)[i], John Coupere, all except Hannay of Bampton, Henry Barriour of Witney, Simon [Taylor Welshman of Witney, Philip] Webbe of West End, William Bakere parson of South Leigh, John Milford weaver, John Paradys both of Cogges, William Nasshe collier of Ascot, William clerk of the church of Cogges, and one hundred others feloniously and treasonably rose against the crown and their allegiance, shouting their slogan.

11. Chadlington Hundred, Easter 1398 (K. B. 9/100, m. 6)
William atte Nasshe, William Hannay of Swinbrook, and John [*torn*] at Ducklington Wood with others rose in new insurrection to kill supporters of the king who opposed them.

12. Grand Jury of the County of Oxford, Easter 1398 (K. B. 9/100, m. 14)
Henry Ropere, Thomas Gildesowe of Witney, John Milford, [Gilbert] Vaughan, William Hannay bailiff of Brize Norton, and William Makerell of Eynsham, joined by John Bedemansone of Witney, John [*illegible*] of the abbot of Eynsham, John Malmesbury of Kidlington, Henry Barriour, ?Philip Webbe of West End, Simon Taillour Welshman of Witney, John Warner, and others [*names torn*]; details as in record of trial of John Milford, above no. 1.

II Process on Those Indicted in the Bampton Uprising

In all thirty-two men are known to have been presented one or more times for involvement in the Bampton uprising on Palm Sunday 1398. Twenty-five were indicted before the justices of the peace (Roll B, nos. 4, 6, 11); seven others were named in the presentments by the grand jury and the local juries before the king's bench (App. I, nos. 8-12). In order to bring together all the information available concerning the punishment of these men and to avoid lengthy and repetitious notes on the indictments in the text, the following table has been prepared.

In the left-hand column are the names of those indicted in the uprising arranged in the first three groups as the names appear in the indictments before the justices of the peace; the names in the last group appear only in the presentments before the king's bench.

	1	2	3	4	5	6	7	8	
Roll B, no. 4									
Henry Barriour	x	x	x	x			2	x	
John Milleford	x	x	x	x		x	3	x	9
Thomas Gildeslowe	x	x	x			x	2	x	
William Hannay	x	x	x	x	x		3		
Gilbert Vaughan	x	x		x			1		10
John Kirkeby	x			x			1		11
Thomas Boucher	x			x			1		12
John Coupere	x			x			1		13
William Wawe	x			x			1	x	12
Henry Ropere		x							14
Roll B, no. 6									
John Paradys	x			x		x	2		15
John Leche	x								
William Makerel	x	x				x	1		
John Donnyng	x					x	1		
John Smyth	x					x	1		16
John, servant of John Yerby	x					x	1		
William Shoppe	x					x	1		
Edward Underhorn	x								
John Cadewell	x								
Roll B, no. 11									
Simon Taillour	x	x		x			1	x	
John Warner	x	x	x				1		17
John Bellebroughton	x		x				1		
Philip Welynton	x		x				1	x	
John Redeman, jr.			x				1		18
William atte Nasshe	x			x	x		2	x	19
Presented coram rege									
John Bedemansone		x							20
John . . of abbot of Eynsham		x							
John Malmesbury		x				x			
Philip Webbe		x		x			1		21
William Bakere				x			1		
William, clerk of Cogges church				x			1		
John. .					x				

The numbers on the preceding eight columns may be explained as follows; they also refer to notes containing references.

Column 1 A check indicates failure to appear before the king's bench for trial, Easter 1398; unless further process is noted the accused was presumably outlawed.

Column 2 A check indicates presentment by the county grand jury.

Column 3 A check indicates presentment by a jury from the town of Witney.

Column 4 A check indicates presentment by a jury from Bampton hundred.

Column 5 A check indicates presentment by a jury from Chadlington hundred.

Column 6 A check indicates presentment by a jury from Wootton hundred.

Column 7 A number indicates the number of times the name is listed for failure to appear before the king's bench for trial, Easter 1398, on presentment by a local jury; unless further process is noted the accused was presumably outlawed.

Column 8 The property of those marked in this column was forfeited because they had been convicted of treason; no record of these convictions has been found; two were eventually pardoned.

The numbers 9-21 in the right-hand column refer to notes providing information on the process on the individual noted.

1 In exigend in the king's bench at Oxford on indictment before the justices of the peace, Easter 1398; K. B. 27/548, Rex, m. 19.

2 Presented before the king's bench at Oxford by the grand jury of the county of Oxford, Easter 1398; K. B. 9/100, m. 14.

3 Presented by the jury of the town of Witney before the king's bench at Oxford, Easter 1398; *ibid.*, m. 3. Missing names supplied from K. B. 27/548, Rex, m. 19.

4 Presented by the jury from Bampton hundred before the king's bench at Oxford, Easter 1398; K. B. 9/100, m. 5. Missing names supplied from K. B. 27/548, Rex, m. 19.

5 Presented by the jury from Chadlington hundred before the king's bench at Oxford, Easter 1398; K. B. 9/100, m. 6.

6 Presented by the jury from Wootton hundred before the king's bench at Oxford, Easter 1398; *ibid.*, m. 9. Missing names supplied from K. B. 27/548, Rex, m. 19.

7 In exigend in the king's bench at Oxford on indictment coram rege, Easter 1398; *ibid.* The figures indicate the number of times a name is listed. This list contains only the names presented by the three hundred juries and the jury from Witney, not the names presented by the grand jury.

8 Property forfeited for treason, 12 April 1398; total yearly value of lands, 40*s.*, goods and chattels, £20; *C. P. R.* 1396-1399, p. 328.

9 Tried before the king's bench at Westminster, Michaelmas 1398 on presentment before the bench at Oxford, Easter 1398, by juries from the hundreds; pled not guilty; released *sine die*, Michaelmas 1403, because pardoned, 15 September 1403; K. B. 27/550, Rex, m. 23. For the pardon see Pardon Roll 32, m. 10. For summons prior to acquittal see K. B. 27/555, Rex, m. 5; 556, Rex, m. 2; 558, Rex, m. 6; 559, Rex, m. 1; 568, Rex, m. 9; 569, Rex, m. 2d. For payment of fines for non-appearance, *ibid.*, 559, Fines, m. 1; 570, Fines,

m. 1d. See also *C. C. R.* 1399-1402, p. 45. I have found no record that his property was restored to him.

10 See also K. B. 27/550, Rex, m. 23. For another offence see Roll B, no. 21.

11 A John Kirkeby clerk was pardoned, 15 April 1399; Pardon Roll 31, m. 10.

12 Bocher and Wawe appeared for trial before the king's bench at Westminster, Hilary 1399, on presentment before the bench at Oxford, Easter 1398, by juries from the hundreds; pled not guilty; mainperned for trial, Easter 1399 and subsequently; in exigend, Trinity 1401 and subsequently; K. B. 27/551, Rex, m. 1d.; 552, Rex, m. 2; 554, Rex, m. 3d.; 555, Rex, m. 2d.; 558, Rex, m. 13; 561, Rex, m. 9d.; 563, Rex, m. 16d.; 566, Rex, m. 19; see also *C. C. R.* 1396-1399, p. 475. According to notation on the file of the Bampton hundred jury presentment they were at some point released *sine die* because of insufficient evidence; K. B. 9/100, m. 5.

13 Pardoned, 14 October 1413; Pardon Roll 36, m. 28.

14 Tried before the king's bench delivering Oxford Castle gaol on indictment before the justices of the peace, Easter 1398; pled not guilty; acquitted; tried before the king's bench at Oxford, Easter 1398, on presentment before the bench by juries from the hundreds; pled not guilty; sentenced to be drawn, hanged, and quartered, his head to be sent to Reading, the quarters to Colchester, Norwich, Northampton, and Coventry; no chattels; K. B. 27/548, Rex, mm. 9, 22d.

15 Fine paid for his escape from Maidenhead gaol, 21 September 1398; *C. P. R.* 1396-1399, p. 417.

16 Tried before the king's bench at Westminster, Easter 1400, on presentment before the justices of the peace of Oxfordshire; released *sine die* on offering pardon, dated 10 February 1400; K. B. 27/566, Rex, m. 7d. For the pardon see Pardon Roll 32, m. 22.

17 Appeared for trial before the king's bench at Westminster, Hilary 1399, on presentment before the bench at Oxford, Easter 1398, by juries from the hundreds; outlawry having been pronounced in error quashed; mainperned for subsequent appearance; K. B. 27/551, Rex, m. 5; pardoned, 15 January 1414; Pardon Roll 36, m. 27.

18 Tried before the king's bench delivering Oxford Castle gaol on indictment before the justices of the peace, Easter 1398; pled not guilty; acquitted; K. B. 27/548, Rex, m.9.

19 Pardoned, 15 June 1398; Pardon Roll 30, m. 15.

20 Tried with Milford before the king's bench at Westminster, Michaelmas 1398, on presentment before the bench at Oxford, Easter 1398, by juries from the hundreds; pled not guilty; mainperned; K. B. 27/550, Rex, m. 23.

21 Tried before the king's bench at Westminster, Michaelmas 1398 having been outlawed for failure to appear before the bench as an indicted felon and traitor; sentenced to be drawn and hanged; K. B. 27/551, Rex, m. 5; see also above n. 7.

GAOL DELIVERIES
1389-1398

ROLL C

GAOL DELIVERY ROLL 180

[*m. 1*]

Rex mandauit dilectis et fidelibus suis Roberto de Cherlton' et Iohanni Hull' iusticiarijs suis breue suum patens in hec verba. Ricardus dei gratia rex Anglie et Francie et dominus Hibernie dilectis et fidelibus suis Roberto de Cherlton' et Iohanni Hull' salutem. Sciatis quod constituimus vos iusticiarios nostros ad gaolam nostram castri Oxon' de prisonibus in ea existentibus deliberandam. Et ideo vobis mandamus quod ad certum diem quem vos ad hoc prouideritis conueniatis apud Oxon' ad gaollam illam deliberandam facturi inde quod ad iusticiam pertinet secundum legem et consuetudinem regni nostri Anglie saluis nobis amerciamentis et alijs ad nos inde spectantibus. Mandauimus enim vicecomiti nostro Oxon' quod ad certum diem quem ei scire facietis omnes prisones eiusdem gaole et eorum attachiamentos coram vobis ibidem venire faciat. In cuius rei testimonium has litteras nostras fieri fecimus patentes. Teste me ipso apud Westm' xxiiij die Aprilis anno regni nostri duodecimo [24 April 1389].

Deliberacio gaole domini regis castri Oxon' et Berk' facta apud Oxon' coram Roberto de Cherlton' et Iohanne Hull' iusticiarijs domini regis ad gaolam illam deliberandam assignatis die Veneris proximo post festum sancti Marci euangeliste anno regni regis Ricardi secundi post conquestum Anglie duodecimo [30 April 1389].

1. *Marg:* Oxon' Iohannes Randolf de Marleburgh' captus pro eo quod indictatus fuit coram Ricardo Abberbury et socijs suis iusticiarijs domini regis ad pacem in comitatu predicto conseruandam assignatis de eo quod ipse die Martis proximo ante festum apostolorum Philipi et Iacobi anno regni domini regis nunc Anglie nono felonice et proditiose construxit falsam monetam videlicet quadrantes de copere simulatas auro et grota de peutre simulata argento ad summam quadraginta solidorum in domo Walteri Lydrerd' de Bageslade; et quod est communis latro; quod quidam indictamentum prefati iusticiarij pacis iusticiarijs hic liberarunt venit coram iusticiarijs hic per vicecomitem ductus et allocutus qualiter se

velit de felonia predicta acquietare dicit quod ipse in nullo est inde culpabilis et de hoc ponit se de bono et malo super patriam. Ideo fiat inde iurata. Iuratores veniunt qui ad hoc electi triati et iurati dicunt super sacramentum suum quod predictus Iohannes culpabilis est de felonia predicta. Catalla ipsius Iohannis nulla. Ideo idem Iohannes trahiatur et suspendeatur. *Marg:* Suspendeatur et trahiatur

John Randolf of Marlborough [*Wilts.*] *indicted before Richard Abberbury and fellow justices of the peace for on 24 April 1386 feloniously and treasonably making false money, farthings of copper to look like gold and groats of pewter to look like silver, to the amount of 40s. in the house of William Lydrerd of Bagley* [*Berks*]; *being a common thief; pled not guilty, was tried, found guilty, and sentenced to be drawn and hanged; no chattels.*

2. *Marg:* Oxon' Ricardus Sclattere captus pro eo quod indictatus fuit coram Gilberto Wace et socijs suis iusticiarijs domini regis ad pacem in comitatu predicto conseruandam assignatis de eo quod ipse die Sabati proximo ante diem Dominicam in medio quadragesime anno regni domini regis nunc Anglie vndecimo felonice furatus fuit vnam ollam eneam precij trium solidorum apud Northlye de Ricardo Chaundeler de Northlye; quod quidem indictamentum prefati iusticiarij pacis iusticiarijs hic liberarunt venit coram iusticiarijs hic per vicecomitem ductus et allocutus qualiter se velit de felonia predicta acquietare dicit quod ipse in nullo est inde culpabilis et de hoc ponit se de bono et malo super patriam. Ideo fiat inde iurata. Iuratores veniunt qui ad hoc electi triati et iurati dicunt super sacramentum suum quod predictus Ricardus culpabilis est de felonia predicta. Catalla ipsius Ricardi nulla. Ideo idem Ricardus suspendeatur etc. *Marg:* Suspendeatur

Richard Sclattere indicted before Gilbert Wace and fellow justices of the peace for on 7 March 1388 feloniously stealing a brass pot, price 3s., at North Leigh from Richard Chaundeler of North Leigh; pled not guilty, was tried, found guilty, and sentenced to be hanged; no chattels.

3. *Marg:* Oxon' Ricardus Tauenour de Faldo captus pro eo quod indictatus fuit coram Gilberto Wace et socijs suis iusticiarijs domini regis ad pacem in comitatu predicto conseruandam assignatis de eo quod ipse die Iouis quarto die Marcij anno regni domini regis nunc Anglie duodecimo felonice furatus fuit duo paria caligarum precij duorum solidorum et vnam vlnam panni de russeto precij decem et octo denariorum de Ricardo Forest de Bannebury; et tres libras cere precij decem et octo denariorum de Thoma Spycer de Bannebury apud Bannebury; et de eo quod ipse die et anno supradictis apud Bannebury in pleno foro felonice furatus fuit duos salmones precij duodecim

denariorum de vno homine ignoto; quod quidem indictamentum prefati iusticiarij pacis iusticiarijs hic liberarunt venit coram iusticiarijs hic per vicecomitem ductus et allocutus qualiter se velit de felonia predicta acquietare dicit quod ipse in nullo est inde culpabilis et de hoc ponit se de bono et malo super patriam. Ideo fiat inde iurata. Iuratores veniunt qui ad hoc electi triati et iurati dicunt super sacramentum suum quod predictus Ricardus culpabilis est de felonia predicta. Catalla ipsius Ricardi nulla. Ideo idem Ricardus suspendeatur etc. *Marg:* Suspendeatur

Richard Tavenour of Leafield indicted before Gilbert Wace and fellow justices of the peace for on 4 March 1389 feloniously stealing two pairs of hose, price 2s., and one ell of russet cloth, price 18d., from Richard Forest of Banbury; three lbs. of wax, price 18d., from Thomas Spycer of Banbury, at Banbury; and in the market at Banbury two salmon, price 12d., from an unknown man; pled not guilty, was tried, found guilty, and sentenced to be hanged; no chattels.

4. *Marg:* Oxon' Iohannes Roys de Totebaldyndon' et Iohannes Brasyere de Laurence Baldyngdon' capti pro eo quod indictati fuerunt coram prefatis iusticiarijs pacis de eo quod vbi Iohannes Broun de Hibernia et Iohannes Brasiere de Baldyndon' iunior indictati fuerunt de eo quod ipsi die Mercurij in prima septimana quadragesime anno regni domini regis nunc Anglie decimo venerunt ad domum Ricardi Bailly de Newenham et ibidem vnum coopertorium precij duodecim denariorum vnum quadrantem de auro et quinque solidos argenti in pecunia numerata eiusdem Ricardi noctanter felonice furati fuerunt; et de eo quod predicti Iohannes Broun et Iohannes Brasyere die [et] anno supradictis domum eiusdem Ricardi Bailly apud Newenham noctanter felonice fregerunt et ibidem duas mappas mensales precij quatuor solidorum vnam tunicam precij duorum solidorum et alia bona et catalla ad valenciam tresdecim solidorum et quatuor denariorum felonice furati fuerunt et asportauerunt; et de [eo] quod predicti Iohannes Broun et Iohannes Brasyere venerunt super Haryndon' inter villam de Hasele et villam de Rycot die Sabati in vigilia pasche regni predicti regis Ricardi supradicto et ibidem Hugonem Cormonger de vno equo precij duorum solidorum vno sacco precij duodecim denariorum et de duodecim denarijs argenti in pecunia numerata eiusdem Hugonis felonice depredauerunt; et de eo quod predicti Iohannes Broun et Iohannes Brasiere in vigilia pasche venerunt apud Combe et ibidem vnum iumentum precij quinque solidorum vnum couerlyt precij duodecim denariorum vnum canauas precij octo denariorum de Thoma Caymoys noctanter felonice furati fuerunt; et quod sunt communes latrones. Ijdem Iohannes Roy [et] Iohannes Brasyere de Laurencebaldyndon' predictos Iohannem Broun et

Iohannem Brasiere de Baldyndon' apud Laurence Baldyndon' postea die Mercurij proximo post festum pasche anno regni domini regis nunc Anglie decimo receptauerunt scientes ipsos feloniam predictam fecisse pro qua quidem felones predicti [Iohannes] Broun et Iohannes Brasiere de Baldyngdon' coram prefatis Ricardo Abberbury et socijs suis iusticiarijs conuicti et suspensi fuerunt; quod quidem indictamentum prefati iusticiarij pacis iusticiarijs hic l[iberarunt] ac eciam recordum deliberacionis predictorum Iohannis Broun et Iohannis Brasiere coram Ricardo Abberbury et [socijs] suis iusticiarijs pacis in comitatu predicto de principali felonia predicta iusticiarijs hic ostenderunt veniunt coram iusticiarijs hic per vicecomitem ducti et allocuti qualiter se velint de accessorio felonie predicte acquietare [dicunt] quod ipsi in nullo sunt inde culpabiles et de hoc ponunt se de bono et malo super patriam. [Ideo] fiat inde iurata. Iuratores veniunt qui ad hoc electi triati et iurati dicunt super sacramentum suum quod [predicti] Iohannes Roys et Iohannes Brasyere in nullo sunt culpabiles de receptamento predicto nec [ea] occasione vnquam se retraxerunt. Ideo ijdem Iohannes Roys et Iohannes Brasiere eant inde quieti etc. *Marg:* Quieti

John Roys and John Brasyere, both of Toot Baldon were indicted before the said justices of the peace as accessories to the following: John Broun of Ireland and John Brasiere, jr., of Baldon were indicted for on the night of 27 February 1387 feloniously stealing a coverlet, price 12d., a quarter of a gold florin, and five silver shillings from Richard Bailly of Newnham Murren; on the same night they feloniously broke into his house and stole two table-cloths, price 4s., a coat, price 2s., and other goods valued at 13s. 4d.; on 6 April 1387 at Haryndon between Haseley and Rycote they feloniously robbed Hugh Cormonger of a horse, price 2s., a sack, price 12d., and 12d. in cash; on the same night at Combe they feloniously stole a draught animal, price 5s., a coverlet, price 12d., and a piece of canvas, price 8d., from Thomas Caymoys; they are common thieves. On 10 April 1387 John Roys and John Brasyere received Broun and Brasyere, jr., knowing that they had committed the aforesaid felonies. It was shown that the latter had been tried and sentenced to be hanged before Richard Abberbury and his fellow justices of the peace. Roys and Brasyere, sr., tried as accessories, pled not guilty, and were acquitted.

[*For the trial and conviction of John Broun and John Brasiere, jr., before the justices of the peace see above Roll A, no. 10.*]

[*m. 1d.*]

5. *Marg:* Oxon' Ricardus Pynnere captus pro eo quod indictatus fuit coram Gilberto Wace et socijs suis iusticiarijs domini regis ad pacem in comitatu predicto conseruandam assignatis de eo quod ipse die Mercurij proximo ante festum conuersacionis sancti Pauli anno regni domini regis

nunc Anglie duodecimo apud Dadyngton' domum Andree Drapere de Dadyngton' noctanter felonice fregit et viginti libras argenti ipsius Andree in pecunia numerata felonice furatus fuit; quod quidem indictamentum prefati iusticiarij pacis iusticiarijs hic liberarunt venit coram iusticiarijs hic per vicecomitem ductus et allocutus qualiter se velit de felonia predicta acquietare dicit quod ipse clericus est et quod ipse non potest [*blank*] sine Iohanne episcopo Lincoln' loci illius ordinario respondere. Et super hoc venit quidam Stephanus Brakkale decanus Oxon' (commissorius generalis ipsius episcopi)[i] et profert hic in curia litteras Iohannis episcopi Lincoln' eidem Stephano directi ad omnes clericos de quocumque crimine felonico coram quibuscumque iusticiarijs domini regis irrititos petendos et calumpniandos et super hoc predictus Ricardus petit examinacionem sibi fieri vtrum ipse clericus sit nec ne et per examinacionem predicti Stephani clericus inuenitur. Et super hoc predictus Stephanus petit predictum Ricardum tanquam clericum etc. sibi deliberari set vt prius sciatur pro quali idem Ricardus deliberari debeat rei veritas inquiratur per patriam. Ideo fiat inde iurata. Iuratores veniunt qui ad hoc electi triati et iurati dicunt super sacramentum suum quod predictus Ricardus culpabilis est de felonia predicta. Catalla ipsius Ricardi duodecim denarijs vnde prior de Burcestre oneratur. Et super hoc predictus Ricardus deliberatur hic in curia prefato ordinario ad ipsum saluo ducendum vsque ad gaolam predicti episcopi de Bannebury ibidem moraturum periculo quo incombit etc. *Marg:* catalla (xij d.)[e]

Richard Pynnere, indicted before Gilbert Wace and fellow justices of the peace for on 20 January 1389 at night feloniously breaking into the house of Andrew Drapere of Deddington at Deddington and feloniously stealing £20 in silver, proved clergy; after the jury had found him guilty, he was released to the ordinary for imprisonment in the bishop's gaol at Banbury; chattels, 12d., in charge to the prior of Bicester.

6. *Marg:* Oxon' William Ropere de Sibford' captus pro eo quod indictatus fuit coram prefatis iusticiarijs pacis de eo quod ipse die Sabati proximo post festum epiphanie domini anno regni domini regis nunc Anglie duodecimo in campo de Berford Seint Iohan vnum vomerem et vnum cultrum precij sexdecim denariorum pro caruca de bonis et catallis Ricardi Chestre felonice furatus fuit; et quod ipse est communis latro; quod quidem indictamentum prefati iusticiarij pacis iusticiarijs hic liberarunt venit coram iusticiarijs hic per vicecomitem ductus et allocutus qualiter se velit de felonia predicta acquietare dicit quod ipse in nullo est culpabilis de felonia predicta et de hoc ponit se de bono et malo super patriam. Ideo fiat inde iurata. Iuratores veniunt qui ad hoc electi triati et iurati dicunt super sacramentum suum quod predictus Willelmus

culpabilis est de felonia predicta. Catalla ipsius Willelmi quinque solidi et quatuor denarij (vnde)[i] Iohannes Louell' oneratur de duobus solidis prior hospitalis sancti Iohannis de duodecim denarijs et Almaricus de sancto Amando de duodecim denarijs et Thomas Poyle vicecomes comitatus predicti de sexdecim denarijs. Ideo idem Willelmus suspendeatur etc. *Marg:* (catalla v s. iiij d.)[c] Suspendeatur

William Ropere of Sibford indicted before the aforesaid justices of the peace for on 9 January 1389 feloniously stealing in a field at Barford St John one ploughshare and one coulter for a plough, price 16d., from Richard Chestre, being a common thief: pled not guilty, was tried, found guilty, and sentenced to be hanged; chattels, 5s. 4d., 2s. in charge to John Lovell, 12d. to the prior of the hospital of St John, 12d. to Amaury de St Amand, 16d. to Thomas Poyle, sheriff.

[*m. 2*]
Dominus rex mandauit dilectis et fidelibus suis Roberto Bardolf Roberto Cherlton' Thome Paynell' Thome Power Iohanni Hull' Thome Barentyn Nicholao Somerton' et Ricardo Ouerton' breue suum patens in hec verba. Ricardus dei gratia rex Anglie et Francie et dominus Hibernie dilectis et fidelibus suis Roberto Bardolf Roberto Charlton' Thome Paynell' Thome Power Iohanni Hull' Thome Barentyn Nicholao Somerton' et Ricardo Ouerton' salutem. Sciatis quod assignauimus vos coniunctim et diuisim ad pacem nostram necnon ad statuta apud Wynton' Norht' et Westm' pro conseruacione pacis eiusdem edita in omnibus et singulis suis articulis in comitatu Oxon' tam infra libertates quam extra custodienda et custodiri facienda et omnes illos quos contra formam statutorum predictorum delinquentes inueneritis castigandos et puniendos prout secundum formam statutorum predictorum fuerit faciendum et omnes qui aliquibus de populo nostro de corporibus suis vel de incendio domorum suarum minas fecerint et sufficientem securitatem de pace et bono gestu erga nos et populum nostrum inueniendam coram vobis venire et si huiusmodi securitatem inuenire recusauerint tunc eos in prisonis nostris quousque huiusmodi securitatem inuenerint saluo custodiri faciendos. Assignauimus eciam vos septem sex quinque quatuor tres et duos vestrum iusticiarios nostros ad inquirendum per sacramentum proborum et legalium hominum de comitatu predicto tam infra libertates quam extra per quos rei veritas melius sciri poterit de omnibus felonijs transgressionibus forstallarijs regratarijs et extorsionibus in comitatu predicto infra libertates et extra per quoscumque et qualitercumque factis seu perpetratis et que exnunc ibidem fieri contigeret et eciam de omnibus illis qui in conuenticulis contra pacem nostram et in perturbacionem populi nostri seu vi armata ierint vel equitauerint seu exire vel equitare presumpserint et eciam qui ininsidijs

ad gentem nostram mahemiandam vel interficiendam iacuerint vel exnunc iacere presumpserint et eciam de hijs qui capicijs et alia liberata de vnica secta per confederacionem et pro manutenencia contra defencionem ac formam ordinacionum et statutorum inde ante hec tempora factorum vsi fuerint et alijs huiusmodi liberata imposterum vtentibus et eciam de hostilarijs et alijs qui in abusu mensurarum et pondorum aut in vendicione victualium et eciam de quibuscumque operarijs artificibus et seruitoribus et alijs qui contra formam ordinacionum statutorum pro communi vtilitate regni nostri Anglie de huisusmodi operarijs artificibus seruitoribus hostilarijs et alijs inde ante festum natiuitatis beate Marie vltimo elapsum factorum delinquerint vel attemptauerint in comitatu predicto seu exnunc delinquere vel attemptare presumpserint et ad processus versus omnes quos coram vobis in hac parte indictari contigerit quousque capiantur reddantur vel vtlagentur faciendos et ad omnia breuia et precepta per nuper custodes pacis nostre et iusticiarios nostros ad huiusmodi felonias transgressiones et malefacta in hac parte audienda et terminanda assignandos facta et coram eis ad certos terminos futuros retornabilia ad terminos illos recipienda et continuanda ad eosdem operarios artifices et seruitores iuxta formam statutorum predictorum castigandos et puniendos. Assignauimus vos septem sex quinque quatuor tres et duos vestrum quorum alterum vestrum vos prefati Roberte Cherlton' et Iohannes vnum esse volumus iusticiarios nostros ad felonias predictas ac ea omnia et singula que per huiusmodi conuenticula contra pacem nostram et perturbacionem populi nostri et ea eciam que per huiusmodi insidias ad gentem nostram mahemiandam vel interficiendam et ea eciam que per vsum huiusmodi capiciorum et aliarum liberatarum per confederacionem et per manutencia sicut predictum est attemptata fuerint vel attemptari contigerit ac transgressiones et forstallarias predictas audiendas et premissa omnia ac indictamenta quecumque coram prefatis nuper custodibus pacis nostre et iusticiarijs nostris virtute litterarum nostrarum sibi in hac parte factarum facta et non dum terminata inspicienda et debito modo terminanda ad sectam nostram tantum ac extorsiones et regratarias predictas et omnia alia que per huiusmodi hostilarios et alios in abusu mensurarum et pondorum ac in vendicione victualium et omnia alia que per huiusmodi operarios artifices et seruitores contra formam ordinacionum et statutorum predictorum seu in eneruacionem in aliquo presumpta vel attemptata fuerint tam ad sectam nostram quam aliorum quorumcumque coram vobis pro vobis vel pro se ipsis conqueri vel prosequi volencium audienda et terminanda et ad eosdem operarios artifices et seruitores per fines redempciones et amerciamenta et alio modo pro delictis suis prout ante ordinacionem de punicione corporali huiusmodi operarijs artificibus et seruitoribus pro delictis suis exhibendis factam fieri consueuit castigiandos et puniendos secundum legem et consuetudinem regni nostri Anglie ac formam ordinacionum et statutorum predictorum. Prouiso semper quod si casus difficultatis super determinacione extorcionum huiusmodi coram vobis euenire contigerit quod ad iudicium inde reddendum nisi in presencia vnius iusticiariorum nostrorum de vno vel altero banco aut iusticiariorum nostrorum ad assisas in comitatu predicto capiendas assignatorum coram vobis minime procedatur. Et ideo vobis et cuilibet vestrum mandamus quod circa custodiam pacis et statutorum predictorum diligenter intendatis et ad certos dies et loca quas vos septem sex quinque quatuor tres vel duo vestrum ad hoc prouideritis inquisiciones super premissis faciatis et premissa omnia et singula audiatis et terminetis ac modo debito et effectualiter expleatis in forma predicta facturi inde quod ad iusticiam pertinet secundum legem et consuetudinem regni nostri Anglie saluo nobis amerciamentis et alijs ad nos inde spectantibus. Mandamus enim vicecomiti nostro comitatus predicti quod ad certos dies et loca quos vos septem sex quinque quatuor tres vel duo vestrum ei scire faciatis venire faciat coram vobis septem sex quinque quatuor tribus vel duobus vestrum tot et tales probos et legales homines de balliua tua tam infra libertates quam extra per quos rei veritas in premissis melius sciri poterit et inquiri. In cuius rei testimonium has litteras nostras fieri fecimus patentes. Teste me ipso apud Westm' xv die Iulij anno regni nostri terciodecimo [15 July 1389].

Deliberacio gaole domini regis castri Oxon' facta apud Oxon' coram Iohanne Hulle et socijs suis iusticiarijs domini regis ad pacem in comitatu Oxon' conseruandam assignatis die Veneris proximo ante festum sancti Petri in cathedra anno regni regis Ricardi secundi post conquestum terciodecimo [18 February 1390].

7. *Marg:* Oxon' Willelmus Gymel et Petrus Ardach' capti pro eo quod indictati fuerunt coram Roberto Cherlton' et socijs suis iusticiarijs domini regis ad pacem in comitatu predicto conseruandam assignatis de eo quod ipsi simul cum alijs ignotis felonibus eis armatis alligatis modo guerrino arraiatis apud Oxon' die Iouis et die Veneris in quarta septimana quadragesime anno regni domini regis nunc Anglie duodecimo ordinauerunt inter eos certos capitaneos et gubernatores insurgendo contra

Plus in tergo de eodem recordo

[*m. 2d.*]

[pacem domini regis et quesiuerunt][1] Wallicos quoscumque in villa Oxon' existentes sagittando in diuersis vicis et venellis ante se

[1]A blank in the record; supplied from no. 14.

clamando ware ware ware sle sle sle the Walsh dogges and here helpes and ho so loketh' out of his hous he shal be ded et quosdam occiderunt vt inferius et quosdam grauiter vulnerauerunt et quosdam Wallicos genuflexebant abiurare villam fecerunt ducentes eos ad portas dicte ville et super eas fecerunt eos mingere et osculare portam et sic osculando tundebant capita ad portam ita quod quandoque sanguis de naso interdum lacrime exibant ab oculis eorundem; et quandam aulam in Oxon' vocatam Depehalle felonice fregerunt et ibidem vnum librum vnum pennare cum cornu vnum par bractarum Willelmi Whetehull' et vnum gladium et libros Iohannis Hoby ad valenciam triginta et octo solidorum felonice furati fuerunt et asportauerunt; et quod (dicto)[i] die Veneris noctanter cameram Thome Frenssh' in dicta aula situatam felonice fregerunt et duos gladios vnam parmam duos arcus cum viginti et sex sagittis vnum iak de fustian vnam togam rubeam duo paria manicarum albarum vnum par linthiaminum vnam armilausam dupplicatam quinque paria caligarum et duas vlnas de caneuas vnum par linee tele et alia bona et catalla ipsius Thome French' precij sexaginta solidorum felonice furati fuerunt et asportauerunt; et alias cameras diuersorum scolarium in aula predicta manencium predicto die Veneris felonice fregerunt et bona et catalla ibidem inuenta videlicet libros pannos lineos et laneos felonice furati fuerunt; et dicto die Veneris noctanter introitum nuncupatum Neuylesentre in Oxon' felonice fregerunt et bona et catalla videlicet hostia fenestras ac libros gramaticales ac pannos lineos et laneos Willelmi Dannay principalis eiusdem introitus Iohannis Halkyn scolaris ibidem et aliorum scolarium ibidem morancium ad valenciam sexaginta solidorum felonice furati fuerunt et asportauerunt; et eodem die Veneris noctanter aulam vocatam seint Agase halle in Oxon' felonice fregerunt et bona et catalla ibidem inuenta videlicet pannos lineos et laneos libros gramaticales simul diolecticales gladios arcus citheras Willelmi Getton' Iohannis Mulle Iohannis Gloiue et aliorum scolarium ibidem existencium ad valenciam quatuor librarum felonice furati fuerunt; et quod die Sabati in dicta quarta septimana quadragesime anno supradicto predicti Willelmus Gymel et Petrus simul cum alijs felonibus ignotis aulam vocatam Pyrihalle in Oxon' felonice fregerunt et bona principalis eiusdem aule Mathei Alco et Ricardi Olyuere videlicet duos gladios clocos dupplicatos diuersorum colorum vnum baselard vnam securim ac arcus et sagittas ad valenciam quatuor librarum felonice furati fuerunt; et alias aulas et introitus ibidem eodem die intrauerunt videlicet Mildredhalle Hampton'-halle Bastaplesentre et diuersa bona diuersorum scolarium in dicta aula manencium ad valenciam quinquaginta solidorum felonice furati fuerunt; et quod in dicta surexione occisi fuerunt per dictos felones videlicet Edwardus Nuton' Galfridus Hanlane de Wall' Thomas Repton' et

Iohannes Bowman; et quod dicto die Iouis predicti felones et diuersi ignoti exportauerunt ostia tabulas et petras de dictis aulis spoliata in altum vicum iuxta ecclesiam beate Marie et acceperunt lignum truncos et hostia laicorum inuitis illis et clauserunt se a Cherltonesyn vsque ad Penchurclane et ibi de nocte permanserunt; veniunt coram iusticiarjis hic per vicecomitem ducti et allocuti qualiter se velint de felonijs predictis acquietare dicunt quod ipsi in nullo sunt culpabiles et de hoc ponunt se de bono et malo super patriam. Ideo fiat inde iurata. Iuratores veniunt qui ad hoc electi triati et iurati dicunt super sacramentum suum quod predicti Willelmus Gymel et Petrus non sunt culpabiles de felonijs predictis nec ea occasione vnquam se retraxerunt. Ideo consideratum est quod predicti Willelmus Gymel et Petrus eant inde quieti etc. *Marg:* Quieti

William Gymel and Peter Ardach indicted before Robert Cherlton and fellow justices of the peace for the following: on 1-2 April 1389 they with others unknown, armed and leagued together, sought out Welshmen in Oxford shouting ware ware ware sle sle sle the Walsh dogges and here helpes and ho so loketh out of his hous he shal be ded, killing some as below, wounding others, forcing them to abjure the town, and inflicting indignities on them at the gates; they broke into Deep Hall taking from William Whetehull a book, a pen, an inkhorn, and a pair of breeches, and from John Hoby a sword and books, all this valued at 38s.; they feloniously broke into the chamber of Thomas Frenssh in the same hall and feloniously took two swords, a buckler, two bows with twenty-six arrows, a fustian jacket, a red coat, two pairs of white gloves, a pair of sheets, a lined cloak, five pairs of hose, two ells of canvas, a pair of linen ?curtains and other goods, price 60s.; from rooms of other scholars in the same hall, books and linen and woollen cloth; they feloniously broke into Neville's Entry taking doors, windows, grammar books, and linen and woollen cloth from William Dannay principal, John Haklyn scholar and others to the value of 60s.; they feloniously broke into St Agate Hall took linen and woollen cloth, grammar and dialectic books, swords, bows, and cithers from William Getton, John Mulle, John Gloive, and other scholars valued at £4; on 3 Aril they feloniously broke into Pyry Hall and took goods of the principal and Mathew Alco and Richard Olyvere, swords, lined cloaks of different colours, a dagger, an axe, and bows and arrows valued at £4; and from Mildred Hall, Hampton Hall, and Bastaple's Entry goods of scholars valued at 50s.; they killed Edward Nuton, Geoffrey Hanlane of Wales, Thomas Repton and John Bowman; they took doors, tables, and stones from the said halls into the High Street by St Mary's church and with wood, trunks, and doors taken from unwilling laymen barricaded themselves from Charlton's Inn to Pentrich Lane and remained the night; they pled not guilty, were tried, and acquitted.

[*See also below nos. 14, 20; for the coroners' inquests on the deaths of Geoffrey* [*Hanlane*] *of Wales and Thomas Repone see Records of Mediaeval Oxford, Coroners' Inquests, etc. ed. by H. E. Salter (Oxford, 1912), p. 48. Neither of the men named as killer appeared among those indicted before the justices of the peace in connection with the riot*].

8. *Marg:* Oxon' Willelmus Norton' capellanus captus pro eo quod indictatus fuit coram Roberto Bardolf et socijs suis iusticiarijs domini regis ad pacem in comitatu predicto conseruandam assignatis de eo quod ipse felonice fregit domum Iohannis Rammesden' apud Shipton' subtus Whychewod noctanter die Lune proximo ante festum sancte Marie Magdalane anno regni domini regis nunc duodecimo et ibidem cum vxore dicti Iohannis concubuit et eam rapuit contra voluntatem viri sui; et de eo quod ipse felonice noctanter fregit domum Iohannis Taillour apud Shipton' subtus Whychewod in festo circumcisionis domini anno regni domini regis nunc supradicto et ibidem Isabellam vxorem suam rapuisse voluisset et cum ea concubuisset; venit coram iusticiarijs hic per vicecomitem ductus et allocutus qualiter se velit de felonijs predictis acquietare dicit quod ipse in nullo est (inde)[i] culpabilis et de hoc ponit se de bono et malo super patriam. Ideo fiat inde iurata. Iuratores veniunt qui ad electi triati et iurati dicunt super sacramentum suum quod predictus Willelmus in nullo est culpabilis de felonijs predictis nec ea occasione vnquam se retraxit. Ideo consideratum est quod predictus Willelmus eat inde quietus etc. *Marg:* Quietus

William Norton chaplain indicted before Robert Bardolf and fellow justices of the peace for on the night of 20 July 1388 feloniously breaking into the house of John Rammesden at Shipton under Wychwood and raping the wife of John, and on the night of 1 January 1389 feloniously breaking into the house of John Taillour at Shipton under Wychwood and attempting to rape his wife, Isabel; pled not guilty, was tried, and acquitted.

9. *Marg:* Oxon' Thomas Dababom et Iohannes Wilteshire capti pro eo quod indictati fuerunt coram Roberto Cherlton' et socijs suis iusticiarijs domini regis de pace de eo quod ipsi die Veneris in vigilia apostolorum Philipi et Iacobi anno regni domini regis nunc Anglie duodecimo apud Burwardescote decem et nonem oues precij triginta solidorum Iohannis Muleward de parochia de Burwardescote et viginti oues precij viginti et sex solidorum Iohannis othe Mone de parochia de Burwardescote noctanter felonice furati fuerunt; veniunt coram iusticiarijs hic per vicecomitem ducti et allocuti qualiter se velint de felonia predicta acquietare dicunt quod ipsi in nullo sunt inde culpabiles et de hoc ponunt se de bono et malo super patriam. Ideo fiat inde iurata. Iuratores veniunt qui ad hoc electi triati et iurati dicunt super sacramentum suum quod

predicti Thomas et Iohannes culpabiles sunt de felonia predicta. Ideo ijdem Thomas et Iohannes suspendeantur. Catalla ipsorum Thome et Iohannis quinquaginta et sex solidi vnde Thomas Barentyn oneratur etc. *Marg:* Suspendeantur (catalla lvj s.)[c]

Thomas Dababom and John Wilteshire indicted before Robert Cherlton and fellow justices of the peace for on 30 April 1389 feloniously stealing nineteen sheep, price 30s., f·om John Muleward and twenty sheep, price 26s., from John othe Mone, both of Buscot parish [*Berks.*], *at night; pled not guilty; were tried, found guilty, and sentenced to be hanged; chattels, 56s., in charge to Thomas Barentyn.*

[*m. 3*]
Deliberacio gaole domini regis castri Oxon' facta apud Oxon' coram Roberto de Cherlton' et Iohanne Hulle iusticiarijs domini regis ad gaolam illam deliberandam assignatis die Veneris proximo ante festum sancte Margarete virginis anno regni regis Ricardi secundi post conquestum Anglie quartodecimo [15 July 1390].

10. *Marg:* Oxon' Christoforus atte Nasshe captus pro eo quod indictatus fuit coram Thoma Poure et socijs suis iusticiarijs domini regis ad pacem in comitatu predicto conseruandam assignatis de eo quod ipse venit apud Stratton' Audele iuxta molendinum aquaticum ibidem die Lune proximo post festum anunciacionis beate Marie anno regni domini regis nunc Anglie terciodecimo et ibidem Iohannem Craweton' capellanum de quinquaginta solidis auri et argenti vna zona argenti precij decem solidorum vno portiforo precij quadraginta solidorum duabus tegis tallaribus precij viginti solidorum vna cella precij quadraginta denariorum calciamenta precij duorum solidorum et vno gladio cum vno bokelario precij duorum solidorum felonice depredauit; et de eo quod ipse simul cum alijs die Sabati proximo ante festum pasche anno eiusdem domini regis nunc nono Robertum Chapman de decem et octo solidis et vno equo rubio precij triginta solidorum apud Bekebrok felonice depredatus fuit; et quod est communis latro; quod quidem indictamentum prefati iusticiarij pacis iusticiarijs hic liberarunt venit coram iusticiarijs hic per vicecomitem ductus et allocutus qualiter se velit de felonia predicta acquietare dicit quod ipse clericus est et dicit quod ipse non potest sine Iohanne episcopo Lincoln' loci illius ordinario respondere. Et super hoc venit quidam Iohannes vicarius ecclesie beate Marie Magdalene decanus Christianitatis Oxon' et profert hic in curia litteras Iohannis episcopi Lincoln' eidem decano directi ad omnes clericos de quocumque crimine felonico coram quibuscumque iusticiarijs domini regis irrititos petendos et calumpniandos quarum datum est apud vetus templum London' decimo die mensis Februarij anno regni domini regis

nunc Anglie terciodecimo [10 February 1390]. Et super hoc predictus Christoforus petit examinacionem sibi fieri vtrum ipse clericus sit nec ne et per examinacionem predicti decani clericus inuentur. Et super hoc idem decanus petit predictum Christoforum tamquam clericum etc. sibi deliberari set prius sciatur pro quali idem Willelmus [*sic*] deliberari debeat rei veritas inquiratur per patriam. Ideo fiat inde iurata. Iuratores veniunt qui ad hoc electi triati et iurati dicunt super sacramentum suum quod predictus Christoforus culpabilis est de felonia predicta. Catalla ipsius Christofori viginti et sex solidi et octo denarij vnde Willelmus Grims oneratur. Et super hoc predictus Christoforus deliberatur hic in curia prefato ordinario ad ipsum saluo ducendum vsque gaolam predicti episcopi ad Bannebury ibidem moraturum periculo quo incumbit etc. *Marg:* clericus conuictus catalla (ij marce)[e]

Christopher atte Nasshe indicted before Thomas Poure and fellow justices of the peace for on 28 March 1390 feloniously robbing John Craweton chaplain at Stratton Audley of 50s. in gold and silver, a silver belt, price 10s., a portable breviary, price 40s., two covers, price 20s., a saddle, price 40d., shoes, price 2s., and a sword with a buckler, price 2s.; and on 21 April 1386 with others feloniously robbing Robert Chapman at Begbroke of 18s. and a red horse, price 30s., being a common thief, proved clergy; after the jury found him guilty, he was released to the ordinary for imprisonment in the bishop's gaol at Banbury; chattels, 26. 8d., in charge to William Grims.

11. *Marg:* Iohannes Abraham de Clanefeld captus pro eo quod indictatus fuit coram Thoma Paynell' et socijs suis iusticiarijs domini regis ad pacem in comitatu predicto conseruandam assignatis de eo quod ipse die Sabati proximo post festum sancti Barnabe apostoli anno regni domini regis nunc Anglie octauo venit apud Bampton' et ibidem vnum pullum nigrum precij decem solidorum de Gilberto Talbot tunc domino de Bampton' felonice furatus fuit et abduxit; quod quidem indictamentum prefati iusticiarij pacis iusticiarijs hic liberarunt venit coram iusticiarijs hic per vicecomitem ductus et allocutus qualiter se velit de felonia predicta acquietare dicit quod ipse in nullo est inde culpabilis et de hoc ponit se de bono et malo super patriam. Ideo fiat inde iurata. Iuratores veniunt qui ad hoc electi triati et iurati dicunt super sacramentum suum quod predictus Iohannes non est culpabilis de felonia predicta nec ea occasione vnquam se retraxit. Ideo idem Iohannes eat inde quietus etc. *Marg:* Quietus

John Abraham of Clanfield indicted before Thomas Paynell and fellow justices of the peace for on 17 June 1385 feloniously stealing a black colt, price 10s., from Gilbert Talbot then lord of Bampton, at Bampton; pled not guilty, was tried, and acquitted.

12. *Marg:* Oxon' Robertus Emmeson' et Thomas Webbe de Chynnore capti pro eo quod indictati sunt coram prefatis iusticiarijs pacis de eo quod ipsi die Sabati in vigilia assumpcionis beate Marie anno regni domini regis nunc Anglie terciodecimo cameram Ade vicarij ecclesie de Shirburn' apud Shirburn' felonice fregerunt et ibidem quindecim solidos et decem denarios in pecunia numerata nonem coclearia argenti precij nonem solidorum vnum monile argenti precij quatuor solidorum duo paria de paternostres de lambre vnam bursam de serico precij quatuor solidorum felonice furati fuerunt; quod quidem indictamentum prefati iusticiarij pacis iusticiarijs hic liberarunt veniunt coram iusticiarijs hic per vicecomitem ducti et allocuti qualiter se velint de felonia predicta acquietare dicunt quod ipsi in nullo sunt inde culpabiles et de hoc ponunt se de bono et malo super patriam. Ideo fiat inde iurata. Iuratores veniunt qui ad hoc electi triati et iurati dicunt super sacramentum suum quod predicti Robertus et Thomas non sunt culpabiles de felonia predicta nec ea occasione vnquam se retraxerunt. Ideo ijdem Robertus et Thomas eant inde quieti etc. *Marg:* Quieti

Robert Emmeson and Thomas Webbe of Chinnor indicted before the aforesaid justices for on 14 August 1389 feloniously breaking into the chamber of Adam vicar of Shirburn, at Shirburn and stealing 15s. 10d. in cash, nine silver spoons, price 9s., a silver necklace, price 4s., two rosaries of amber, and a silk purse, price 4s.; pled not guilty, were tried, and acquitted.

[*See below no. 16.*]

13. *Marg:* Oxon' Iohannes Toimnes de Netherenstan' captus pro eo quod indictatus fuit coram prefatis iusticiarijs pacis de eo quod ipse die Lune proximo post festum natiuitatis sancti Iohannis baptiste anno regni domini regis nunc Anglie sexto venit in campo de Netherenston' et ibidem Iohannam seruientem Thome Mulleward felonice rapuit; quod quidem indictamentum prefati iusticiarij pacis iusticiarijs hic liberarunt venit coram iusticiarijs hic per vicecomitem ductus et allocutus qualiter se velit de felonia predicta acquietare dicit quod ipse in nullo est inde culpabilis et de hoc ponit se de bono et malo super patriam. Ideo fiat inde iurata. Iuratores veniunt qui ad hoc electi triati et iurati dicunt super sacramentum suum quod predictus Iohannes non est culpabilis de felonia predicta nec ea occasione vnquam se retraxit. Ideo idem Iohannes eat inde quietus etc. *Marg:* Quietus

John Toimnes of Enstone indicted before the aforesaid justices of the peace for on 30 June 1382 feloniously raping Johanna servant of Thomas Mulleward in a field at Enstone; pled not guilty, was tried, and acquitted.

14. *Marg:* Oxon' Robertus Wynyngton' Iohannes Leylond' Thomas Speek capellanus Iohannes mancipium de Ouenehalle Iohannes Boner

Iohannes Bourton' et Iohannes Luyde gardyner capti pro eo quod indictati sunt coram Roberto Bardolf et socijs suis iusticiarijs domini regis ad pacem in comitatu predicto conseruandam assignatis de eo quod ipsi simul cum alijs die Iouis et die Veneris in quarta septimana quadragesime anno regni domini regis nunc Anglie duodecimo ordinauerunt inter eos certos capitaneos et gubernatores insurgendo contra pacem domini regis et quesiuerunt Wallicos quoscumque in villa Oxon' existentes sagitando in diuersis vicis et venellis ante se clamando ware ware ware sle sle sle the Walshe dogges and al here helpes and ho so lokes out of his hous he sal be ded et quosdam occiderunt et quosdam grauiter vulnerauerunt et quosdam Wallicos qui genuflexebant abiurare villam fecerunt ducentes eos ad portas dicte ville et super eas fecerunt eos mingere et osculare portam et sic osculando tundebant capita ad portam ita quod quandoque sanguis de naso interdum lacrime exibant ab oculis eorundem; et quandam aulam in Oxon' vocatam Depehalle felonice fregerunt et ibidem vnum librum vnum pennare cum cornu vnum par bractarum Willelmi Wetehull' et vnum gladium et libros Iohannis Hoby ad valenciam triginta et octo solidorum felonice furati fuerunt et asportauerunt; et quod dicto die Veneris noctanter cameram Thome Frensshe in dicta aula situatam felonice fregerunt et duos gladios vnam parmam duos arcus cum viginti et sex sagittis vnum iak de fustian vnam togam rubiam duo paria manicarum albarum vnum par linthiaminum vnam armilausam dupplicatam quinque paria caligarum et duas vlnas de caneuas vnum par linee thele et alia bona et catalla ipsius Thome Frenssh' precij sexaginta solidorum felonice furati fuerunt et asportauerunt; et alias cameras diuersorum scolarium in aula predicta manencium predicto die Veneris felonice fregerunt et diuersa bona et catalla ibidem inuenta videlicet libros pannos lineos et laneos felonice furati fuerunt; et dicto die Veneris noctanter introitum nuncupatum Neuylesentre in Oxon' felonice fregerunt et bona

Plus intergo de eodem recordo

[*m. 3d.*]

et catalla videlicet ostia fenestras ac libros gramaticales ac pannos lineos et laneos Willelmi Dannay principalis eiusdem introitus Iohannis Halkyn scolaris ibidem et aliorum scolarium ibidem morancium ad valenciam sexaginta solidorum felonice furati fuerunt et asportauerunt; et eodem die Veneris noctanter aulam vocatam Seynteagace halle in Oxon' felonice fregerunt et bona et catalla ibidem inuenta videlicet pannos lineos et laneos libros gramaticales simul diolecticales gladios arcus citheras Willelmi Gitton' Iohannis Mulle Iohannis Gloue et aliorum scolarium ibidem existentium ad valenciam quatuor librarum felonice furati fuerunt; et de eo quod ipsi simul etc. die Sabati in dicta quarta septimana quadragesime anno supradicto aulam vocatam Piryhalle in Oxon' felonice fregerunt et bona principalis eiusdem aule et Mathei Alco et Ricardi Olyuere videlicet duos gladios clocos dupplicatos diuersi coloris vnum baselard vnum securim ac arcus et sagittas ad valenciam quatuor librarum felonice furati fuerunt; et alias aulas et introitus eodem die ibidem intrauerunt videlicet Mildredehalle Hampton' halle Bastaplesentre et diusersa bona et catalla diuersorum scolarium in dicta aula manencium ad valenciam quinquaginta solidorum felonice furati fuerunt; et quod in dicta insureccione occisi fuerunt per dictos felones videlicet Edwardus Nuton' Galfridus Hanlane de Wall' Thomas Rypon' et Iohannes Bowman; et de eo quod ipsi predicto die Iouis exportauerunt hostia tabulas et portas de dictis aulis spoliata in altum vicum iuxta ecclesiam beate Marie et acceperunt lignum truncos et hostia laicorum inuitis illis et clauserunt se a Cherltonesyn vsque ad Pentrithlane et ibidem de nocte permanserunt; quod quidem indictamentum prefati iusticiarij pacis iusticiarijs hic liberarunt veniunt coram iusticiarijs hic per vicecomitem ducti et allocuti qualiter se velint de felonijs predictis acquietare dicunt quod ipsi in nullo sunt inde culpabiles et de hoc ponunt se de bono et malo super patriam. Ideo fiat inde iurata. Iuratores veniunt qui ad hoc electi triati et iurati dicunt super sacramentum suum quod predicti Robertus Iohannes Thomas Iohannes Iohannes Iohannes et Iohannes non sunt culpabiles de felonijs predictis. Ideo consideratum est quod ijdem Robertus et omnes alij eant inde quieti etc. *Marg:* Quieti

Robert Wynyngton, John Leylond, Thomas Speek chaplain, John manciple of Oven Hall, John Boner, John Bourton, and John Luyde gardener indicted before Robert Bardolf and fellow justices of the peace for the following: on 1-2 April 1389 with others unknown they chose leaders and rose against the king's peace, sought out Welshmen in Oxford, shooting at them in various streets shouting ware ware ware sle sle sle the Walshe dogges and al here helpes and ho so loketh out of his hous he sal be ded; some they killed, others seriously wounded, and others who renounced the town they led to the gates where they inflicted indignities on them; they feloniously broke into Deep Hall and feloniously stole a book, a pen with an inkhorn, and a pair of breeches from William Wetehull and a sword and books from John Hoby valued at 38s.; at night they feloniously broke into the chamber of Thomas Frensshe in the same hall and feloniously stole two swords, a buckler, two bows with twenty-six arrows, a fustian jacket, a red coat, two pairs of white gloves, a pair of sheets, a lined cloak, five pairs of hose, two ells of canvas, a pair of linen ?curtains, and other goods, price 60s.; they broke into chambers of other scholars in the same hall and took books and linen and woollen cloth; at night they feloniously broke into Neville's Entry and feloniously stole doors, windows, grammar books, linen and woollen cloth from William Dannay principal, John Hakkyn and other scholars valued at 60s.; at night they broke into St Agate Hall and feloniously stole linen and woollen cloth, grammar and dialectic books, swords, bows, and cithers belonging to William Gitton, John Mulle, John Glove, and other scholars valued at £4; on 3 April they broke in Pyry Hall and took from the principal and Mathew Alco and Richard Olyvere two swords, lined cloaks of various colours, a dagger, an axe, and bows and arrows valued at £4, they took goods valued at 50s. from scholars in Mildred Hall, Hampton Hall, and Bastaple Entry: in this insurrection Edward Nuton, Geoffrey Hanlane of Wales, Thomas Rypon, and John Bowman were killed; they carried doors, tables, and gates from these halls into the High Street by St Mary's church and with wood, trunks, and doors taken from unwilling laymen barricaded themselves from Charlton Inn to Pentrich Lane and remained for the night; pled not guilty, were tried, and acquitted.

[*See above Roll C, no. 7; below no. 20. For the involvement of Thomas Speek see: H. C. M. Lyte, History of the University of Oxford (Oxford, 1886), pp. 308-309; History and Antiquities of the University of Oxford by A. Wood, now first published in English by J. Gutch, i (Oxford, 1792), 519 ff.*]

15. *Marg:* Oxon' Walterus Gun manciple Willelmus Lokcombe et Iohannes Lude gardyner capti pro eo quod indictati sunt coram prefatis iusticiarijs pacis de eo quod ipsi simul cum alijs ignotis die Dominica in festo decollacionis sancti Iohannis baptiste anno regni domini regis nunc Anglie terciodecimo noctanter apud Oxon' in parochia Omnium Sanctorum felonice depredauerunt quendam Robertum Mayde mancipium aule sancti Laurencij de vno torche precij quinque solidorum et ipsum verberauerunt vulnerauerunt et male tractauerunt et ad exitacionem procuracionem et abbetorimentum Agnetis filie Iohannis Punfold' cum secure et alijs instrumentis ostia et fenestras domus Ricardi Bowyere super Grauntpount in suburbio Oxon' felonice fregerunt eadem nocte et voluerunt dictam domum intrasse et dictum Ricardum Bowiere per voluntatem eorum occidisse et sic dicta Agnes fuit abbetata et excitata istius malefacti; et quod predictus Willelmus Lokcombe die Lune proximo post festum anunciacionis beate Marie anno regni predicti domini regis nunc duodecimo felonice dispoliauit Iohannem Coke sclattere in parochia sancte Ebbe Oxon' de viginti denarijs in auro; et quod idem Willelmus circa festum sancti Luce euangeliste anno regni eiusdem domini regis nunc vndecimo receptauit in domo sua in parochia sancte Ebbe Oxon' quendam Robertum Pelliparium de London' cum vna rubia tunica precij octo solidorum vna furrura de popul precij sexdecim solidorum et vna tunica de russeto precij quinque solidorum scientes dictum Robertum Pellipar' cum alijs felonibus ignotis quandam

Elizabeth' Woluesham de eisdem bonis iuxta Boteley felonice depredasse et eciam sciens ipsum Robertum esse indictatum de morte cuiusdam mulieris de Cokkeslane in London; quod quidem indictamentum prefati iusticiarij pacis iusticiarijs hic liberarunt veniunt coram iusticiarijs hic per vicecomitem ducti et allocuti qualiter se velint de felonijs predictis acquietare dicunt quod ipsi in nullo sunt inde culpabiles et de hoc ponunt se de bono et malo super patriam. Ideo fiat inde iurata. Iuratores veniunt qui ad hoc electi triati et iurati dicunt super sacramentum suum quod predicti Walterus Willelmus et Iohannes non sunt culpabiles de felonijs predictis (nec eis occasionibus vnquam se retraxerunt)[i]. Ideo consideratum est quod ijdem Walterus Willelmus et Iohannes eant inde quieti etc. *Marg:* Quieti

Walter Gun manciple, William Lokcombe, and John Lude gardener indicted before the aforesaid justices of the peace for the following: with others unknown at night on 29 August 1389 in the parish of All Saints Oxford they feloniously robbed Robert Mayde manciple of St Lawrence Hall of a torch, price 5s., beating, wounding, and maltreating him; also incited and abetted by Agnes daughter of John Punfold with an axe and other tools they feloniously broke the doors and windows of the house of Robert Bowyere on Grandpont in the suburbs of Oxford, wishing to enter the house and kill Robert Bowyere; on 28 March 1390 the said William Lokcombe feloniously robbed John Coke slater in the parish of St Ebbe Oxford of 20d. in gold and he received in his house in the parish of St Ebbe Robert Pelliparius of London with a red tunic, price 8s., a popul fur, price 16s., and a red tunic, price 5s., knowing that Robert Pelliparius with other felons robbed Elizabeth Wolvesham of certain goods near Botley [*Berks.*] *and knowing he was under indictment for the death of a woman of Cock Lane, London; pled not guilty, were tried, and acquitted.*

[*See below no. 19.*]

[*m. 5*]

Deliberacio gaole domini regis castri Oxon' facta apud Oxon' coram Roberto de Cherlton' et Iohanne Hulle iusticiarijs domini regis ad gaolam ilam deliberandam assignatis die Lune proximo ante festum sancti Petri in cathedra anno regni regis Ricardi secundi post conquestum Anglie quartodecimo [20 February 1391].

16. *Marg:* Oxon' Robertus Emmesson' et Thomas Webbe de Chynnore capti pro eo quod indictati sunt coram Ricardo Abberbury et socijs suis iusticiarijs domini regis ad pacem in comitatu predicto conseruandam assignatis de eo quod ipsi felonice furati fuerunt die Dominica in festo pentecoste anno regni domini regis nunc Anglie terciodecimo apud Shirborn' vnum vitulum Willelmi Cayme precij quatuor solidorum; et de eo quod ipsi simul cum alijs in vigilia natalis domini anno regni domini

regis nunc supradicto apud Stokenchurche felonice venerunt et ymaginauerunt mortem Iohannis Hordewyk senioris et Iohannis Bedewynde capellani et eos de omnibus bonis et catallis suis felonice depredasse voluerunt; quod quidem indictamentum prefati iusticiarij pacis iusticiarijs hic liberarunt veniunt coram iusticiarijs hic per vicecomitem ducti et allocuti qualiter se velint de felonijs predictis acquietare dicunt quod ipsi in nullo sunt inde culpabiles et de hoc ponunt se de bono et malo super patriam. Ideo fiat inde iurata. Iuratores veniunt qui ad hoc electi triati et iurati dicunt super sacramentum suum quod predicti Robertus et Thomas culpabiles sunt de felonijs predictis. Ideo consideratum est quod predicti Robertus et Thomas suspendeantur etc. Catalla ipsorum Roberti et Thome nulla etc. *Marg:* Suspendeantur catalla nulla

Robert Emmesson and Thomas Webbe of Chinnor indicted before Richard Abberbury and fellow justices of the peace for on 22 May 1390 feloniously stealing at Shirburn a calf price 4s., from William Cayme; at Stokenchurch [*Bucks.*] *on 24 December 1389 they planned the death of John Hordewyk, sr., and John Bedewynde chaplain and wished to rob them of all their goods; pled not guilty, were tried, convicted, and sentenced to hang; no chattels.*

[*See above Roll C, no. 12*].

17. *Marg:* Oxon' Willelmus Shethere capellanus de Kyrtlyngton' captus pro eo quod indictatus fuit coram Thoma Paynell' et socijs suis iusticiarijs domini regis ad pacem in comitatu predicto conseruandam assignatis de eo quod ipse venit in vigilia purificacionis beate Marie anno regni domini regis nunc Anglie terciodecimo apud Kirtlyngton' et ibidem fregit domum Thome Dycon' de Kirtlyngton' et bona et catalla dicti Thome de domo sua ad valenciam quadraginta solidorum felonice asportauit et Feliciam vxorem dicti Thome ibidem felonice rapuit et eam abduxit cum bonis et catallis suis; quod quidem indictamentum prefati iusticiarij pacis iusticiarijs hic liberarunt venit coram iusticiarijs hic per vicecomitem ductus et allocutus qualiter se velit de felonia predicta acquietare dicit quod ipse in nullo est inde culpabilis et de hoc ponit se de bono et malo super patriam. Ideo fiat inde iurata. Iuratores veniunt qui ad hoc electi triati et iurati dicunt super sacramentum suum quod predictus Willelmus in nullo est culpabilis de felonia predicta nec ea occasione vnquam se retraxit. Ideo idem Willelmus eat inde quietus etc. *Marg:* Quietus

William Shethere chaplain of Kirtlington indicted before Thomas Paynell and fellow justices of the peace for on 1 February 1390 breaking into the house of Thomas Dycon of Kirtlington, at Kirtlington, feloniously taking goods valued at 40s., raping Felicia wife of Thomas and abducting her with the goods; pled not guilty, was tried, and acquitted.

18. *Marg:* Oxon' Iohannes Harald' de Whatele captus pro eo quod indictatus fuit coram Ricardo Abberbury et socijs suis iusticiarijs domini regis ad pacem in comitatu predicto conseruandam assignatis de eo quod ipse simul cum alijs venit die Martis proximo ante festum pentecoste ad noctem anno regni domini regis nunc Anglie vndecimo in campis de Hedyngdon' iuxta Shottouere in Thomam seruientem Iohannis Diere de Oxon' insultum fecit et ipsum de vno equo precij viginti solidorum et panno laneo precij triginta solidorum et viginti solidis in pecunia numerata ipsius Iohannis Diere ibidem felonice depredauit; quod quidem indictamentum prefati iusticiarij pacis iusticiarijs hic liberarunt venit coram iusticiarijs hic per vicecomitem ductus et allocutus qualiter se velit de felonia predicta acquietare dicit quod ipse in nullo est inde culpabilis et de hoc ponit se de bono et malo super patriam. Ideo fiat inde iurata. Iuratores veniunt qui ad hoc electi triati et iurati dicunt super sacramentum suum quod predictus Iohannes in nullo est culpabilis de felonia predicta nec ea occasione vnquam se retraxit. Ideo idem Iohannes Harald eat inde quietus etc. *Marg:* Quietus

John Harald of Wheatley indicted before Richard Abberbury and fellow justices of the peace for at night on 12 May 1388 in the fields of Headington near Shotover assaulting Thomas servant of John Diere of Oxford and feloniously robbing him of one horse, price 20s., woollen cloth, price 30s., and 20s. in cash; pled not guilty, was tried, and acquitted.

19. *Marg:* Oxon' Robertus Hethe captus pro eo quod indictatus fuit coram prefatis iusticiarijs pacis[1] de eo quod ipse simul cum alijs die Dominica in festo decollacionis sancti [Iohannis] baptiste anno regni domini regis nunc[2] noctanter apud Oxon' in parochia Omnium Sanctorum felonice depredauit quendam Robertum Mayde mancipium aule sancti Laurencij de vno torche precij quinque solidorum et ipsum verberauit vulnerauit et male tractauit ad excitacionem procuracionem et abettamentum Agnetis filie Iohannis Ponfeld' cum secure et alijs instrumentis ostia et fenestras domus Ricardi Bowyer super Grauntpount in suburbio Oxon' felonice fregit eadem nocte et voluit dictam domum intrasse et dictum Ricardum Bowyer per voluntatem suam occidisse; quod quidem indictamentum prefati iusticiarij pacis iusticiarijs hic liberarunt venit coram iusticiarijs hic per vicecomitem ductus et allocutus qualiter se velit de felonia predicta acquietare dicit quod ipse in nullo est inde culpabilis et de hoc ponit se de bono et malo super patriam. Ideo fiat inde iurata. Iurtores veniunt qui ad hoc electi triati et iurati dicunt super

[1]The justices named in the previous case were Berkshire justices of the peace; since this case involves the same offence as that in no. 15 above, it is included here.

[2]The year is omitted but was probably *terciodecimo;* see above no. 15.

sacramentum suum quod predictus Robertus non est culpabilis de felonia predicta nec ea occasione vnquam se retraxit. Ideo predictus Robertus eat inde quietus etc. *Marg:* Quietus

Robert Hethe indicted before the aforesaid justices of the peace for the following: with others at night on 29 August 1389 in the parish of All Saints Oxford he feloniously robbed Robert Mayde manciple of St Lawrence Hall of a torch, price 5s., beating and wounding him; incited by Agnes daughter of John Ponfold with an axe and other tools he feloniously at night broke into the house of Richard Bowyer on Grandpont in the suburbs of Oxford, wishing to enter the house and kill the said Richard; pled not guilty, was tried, and acquitted.

[*m. 5d.*]

20. *Marg:* Oxon' Nicholaus Peershale Robertus Alynton' Iohannes Alkebarwe Henricus Corbrigge Adam Vsk Robertus Ampelford' Iohannes Oswalkirke et Nicholaus Stanley capti pro eo quod indictati fuerunt coram Roberto de Cherlton' et socijs suis iusticiarijs domini regis ad pacem in comitatu predicto conseruandam assignatis de eo quod predictus Nicholaus Stanley simul cum Iohanne Kirkeby Iohanne Middelton' Iohanne Lambard Willelmo Hayton' Iohanne Swale Roberto Pyk Iohanne Russeley Iohanne Baron' Philipo Mayhewe Dauid Crane Willelmo Smyth' de Hibernia Willelmo Yonge de Hibernia Iohanne Darcy Henrico Milton' Iohanne White de Hibernia Dauid Thloot Willelmo Gough' de Wallia Rogero Brond' Iohanne Bulfote Iohanne Essold Iohanne Ardyngton' Rogero Pynchyn Iohanne Morpath' Roberto Wynwyk Willelmo Kirkeby Iohanne Castell' Roberto Newham Thoma Westwyk Willelmo Herand' Roberto Shirbourn' Iohanne Gaunt Ricardo Blake et Iohanne Feston et pluribus alijs malefactoribus et felonibus ignotis eis iuratis et alligatis modo guerrino arraiatis apud Oxon' die Iouis et die Veneris in quarta septimana quadragesime anno regni domini regis nunc Anglie duodecimo ordinauit certos capitaneos et gubernatores insurgendo contra pacem domini regis quesiuit Wallicos quoscumque in villa Oxon' existentes sagittando in diuersis vicis et venellis ante se clamando ware ware ware sle sle sle the Walshe dogges and here helpes and ho so loketh out of his hous he shal be ded et quosdam occidit vt patet inferius et quosdam grauiter vulnerauit et quosdam Wallicos qui genuflexebant abiurare villam fecit ducens eos ad portas dicte ville et super eas fecit eos mingere et osculare portam et sic osculando tundebat capita ad portam ita quod quandoque sanguis de naso interdum lacrime exibant ab oculis eorundem; et quandam aulam in Oxon' vocatam Dephalle felonice fregit et ibidem vnum librum vnum pennare cum cornu vnum par bractarum Willelmi Wetehull' et vnum gladium et libros Iohannis Hoby ad valenciam triginta et octo solidorum felonice furatus fuit et asportauit; et quod ipse simul etc. dicto die Veneris noctanter

cameram Thome Frenssh' in dicta aula situatam felonice fregit et duos gladios vnam parmam duas arcus cum viginti et sex sagittis vnum iakke de fustiane vnam togam rubiam duo paria manucarum albarum vnum par linthiaminum vnam armilausam dupplicatam quinque paria caligarum et duas vlnas de caneuas vnum par linie tele et alia bona et catalla ipsius Thome Frenssh' precij sexaginta solidorum felonice furatus fuit et asportauit; et alias cameras diuersorum scolarium in aula predicta manencium predicto die Veneris felonice fregit et diuersa bona at catalla ibidem videlicet libros pannos lineos et laneos felonice furatus fuit; et dicto die Veneris noctanter introitum nuncupatum Neuylesentre in Oxon' felonice fregit et bona et catalla videlicet ostia fenestras ac libros gramaticales ac pannos lineos et laneos Willelmi Dannay principalis eiusdem introitus Iohannis Halkyn scolaris ibidem et aliorum scolarium ibidem morancium ad valenciam sexaginta solidorum felonice furatus fuit et asportauit; et eodem die Veneris noctanter aulam vocatam Seynt Agace halle in Oxon' felonice fregit et bona et catalla ibidem inuenta videlicet pannos lineos et laneos libros gramaticales ciuiles diolecticales gladios arcus citheras Willelmi Gitton' Iohannis Mulle Iohannis Gloue et aliorum scolarium ibidem existencium ad valenciam quatuor librarum felonice furatus fuit; et de eo quod ipse simul etc. die Sabati in predicta quarta septimana quadragesime anno regni domini regis nunc supradicto predictus Nicholaus Stanley simul etc. aulam vocatam Piryhalle in Oxon' felonice fregit et bona principalis eiusdem aule et Mathei Alco et Ricardi Olyuer videlicet duos gladios clocos dupplicatos diuersi coloris vnum baselard vnam securim ac arcus et sagittas ad valenciam quatuor librarum felonice furatus fuit; et alias aulas et introitus eodem die ibidem intrauerunt videlicet Mildredhalle Hampton' halle Bastaplesentre et diuersa bona et catalla diuersorum scolarium in dicta aula manencium ad valenciam quinquaginta solidorum felonice furatus fuit; et quod in dicta insurrecione occisi fuerunt per predictum Nicholaum simul etc. videlicet Edwardus Nuton' Galfridus Hanlane de Wallia Thomas Repon' et Iohannes Bowman; et de eo quod predictus Nicholaus Stanley simul etc. predicto die Iouis exportauit ostia tabulas et portas de dictis aulis spoliata in altum vicum iuxta ecclesiam beate Marie et accepit lignum truncos et ostia laicorum inuitis illis et clausit se a Charltonesyn vsque ad Penchrich' lane et ibi de nocte permansit; et quod predicti Nicholaus Pershale Robertus Alyngton' Iohannes Alkebarwe Henricus Corbrigge Adam Vske Robertus Ampelford' et Iohannes Oswalkirke fuerunt manutentes fautores et confortatores dictorum felonium ad felonias predictas faciendas; quod quidem indictamentum prefati iusticiarij pacis iusticiarijs hic liberarunt necnon vtlagaria versus predictos Iohannem Kirkeby Iohannem Middelton' Iohannem Lambard Willelmum Hayton' Iohannem Swale Robertum Pyk Iohannem Russeley Iohannem Baron'

Philippum Mayhewe Dauid Crane Willelmum Smyth' de Hibernia Willelmum Yonge de Hibernia Iohannem Darcy Henricum Milton' Iohannem White de Hibernia Dauid Thloot Willelmum Gough' de Wallia Rogerum Brond Iohannem Bulfote Iohannem Essold Iohannem Ardyngton' Rogerum Pynchyn Iohannem Morpath' Robertum Wynwyk Willelmum Kirkeby Iohannem Castell' Robertum Newham Thomam Westwyk Willelmum Herand Robertum Shirbourne Iohannem Gaunt Ricardum Blake et Iohannem Feston' promulgatur per processum coram eis factum ostenderunt veniunt coram iusticiarijs hic per vicecomitem ducti et predictus Nicholaus Stanley allocutus qualiter se velit de principalibus felonijs predictis acquietare dicit quod ipse in nullo est inde culpabilis et de hoc ponit se de bono et malo super patriam. Ideo fiat inde iurata. Iuratores veniunt qui ad hoc electi triati et iurati dicunt super sacramentum suum quod predictus Nicholaus Stanley in nullo est culpabilis de principalibus felonijs predictis nec ea occasione vnquam se retraxit. Ideo idem Nicholaus Stanley eat inde quietus etc. Et predicti Nicholaus Pershale Robertus Alynton' Iohannes Alkebarwe Henricus Corbrig Adam Vske Robertus Ampulford' et Iohannes Oswalkirke qui indictati sunt de accessorio felonie predicte eant inde quieti etc. *Marg:* Quieti

Nicholas Peershale, Robert Alynton, John Alkebarwe, Henry Corbrigge, Adam Usk, Robert Ampelford, John Oswalkirke, and Nicholas Stanley indicted before Robert de Cherlton and fellow justices of the peace for the following: Stanley together with John Kirkeby, John Middelton, John Lambard, William Hayton, John Swale, Robert Pyk, John Russeley, John Baron, Philip Mayhewe, David Crane, William Smyth of Ireland, William Yonge of Ireland, John Darcy, Henry Milton, John White of Ireland, David Thloot, William Gough of Wales, Roger Brond, John Bulfote, John Essold, John Ardyngton, Roger Pynchyn, John Morpath, Robert Wynwyk, William Kirkeby, John Castell, Robert Newham, Thomas Westwyk, William Herand, Robert Shirbourn, John Gaunt, Richard Blake, and John Feston and others unknown being armed at Oxford on 1-2 April 1389 chose leaders, rose against the king's peace, and sought Welshmen, shooting them in the streets and shouting ware ware ware sle sle sle the Walshe dogges and here helpes and ho so loketh out of his hous he shal be ded; some were killed, some seriously wounded, and some who renounced the town were led to the gates where serious indignities were inflicted on them; Stanley feloniously broke into Deep Hall and feloniously stole a book, a pen with an inkhorn, and a pair of breeches from William Wetehull, and a sword and books from John Hoby valued at 38s.; on Friday night he feloniously broke into the chamber of Thomas Frenssh in the same hall and feloniously stole two swords, a buckler, two bows with twenty-six arrows, a fustian jacket, a red coat, two pairs of white gloves, a pair of sheets, a lined cloak, five pairs of hose, two ells of canvas, a pair of linen ?curtains and other goods, price 60s.; he broke into the chambers of other scholars in the same hall and took books and linen and woollen cloth; the same Friday night he feloniously broke into Neville's Entry and feloniously stole doors, windows, grammar books, and linen and woollen cloth from William Dannay principal and John Halkyn and other scholars valued at 60s.; he broke into St Agate Hall and feloniously stole linen and woollen cloth, grammar, civil law, and dialectical books, swords, bows, and cithers belonging to William Gitton, John Mulle, John Glove, and other scholars valued at £4; on 3 April he feloniously broke into Pyry Hall and took from the principal and Mathew Alco and Richard Olyver two swords, lined cloaks of various colours, a dagger, an axe, and bows and arrows valued at £4; he feloniously stole goods valued at 50s. from scholars in Mildred Hall, Hampton Hall, and Bastaple Entry; in the said insurrection Edward Nuton, Geoffrey Hanlane of Wales, Thomas Repon, and John Bowman were killed; on 1 April he carried doors, tables, and gates from these halls into the High Street by St Mary's church and closed it from Charlton Inn to Penchirch Lane and remained there for the night; the aforesaid Nicholas Pershale, Robert Alyngton, John Alkebarwe, Henry Corbrigge, Adam Uske, Robert Ampelford, and John Oswalkirke were accomplices in the said felonies; outlawry had been pronounced against the said John Kirkeby, John Middelton, John Lambard, William Hayton, John Swale, Robert Pyk, John Russeley, John Baron, Philip Mayhewe, David Crane, William Smyth of Ireland, William Yonge of Ireland, John Darcy, Henry Milton, John White of Ireland, David Thloot, William Gough of Wales, Roger Brond, John Bulfote, John Essold, John Ardyngton, Roger Pynchyn, John Morpath, Robert Wynwyk, William Kirkeby, John Castell, Robert Newham, Thomas Westwyk, William Herand, Robert Shirbourne, John Gaunt, Richard Blake, and John Feston; Stanley and his accomplices appeared; Stanley as principal pled not guilty, was tried, and acquitted; the others were acquitted as accessories.

[*See above Roll C, nos. 7, 14. For the pardon of John Kirkeby see C.P.R. 1391-1396, pp. 605-606; Pardon Roll 31, m. 9; for the pardon of David Thloyte, ibid., 32, m. 22. For another account see E. M. Thompson (ed.), Chronicon Adae de Usk, A.D. 1377-1404, (London, 1904), p. 7*[1].]

[*m. 6*]
Deliberacio gaole domini regis castri Oxon' facta apud Oxon' coram Roberto Cherlton' et Iohanne Hulle iusticiarijs domini regis ad gaolam illam deliberandam assignatis die Lune proximo ante festum sancte

[1]Adam of Usk here admitted his guilt.

Margarete virginis anno regni regis Ricardi secundi post conquestum quintodecimo [17 July 1391].

21. *Marg:* Oxon' Iohannes Charwelton' concanonichus prioris de Coldenorton' captus pro eo quod indictatus fuit coram Roberto Bardolf et socijs suis iusticiarijs domini regis ad pacem in comitatu predicto conseruandam assignatis de eo quod ipse contra defencionem episcopi Lincoln' et predicti prioris die Martis proximo post festum natiuitatis beate Marie anno regni domini regis nunc Anglie terciodecimo felonice fregit noctanter domum eiusdem prioris et ibidem vnum equum precij quinque solidorum furatus fuit; quod quidem indictamentum prefati iusticiarij pacis iusticiarijs hic liberarunt venit coram iusticiarijs hic per vicecomitem ductus et allocutus qualiter se velit de felonia predicta acquietare dicit quod ipse in nullo est inde culpabilis et de hoc ponit se de bono et malo super patriam. Ideo fiat inde iurata. Iuratores veniunt qui ad hoc electi triati et iurati dicunt super sacramentum suum quod predictus Iohannes in nullo est culpabilis de felonia predicta nec ea occasione vnquam se retraxit. Ideo idem Iohannes eat inde quietus etc. *Marg:* Quietus

John Charwelton fellow canon of the prior of Cold Norton indicted before Robert Bardolf and fellow justices of the peace for, in spite of the prohibition of the bishop of Lincoln and the said prior, at night on 14 September 1389 feloniously breaking into the house of the prior and stealing a horse, price 5s.; pled not guilty, was tried, and acquitted.

22. *Marg:* Oxon' Iohanna vxor Iohannis Munstrell' de Chiselhampton' capta pro eo quod indictata fuit coram prefatis iusticiarijs pacis de eo quod ipsa die Dominica in festo Sancti Gregorij pape anno regni domini regis nunc Anglie quartodecimo venit apud Brokhampton' et ibidem domum Iohanne Graunt felonice fregit et vnam tunicam furratam precij quinque solidorum eiusdem Iohanne Graunt felonice furata fuit et asportauit; quod quidem indictamentum prefati iusticiarij pacis iusticiarijs hic liberarunt venit coram iusticiarijs hic per vicecomitem ducta et allocuta qualiter se velit de felonia predicta acquietare dicit quod ipsa in nullo est inde culpabilis et de hoc ponit se de bono et malo super patriam. Ideo fiat inde iurata. Iuratores veniunt qui ad hoc electi triati et iurati dicunt super sacramentum suum quod predicta Iohanna in nullo est culpabilis de felonia predicta nec ea occasione vnquam se retraxit. Ideo eadem Iohanna eat inde quieta etc. *Marg:* Quieta

Johanna wife of John Munstrell of Chislehampton indicted before the aforesaid justices of the peace for on 12 March 1391 feloniously breaking into the house of Johanna Graunt at Brookhampton and feloniously stealing a furred tunic, price 5s.; pled not guilty, was tried, and acquitted.

23. *Marg:* Oxon' Willelmus filius Willelmi Gareford' de Southcote captus pro eo quod indictatus fuit coram Roberto Cherlton' et socijs suis iusticiarijs domini regis ad pacem in comitatu predicto conseruandam assignatis de eo quod ipse die Veneris proximo post festum sancti Michelis archangeli anno regni domini regis nunc Anglie terciodecimo apud Gosey Willelmum Waterman de Gosey et Agnetem vxorem eius noctanter felonice interfecit et eodem die vnam aulam duas cameras vnam grangeam plenam de diuersis bladis et decem quarteria fabarum et pisarum in tassis positis precij viginti librarum ipsorum Willelmi Waterman et Agnetis felonice noctanter combuscit; venit coram iusticiarijs hic per vicecomitem ductus et allocutus qualiter se velit de felonijs predictis acquietare dicit quod ipse in nullo est inde culpabilis et de hoc ponit se de bono et malo super patriam. Ideo fiat inde iurata. Iuratores veniunt qui de hoc electi triati et iurati dicunt super sacramentum suum quod predictus Willelmus culpabilis est de felonia predicta. Catalla ipsius Willelmi nulla. Ideo idem Willelmus suspendeatur etc. *Marg:* catalla nulla Suspendeatur

William son of William Gareford of Southcot [*Berks.*] *indicted before Robert Cherlton and his fellow justices of the peace for at Goosey* [*Berks.*] *on 1 October 138 feloniously killing William Waterman of Goosey and his wife Agnes and burning a hall, two chambers, a grange full of various grains, and ten quarters of beans and peas in stacks, price £20; pled not guilty, was tried, convicted, and sentenced to be hanged; no chattels.*

[*m:* 7]

Deliberacio gaole domini regis castri Oxon' facta apud Oxon' coram Roberto Cherlton' et Iohanne Hulle iusticiarijs domini regis ad gaolam illam deliberandam assignatis die Lune proximo ante festum sancti Petri in cathedra anno regni regis Ricardi secundi post conquestum quintodecimo [19 February 1392].

24. *Marg:* Oxon' Iohannes Broun de Hibernia captus pro eo quod indictatus fuit coram Roberto Cherlton' et socijs suis iusticiarijs domini regis ad pacem in comitatu predicto conseruandam assignatis de eo quod ipse die Sabati proximo post festum natiuitatis beate Marie anno regni domini regis nunc Anglie quintodecimo apud Aston' Doune Iohannem Malpas clericum de vno equo precij tresdecim solidorum et quatuor denariorum vno baselardo cum argento harnessiato precij decem solidorum vna zona argenta arraiata precij sex solidorum et octo denariorum felonice depredatus fuit; quod quidem indictamentum prefati iusticiarij pacis iusticiarijs hic liberarunt venit coram iusticiarijs hic per vicecomitem ductus et allocutus qualiter se velit de felonia predicta acquietare dicit quod ipse in nullo est inde culpabilis et de hoc ponit se de bono et malo super patriam. Ideo fiat inde iurata. Iuratores

veniunt qui ad hoc electi triati et iurati dicunt super sacramentum suum quod predictus Iohannes culpabilis est de felonia predicta. Catalla ipsius Iohannis xl d. vnde Robertus Bullok vicecomes oneratur. Ideo idem Iohannes suspendeatur etc. *Marg:* (catalla xl d.)[c] Suspendeatur

John Broun of Ireland indicted before Robert Cherlton and fellow justices of the peace for on 9 September 1391 at Aston Doune feloniously robbing John Malpas clerk of one horse, price 13s. 4d., one dagger with silver decoration, price 10s., one belt trimmed with silver, price 6s. 8d.; pled not guilty, was tried, convicted, and sentenced to be hanged; chattels, 40d., in charge to Robert Bullok sheriff.

25. *Marg:* Oxon' Iohannes Stuntesfeld' quondam seruiens Lodewin Greuell' de Drayton' captus pro eo quod indictatus fuit coram prefatis iusticiarijs pacis de eo quod ipse simul cum alijs die Dominica proximo ante festum sancti Valentini anno regni domini regis nunc Anglie quintodecimo apud Wroxton' Willelmum White de vndecim virgis blanketi precij sex solidorum et octo denariorum vno cocliar precij decem denariorum et de centum solidis auri et argenti felonice depredatus fuit; quod quidem indictamentum prefati iusticiarij pacis iusticiarijs hic per vice-comitem ductus et allocutus qualiter se velit de felonia predicta acquietare dicit quod ipse in nullo est inde culpabilis et de hoc ponit se de bono et malo super patriam. Ideo fiat inde iurata. Iuratores veniunt qui ad hoc electi triati et iurati dicunt super sacramentum suum quod predictus Iohannes culpabilis est de felonia predicta. Catalla ipsius Iohannis xl d. vnde Robertus Bullok vicecomes oneratur. Ideo idem Iohannes suspendeatur etc. *Marg:* (catalla xl d.)[c] Suspendeatur

John Stuntesfeld former servant of Lodewin Grevell of Drayton indicted before the aforesaid justices of the peace for with others on 11 February 1392 at Wroxton feloniously robbing William White of eleven measures of white woollen cloth, price 6s. 8d., one spoon, price 10d., and 100s. in gold and silver; pled not guilty, was tried, convicted, and sentenced to be hanged; chattels, 40d., in charge to Robert Bullok sheriff

26. *Marg:* Oxon' Edwardus Tannere de Kynbell' captus pro eo quod indictatus fuit coram prefatis iusticiarijs pacis de eo quod ipse in vigilia omnium sanctorum anno regni domini regis nunc Anglie quartodecimo apud Watlyngton' vnum equum Ricardi Kerswell' precij tresdecim solidorum et quatuor denariorum felonice furatus fuit; et quod idem Edwardus die Sabati proximo ante festum sancti Thome apostoli anno regni eiusdem domini regis nunc supradicto apud Watlyngton' vnam vaccam Iohannis Bemond iunioris felonice furatus fuit; quod quidem indictamentum prefati iusticiarij pacis iusticiarijs hic liberarunt venit

coram iusticiarijs hic per vicecomitem ductus et allocutus qualiter se velit de felonijs predictis acquietare dicit quod ipse in nullo est inde culpabilis et de hoc ponit se de bono et malo super patriam. Ideo fiat inde iurata. Iuratores veniunt qui ad hoc electi triati et iurati dicunt super sacramentum suum quod predictus Edwardus culpabilis est de felonijs predictis. Catalla ipsius Edwardi nulla. Ideo idem Edwardus suspendeatur etc. *Marg:* catalla nulla Suspendeatur

Edward Tannere of Kimble [Bucks.] indicted before the aforesaid justices of the peace for on 31 October 1390 feloniously stealing a horse, price 13s. 4d., from Richard Kerswell at Watlington, and on 17 December 1390 at Watlington a cow from John Bemond, jr.; pled not guilty, was tried, convicted, and sentenced to be hanged; no chattels.

27. *Marg:* Oxon' Willelmus Edegar captus pro eo quod indictatus fuit coram prefatis iusticiarijs pacis de eo quod ipse die Lune proximo post festum omnium sanctorum anno regni domini regis nunc Anglie quintodecimo venit apud Dorchestre et ibidem ecclesiam eiusdem ville intrauit et vnam calicem argenti et deaurati parochianam dicte ville precij quadraginta solidorum felonice furatus fuit; et quod est communis latro; quod quidem indictamentum prefati iusticiarij pacis iusticiarijs hic liberarunt venit coram iusticiarijs hic per vicecomitem ductus et allocutus qualiter se velit de felonia predicta acquietare dicit quod ipse clericus est et quod ipse non potest sine Iohanne episcopi Lincoln' loci illius ordinario respondere. Et super hoc venit quidam decanus Christianitatis Oxon' et profert hic in curia litteras ipsius episcopi eidem decano directi ad omnes clericos de quocumque crimine felonico coram quibuscumque iusticiarijs domini regis irrititos petandos et calumpniandos quarum datum est apud Sleford septimo die mensis Iulij anno regni domini regis nunc Anglie quintodecimo [7 July 1391]. Et super hoc predictus Willelmus peti' examinacionem sibi fieri vtrum ipse clericus sit necne et per examinacionem predicti decani clericus inuenitur. Et super hoc idem decanus petit predictum Willelmum tanquam clericum etc. sibi deliberari set prius sciatur pro quali idem Willelmus deliberari debeat rei veritas inquiratur per patriam. Ideo fiat inde iurata. Iuratores veniunt qui ad hoc electi triati et iurati dicunt super sacramentum suum quod predictus Willelmus culpabilis est de felonia predicta. Catalla ipsius Willelmi nulla. Et super hoc predictus Willelmus deliberatur hic in curia prefato decano ad ipsum saluo ducendum vsque gaolam predicti episcopi de Bannebury ibidem moraturum periculo quo incumbit etc. *Marg:* catalla nulla clericus conuictus

William Edegar indicted before the aforesaid justices of the peace for on 6 November 1391 entering the church at Dorchester and feloniously stealing

a chalice of silver and gold, price 40s., being a common thief, proved clergy; after the jury found him guilty, he was released to the ordinary for imprisonment in the bishop's gaol at Banbury; no chattels.

28. *Marg:* Oxon' Thomas Wetley de London' glouer et Robertus Naserton' capti pro eo quod indictati fuerunt coram prefatis iusticiarijs pacis de eo quod ipsi venerunt apud Oxon' die Martis proximo ante festum natiuitatis beate Marie anno regni domini regis nunc Anglie quintodecimo et ibidem ecclesiam beate Marie circa horam nonam eiusdem diei felonice fregerunt et ibidem duas plates argenti de pedibus sancte crucis eiusdem ecclesie cum tribus petris positis in predictis plates precij duorum solidorum felonice depredauerunt; quod quidem indictamentum prefati iusticiarij pacis iusticiarijs hic liberarunt veniunt coram iusticiarijs hic per vicecomitem ducti et allocuti qualiter se velint de felonia predicta acquietare dicunt quod ipsi in nullo sunt inde culpabiles et de hoc ponunt se de bono et malo super patriam. Ideo fiat inde iurata. Iuratores veniunt qui ad hoc electi triati et iurati dicunt super sacramentum suum quod predicti Thomas et Robertus in nullo sunt culpabiles de felonia predicta nec ea occasione vnquam se retraxerunt. Ideo ijdem Thomas et Robertus eant inde quieti etc. *Marg:* Quieti

Thomas Wetley of London glover and Robert Naserton indicted before the aforesaid justices of the peace for at night on 5 September 1391 breaking into the church of St Mary in Oxford and feloniously robbing it of two silver plates from the foot of the cross, with three gems from the plates, price 2s.; pled not guilty, were tried, and acquitted.
[*See below no. 39.*]

[*m. 7d.*]
29. *Marg:* Oxon' Iohannes Eburton' de Swerforde et Ricardus Maydegode vicarius ecclesie de Enston' capti pro eo quod indictati fuerunt coram Thoma Poure et socijs suis iusticiarijs domini regis ad pacem in comitatu predicto conseruandam assignatis de eo quod ipsi simul alijs ignotis de comitatu Warr' circa numerum ducentorum hominum vi et armis scilicet gladijs arcubus et sagittis et quidam eorum in loricis armatorum et modo guerrino arraiatorum hostiliter apud Sewell' insimul congregauerunt die Martis proximo post festum ascencionis domini anno regni domini regis nunc Anglie quartodecimo et ibidem dictus Iohannes Eburton' in presencia dictorum hominum pupplice proclamationem fecit quod nullus eorum a comitiua predicta recederet antequam fecissent id quid propositum fuit ibidem faciendum sub pena amissionis dimidij marce et verberantie et mutulationis membrorum et omnes prenominati ibidem die et anno supradictis cum omnimodis auerijs hominum ville de Swerforde videlict equis bobus vaccis iumentis

et bidentibus pratum et herbam Iohannis Tame ad valenciam viginti marcarum depasturi fuerunt concultauerunt et consumpserunt et Iohannem filium Iohannis Rene de Parua Tywe die et anno supradictis ad portandum focum et stramen de manerio de Dunthrop' vsque dictam villam de Sewell' contra voluntatem suam constrinxerunt ad comburanda spinas et aliud focale dicti Iohannis Tame apud Sewell' predictam inuenta et ibidem homines et seruientes eiusdem Iohannis Tame ad verberandum et interficiendum quesiuerunt et abinde vsque villam de Parua Tywe ad verberandum et interficiendum Iohannem Aces et Willelmum fratrum eius seruientes dicti Iohannis Tame die et anno supradictis equitauerunt et ipsos ibidem contra pacem domini regis et in affraiamentum tocius patrie ibidem supponendos inimicos domini regis ibidem ad ardendum et interficiendum venisse; et quod dictus Iohannes Eburton' et alij de villa de Swerford' ad eandem villam postea quoddam scotium inter se ad manutenendam querelam predictam coligerunt; et quod predicti Iohannes Eberton' et Ricardus Maydegode sunt communes perturbatores pacis et manutentores falsarum querelarum; quod quidem indictamentum prefati iusticiarij pacis iusticiarijs hic liberarunt veniunt coram iusticiarijs hic per vicecomitem ducti et allocuti qualiter se velint de premissis acquietare dicunt quod ipsi in nullo sunt inde culpabiles et de hoc ponunt se de bono et malo super patriam. Ideo fiat inde iurata. Iuratores veniunt qui ad hoc electi triati et iurati dicunt super sacramentum suum quod predicti Iohannes Eburton' et Ricardus Maydegode in nullo sunt culpabiles de premissis. Ideo ijdem Iohannes et Ricardus eant inde quieti etc. *Marg:* Quieti

John Eburton of Swerford and Richard Maydegode vicar of Enstone indicted before Thomas Poure and fellow justices of the peace for the following: on 9 May 1391 they with others unknown from Warwickshire numbering about two hundred armed with swords and bows and arrows in hostile array met at Showell and, in the presence of all John Eburton proclaimed that none would leave until they had accomplished their purpose, under pain of a fine of ½ mark and mutilation, to trample with all the cattle of the village of Swerford the fields and herbage of John Tame valued at 20 marks; they forced John son of John Rene of Little Tew to carry fuel and straw from Dunthrop to Showell to burn the hedges and fuel of John Tame; they sought to wound and kill the servants of John Tame and went to Little Tew to wound and kill John Aces and his brother William, servants of John Tame; they disturbed the countryside coming to burn and kill and they collected money to support their complaints; John Eberton and Richard Maydegode are common disturbers of the peace and supporters of false complaints; they pled not guilty, were tried, and acquitted.

30. *Marg:* Oxon' Patricius Broun de Hibernia captus pro eo quod indictatus fuit coram Roberto Cherlton' et socijs suis iusticiarijs domini regis ad pacem in comitatu predicto conseruandam assignatis de eo quod ipse die Iouis proximo ante festum apostolorum Simonis et Iude anno regni domini regis nunc quintodecimo domum Willelmi Hayton' de Oxon' sadeler apud Oxon' noctanter felonice fregit et ibidem duas togas furratas vnum capucium vnum coopertorium vnum baselardum vnum arcum cum octo sagittis de bonis et catallis eiusdem Willelmi Hayton' precij triginta solidorum felonice furatus fuit; venit coram iusticiarijs hic per vicecomitem ductus et allocutus qualiter se velit de felonijs predictis acquietare dicit quod ipse clericus est et quod ipse non potest sine Iohanne episcopo Lincoln' loci illius ordinario respondere. Et super hoc venit quidam decanus Christianitatis Oxon' et profert hic in curia litteras ipsius episcopi eidem decano directi ad omnes clericos de quocumque crimine felonico coram quibuscumque iusticiarijs domini regis irrititos petandos et calumpniandos quarum datum est apud Sleford septimo die mensis Iulij anno regni domini regis nunc quintodecimo [7 July 1391]. Et super hoc predictus Patricius petit examinacionem sibi fieri vtrum ipse clericus sit necne et per examinacionem predicti decani clericus inuenitur. Et super hoc predictus decanus petit predictum Patricium tanquam clericum etc. sibi deliberari set prius sciatur pro quali idem Patricius deliberari debeat rei veritas inquiratur per patriam. Ideo fiat inde iurata. Iuratores veniunt qui ad hoc electi triati et iurati dicunt super sacramentum suum quod predictus Patricius culpabilis est de felonia predicta. Catalla ipsius Patricij viginti denarij vnde Robertus Bullok vicecomes oneratur etc. Et super hoc predictus Patricius deliberatur hic in curia prefato decano ad ipsum saluo ducendum vsque gaolam dicti episcopi de Bannebury ibidem moraturum periculo quo incumbit etc. *Marg:* catalla (xx d.)[c] clericus conuictus

Patrick Broun of lreland indicted before Robert Cherlton and fellow justices of the peace for at night on 26 October 1391 feloniously breaking into the house of William Hayton saddler of Oxford at Oxford and feloniously stealing two furred coats, a hood, a coverlet, a dagger, and a bow with eight arrows, price 30s., proved clergy; after the jurors found him guilty, he was released to the ordinary for imprisonment in the bishop's gaol at Banbury; chattels, 20d., in charge to Robert Bullok sheriff.

31. *Marg:* Oxon' Ricardus filius Laurencij Abbot captus per suspeccionem apud Waterton' secundum statutum Wynton' etc. Et postea iusticiarij pacis inquisierunt de eo et nichil malum de eo inueniunt etc. venit coram iusticiarijs hic per vicecomitem ductus etc. Et super hoc proclamacio pro domino rege facta est quod si aliquis sit qui prosequi

voluit versus predictum Ricardum veniat et audietur et nullus venit etc. Ideo idem Ricardus deliberatur. *Marg:* deliberatur

Richard son of Lawrence Abbot taken at Water Eaton on suspicion according to the statute of Winchester, having been found by the justices of the peace to be of good repute, was released.

[*m. 8*]
Dominus Rex mandauit dilectis et fidelibus suis Ricardo Abburbury Roberto Bardolf' Roberto Charlton' Iohanni Hill' Thome Poure Thome Barentyne Nicholao Somerton' et Iohanni Rede litteras suas patentes in hec verba. Ricardus dei gratia rex Anglie et Francie et dominus Hibernie dilectis et fidelibus suis Ricardo Abberbury Roberto Bardolf Roberto Cherlton' Iohanni Hull' Thome Poure Thome Barentyne Nicholao Somerton' et Iohanni Rede salutem. Sciatis quod assignauimus vos coniunctim et diuisim ad pacem nostram necnon ad statuta apud Wynton' Northampton' et Westm' pro conseruacione pacis eiusdem ac statuta et ordinaciones ibidem et apud Cantebr' de venatoribus operarijs artificibus seruitoribus hostelarijs mendicantibus et vagabundis ac alijs hominibus mendicantibus qui se nominant trauayllyngmen' necnon omnia alia ordinaciones et statuta pro pono pacis nostre ac quiete regimine et gubernacione populi nostri edita in omnibus et singulis suis articulis in comitatu Oxon' infra libertates et extra iuxta vim formam et effectum eorundem custodienda et custodiri facienda et ad omnes illos quos contra formam ordinacionum et statutorum predictorum delinquentes inueneritis castigandos et puniendos prout secundum formam ordinacionum et statutorum eorundem fuerit faciendum et ad omnes illos qui aliquibus de populo nostro de corporibus suis vel de incendio domorum suarum minas fecerint et ad sufficientem securitatem de pace et bono gestu suo erga nos et populum nostrum inueniendam coram vobis venire et si huiusmodi securitatem inuenire recusauerint tunc eos in prisonis nostris quousque huiusmodi securitatem inuenerint saluo custodiri faciendos. Assignauimus eciam vos septem sex quinque quatuor tres et duos vestrum iusticiarios nostros ad inquirendum per sacramentum proborum et legalium hominum de comitatu tuo infra libertates et extra per quos rei veritas melius sciri poterit de omnimodis felonijs transgressionibus forstallarijs regratarijs et extorcionibus in comitatu tuo predicto infra libertates et extra per quoscumque et qualitercumque factis siue perpetratis et que exnunc ibidem fieri continget et eciam de omnibus illis qui in conuenticulis contra pacem nostram et in perturbacionem populi nostri seu vi armata ierint vel equitauerint seu exnunc ire vel equitare presumpserint et eciam de hijs qui in insidijs ad gentem nostram mahemiandam vel interficiendam iacuerint exnunc iacere presumpserint et eciam de hijs qui capicijs et alia libertata de vnica secta per

confederacionem et per manutenencia contra defencionem ac formam ordinacionum et statutorum inde ante hec tempora factorum vsi fuerint et alijs huiusmodi libertata inposterum vtentibus et eciam de hostelarijs et alijs qui in abusu mensurarum et ponderum ac in vendicione victualium et eciam de quibuscumque operarijs artificibus seruitoribus mendicantibus et vagabundis predictis et alijs qui contra formam ordinacionum et statutorum pro communi vtilitate regni nostri Anglie et populi nostri eiusdem de huiusmodi venatoribus operarijs artificibus seruitoribus hostelarijs mendicantibus vagabundis predictis et alijs inde factorum deliquerint vel attemptauerint in comitatu predicto et exnunc delinquere vel attemptare presumpserint ac eciam de quibuscumque vicecomitibus maioribus balliuis senescallis constabularijs et custodibus gaolarum qui in execucione officiorum suorum erga huiusmodi artifices seruitores laboratores vitelarios mendicantes et vagabundos ac alios predictos iuxta formam ordinacionum et statutorum predictorum facienda indebite se habuerint et exnunc indebite se habere presumpserint aut tepidi fuerint remissi vel necligentes et exnunc tepidos remissos vel necligentes fore contigerit et de omnibus alijs et singulis articulis et circumstancijs premissa omnia et singula ac alijs contra formam ordinacionum et statutorum predictorum per quoscumque et qualitercumque factis siue attemptatis et que exnunc fieri vel attemptari contigerit qualitercumque concernentibus plenius veritatem et ad indictamenta quecumque vobis seu duobus vestrum ac alijs nuper custodibus pacis nostre et iusticiarijs nostris ad huiusmodi transgressiones felonias et malefacta audienda et terminanda assignatis virtute diuersarum litterarum nostrarum vobis et eisdem alijs nuper custodibus pacis nostre et iusticiarijs nostris in hac parte factarum facta et nondum terminata inspicienda et ad omnia breuia et precepta per vos et ipsos alios custodes pacis nostre et iusticiarios nostros virtute litterarum nostrarum predictarum facta et coram vobis et ipsis alijs nuper custodibus pacis nostre et iusticiarijs nostris ad certos terminos futuros retornabilia ad terminos illos recipienda et processus inde inchoatos ac processus versus omnes alios coram vobis et eisdem alijs nuper custodibus pacis nostre et iusticiarijs nostris indictatos et quos (coram)[i] vobis in hac parte indictari contigerit quousque capiantur reddantur vel vtlagarentur faciendos et continuandos. Assignauimus eciam vos septem sex quinque quatuor tres et duos vestrum quorum aliquem vestrum vos prefati Roberte Cherlton' Iohannes Nicholae et Iohannes vnum esse volumus iusticiarios nostros ad ea omnia et singula que per huiusmodi hostelarios et alios in abusu mensurarum et ponderum ac inuendicione victualium et omnia alia que per huiusmodi operarios artifices seruitores mendicantes et vagabundos contra formam ordinacionum et statutorum predictorum seu in eneruacionem eorundem in aliqua presumpta seu attemptata fuerint et attemptari contigerit ac extorciones et regratarias predictas tam ad sectam nostram quam aliorum quorumcumque coram vobis pro nobis vel pro se ipsis conqueri vel prosequi volentium ac transgressiones et forstallarias predictas ad sectam nostram tantum et omnia alia que virtute ordinacionum et statutorum predictorum ac aliorum ordinacionum et statutorum regni nostri Anglie per custodes pacis nostre et iusticiarios nostros huiusmodi discuti et terminari debent audienda et terminanda et ad eosdem operarios artifices et seruitores per fines redempciones et amerciamenta et alio modo pro dilectis suis prout ante ordinacionem de punicione corporali huiusmodi operarijs artificibus et seruitoribus pro delictis suis exibendis factam fieri consueuit necnon eosdem vicecomites maiores balliuos senescallos constabularios custodes gaolarum venatores vitelarios hostelarios mendicantes et vagabundos super hijs qui contra formam ordinacionum et statutorum predictorum attemptata fuerint et attemptari continget castigandos et puniendos secundum legem et consuetudinem regni nostri Anglie ac formam ordinacionum et statutorum eorundem. Assignauimus eciam vos septem sex quinque quatuor tres et duos vestrum quorum alterum vestrum vos prefati Roberte Cherlton' et Iohannes Hull' vnum esse volumus iusticiarios nostros ad felonias predictas et omnia alia superius ad determinanda non declarata ad sectam nostram audienda et terminanda secundum legem et consuetudinem regni nostri Anglie ac formam ordinacionum et statutorum predictorum. Prouiso semper quod si casus difficultatis determinacione extorcionum huiusmodi coram vobis euenire contigerit quod ad iudicium inde reddendum nisi in presencia vnius iusticiariorum nostrorum de vno vel altero banco vel iusticiariorum nostrorum ad assisas in comitatu predicto capiendas assignatorum coram vobis minime procedatur. Et vobis et cuilibet vestrum mandamus quod circa custodiam pacis ac ordinacionum et statutorum predictorum diligenter intendatis et ad certos dies et loca quos vos septem sex quinque quatuor tres vel duo vestrum ad hoc prouideritis inquisiciones super premissis faciatis et premissa omnia et singula audiatis et terminetis ac modo debito et effectualiter expleatis in forma predicta facturi inde quod ad iusticiam pertinet secundum legem et consuetudinem regni nostri Anglie saluis nobis amerciamentis et alijs nobis inde spectantibus. Mandauimus enim vicecomiti nostro comitatus predicti quod ad certos dies et loca quos vos septem sex quinque quatuor tres vel duo vestrum ei scire faciatis venire faciat coram vobis septem sex quinque quatuor tribus et duobus vestrum tot et tales probos et legales homines de balliua sua tam infra libertates quam extra per quos rei veritas in premissis melius sciri poterit et inquiri. Et vos prefate Nicholae ad certos dies et loca per vos et dictos socios vestros super hoc profigendos breuia et precepta processus et indictamenta vt predictum est coram vobis et socijs suis nuper custodibus pacis et iusticiarijs huiusmodi facta et nondum terminata et nunc socijs vestris predictis venire faciatis et ea inspiciatis de debito fine terminetis sicut predictum est. In cuius rei testimonium has litteras nostras fieri fecimus patentes. Teste me ipso apud Westm' xxiiij die Decembris anno regni nostri quartodecimo [24 December 1390].

[*m.8d.*]
Deliberacio gaole domini regis castri Oxon' facta apud Oxon' coram Roberto Cherlton' et socijs suis iusticiarijs domini regis ad pacem in comitatu Oxon' conseruandam assignatis die Lune proximo post clausum pasche anno regni regis Ricardi secundi post conquestum sextodecimo [14 April 1393].

32. *Marg:* Oxon' Robertus Belage Thomas Freman et Henricus Tannere capti pro eo quod indictati fuerunt coram Ricardo Abburbury et socijs suis iusticiarijs domini regis ad pacem etc. de eo quod ipsi cum alijs pluribus ignotis sibi confederati modo guerrino loricis et alijs armaturis die Lune proximo post festum assumpcionis beate Marie anno regni domini regis nunc Anglie sextodecimo apud Chasterton' de nouo insurrexerunt ad interficiendum fratrem Willelmum abbatem de regali loco et ibidem modo guerrino clausum ipsius abbatis fregerunt contra inhibicionem domini regis eisdem directam et ibidem felonicum insultum super eiusdem abbatem fecerunt ad eundem abbatem interficiendum ita quod idem abbas in disperacione vite sue fuit et interfectus fuisset nisi subito fugisset ad manerium suum; et de eo quod ijdem Robertus Thomas et Henricus die Martis extunc proximo sequente modo predicto arraiati de nouo insurgente felonicum insultum in Iacobum seruientem dicti abbatis fecerunt et ibidem verberauerunt et vnum equm precij quadraginta solidorum de bonis et catallis ipsius abbatis in custodia ipsius Iacobi tunc existentis felonice ceperunt et abduxerunt; et de eo quod predicti Robertus Thomas et Henricus sunt communes insurgentes contra pacem et de eo quod predictus Robertus Belage cum alijs felonibus depredauerit Iacobum seruientem abbatis de regali loco de vno equo precij quadraginta solidorum apud Chasterton' et se retraxit occasione felonie predicte; quod quidem indictamentum prefati iusticiarij pacis iusticiarijs hic liberarunt veniunt coram iusticiarijs hic per vicecomitem ducti et allocuti qualiter se velint de felonijs predictis acquietare dicunt quod ipsi in nullo sunt inde culpabiles et de hoc ponunt se de bono et malo super patriam. Ideo fiat inde iurata. Iuratores veniunt qui ad hoc electi triati et iurati dicunt super sacramentum suum quod predicti Robertus Thomas et Henricus in nullo sunt inde culpabiles de felonijs predictis nec ea occasione vnquam se retraxerunt. Ideo eant inde quieti etc. *Marg:* Quietus Quietus Quietus

Robert Belage, Thomas Freman, and Henry Tannere indicted before Richard Abburbury and fellow justices of the peace for the following: on 19 August 1392 with many others unknown armed at Chastleton they rioted to

kill brother William abbot of Rewley and broke into the abbot's close against a royal order, feloniously assaulted the abbot and threatened to kill him so that he fled to his manor; on 20 August 1392 they feloniously assaulted James the abbot's servant and feloniously took a horse, price 40s.; they are common insurgents against the peace; also Robert Belage with others feloniously robbed James servant of the abbot of a horse, price 40s., at Chastleton and withdrew; they pled not guilty, were tried, and acquitted.

33. *Marg:* Oxon' Stephanus Vacgescombe clericus et Willelmus Kent capti pro eo quod indictati fuerunt coram Ricardo Abburbury et socijs suis iusticiarijs domini regis ad pacem etc. de eo quod ipsi quartodecimo die mensis Februarij anno regni domini regis nunc Anglie quintodecimo apud Newenton' Robertum Northlode de vna bulla abbatis de Butlesden' more curie romane bullata ac alia diuersa bona et catalla dicti abbatis ad valenciam centum solidorum in custodia dicti Roberti Northlode inuenta felonice depredauerunt; et de eo quod idem Stephanus Vacgescombe Thomas Croundale et Iohannes Sawyere die Dominica proximo proximo post festum assumpcionis beate Marie anno regni eiusdem domini regis nunc supradicto predicti Stephanus Thomas et Iohannes tres equos precij quinque marcarum de bonis et catallis prioris et conuentus sancte Frydeswyde virginis in regia via apud Halywell extra muros Oxon' felonice ceperunt et abduxerunt; et dictus Stephanus se retraxit; quod quidem indictamentum prefati iusticiarij pacis iusticiarijs hic liberarunt veniunt coram iusticiarijs hic per vicecomitem ducti et allocuti qualiter se velint de felonijs predictis acquietare dicunt quod ipsi in nullo sunt inde culpabiles et de hoc ponunt se de bono et malo super patriam. Ideo fiat inde iurata. Iuratores veniunt qui ad hoc electi triati et iurati dicunt super sacramentum suum quod predicti Stephanus Willelmus Thomas et Iohannes in nullo sunt inde culpabiles de felonijs predictis nec ea occasione vnquam se retraxerunt. Ideo eant inde quieti etc. *Marg:* Quieti Quieti

Stephen Vacgescombe clerk and William Kent indicted before Richard Abburbury and fellow justices of the peace for on 14 February 1392 feloniously robbing Robert Northlode at Newington of a bull of the abbot of Biddlesden sealed in the Roman style and other goods of the abbot valued at 100s.; and the said Stephen, Thomas Croundale, and John Sawyere on 20 September 1391, feloniously took three horses, price 5 marks, from the prior and convent of St. Frideswide; Stephen withdrew; all four pled not guilty, were tried, and acquitted.

[*William Bedell clerk and Robert Bradegare clerk were pardoned, 26 December 1392, for this offence; C. P. R. 1391-1396, p. 198.*]

34. *Marg:* Oxon' Thomas Forst' de Saltford' captus de eo quod indictatus fuit coram Ricardo Abburbury et socijs suis iusticiarijs domini regis ad pacem etc. de eo quod ipse die Lune proximo ante festum ascencionis domini anno regni domini regis nunc Anglie quinto apud Cornwell' tresdecim multones Iohannis de Abburbury precij quadraginta solidorum felonice furatus fuit; et est communis latro; quod quidem indictamentum prefati iusticiarij pacis iusticiarijs hic liberarunt venit coram iusticiarijs hic per vicecomitem ductus et allocutus qualiter se velit de felonijs predictis acquietare dicit quod ipse in nullo est inde culpabilis et de hoc ponit se de bono et malo super patriam. Ideo fiat inde iurata. Iuratores veniunt qui ad hoc electi iurati et triati dicunt super sacramentum suum quod predictus Thomas in nullo est inde culpabilis de felonijs predictis nec ea occasione vnquam se retraxit. Ideo eat inde quietus etc. *Marg;* Quietus

Thomas Forster of Salford indicted before Richard Abburbury and fellow justices of the peace for at Cornwell on 12 May 1382 feloniously stealing thirteen wethers, price 40s., from John de Abburbury, being a common thief; pled not guilty, was tried, and acquitted.

35. *Marg:* Oxon' Iohannes Purkas de Bannebury captus de eo quod indictatus fuit coram prefatis iusticiarijs domini regis ad pacem etc. de eo quod ipse die Iovis proximo post festum sancti Gregorij pape anno regni domini regis nunc Anglie terciodecimo apud Esyndon' iuxta Bannebury trigenta bidentes precij triginta solidorum Ricardi Harryos· felonice furatus fuit; et de eo quod ipse Iohannes vnam vaccam precij sex solidorum et octo denariorum die Veneris proximo post idem festum Iohannis Hoggys de Wykham apud Wykham felonice furatus fuit; quod quidem indictamentum prefati iusticiarij pacis (iusticiarijs)[i] hic liberarunt venit coram iusticiarijs hic per vicecomitem ductus et allocutus qualiter se velit de felonijs predictis acquietare dicit quod ipse in nullo est inde culpabilis et de hoc ponit se de bono et malo super patriam. Ideo fiat inde iurata. Iuratores veniunt qui ad hoc electi triati et iurati dicunt super sacramentum suum quod predictus Iohannes in nullo est inde culpabilis de felonijs predictis nec ea occasione vnquam se retraxit. Ideo eat inde quietus etc. *Marg:* Quietus

John Purkas of Banbury indicted before the aforesaid justices of the peace for on 17 March 1390 feloniously stealing at Easington near Banbury thirty sheep, price 30s., from Richard Harryos and at Wykham a cow, price 6s. 8d., from John Hoggys of Wykham; pled not guilty, was tried, and acquitted.

36. *Marg:* Oxon' Iohannes Howray de Garsyngdon' captus de eo quod indictatus fuit coram prefatis iusticiarijs domini regis ad pacem etc. de eo

quod ipse felonice fregit faldam Thome Spryngald' de Gersyngdon' die Lune proximo post festum sancti Marci euangeliste anno regni domini regis nunc Anglie quintodecimo apud Garsyngdon' predictam et ibidem felonice furatus fuit vnum agnum Thome Scut de Garsyndon' predicta precij quindecim denariorum; quod quidem indictamentum prefati iusticiarij pacis prefatis iusticiarijs hic liberarunt venit coram iusticiarijs hic per vicecomitem ductus et allocutus qualiter se velit de felonijs predictis acquietare dicit quod ipse in nullo est inde culpabilis et de hoc ponit se de bono et malo super patriam. Ideo fiat inde iurata. Iuratores veniunt qui ad hoc electi triati et iurati dicunt super sacramentum suum quod predictus Iohannes in nullo est inde culpabilis nec ea occasione vnquam se retraxit. Ideo eat inde quietus. *Marg:* Quietus

John Howray of Garsington indicted before the aforesaid justices of the peace for on 29 April 1392 feloniously breaking into the fold of Thomas Spryngald of Garsington, at Garsington, and feloniously taking a lamb, price 15d., belonging to Thomas Scut of Garsington; pled not guilty, was tried and acquitted.

[*m. 9*]

37. *Marg:* Oxon' Robertus Mustyll' capellanus captus pro eo quod indictatus fuit coram Ricardo Abberbury et socijs suis iusticiarijs domini regis ad pacem in comitatu predicto conseruandam assignatis de eo quod ipse die Sabati proximo ante primam Dominicam quadragesime anno regni domini regis nunc Anglie quintodecimo venit apud Burford cum diuersis Hibernijs ignotis noctanter circa vndecimam horam noctis et ibidem vicariam et mansionem Henrici Derlyng' vicarij perpetuarij ecclesie de Burford fregit et intrauit necnon bona et catalla predicti Henrici videlicet bordclothes tuwayles et alia vtensilia domus ad valenciam viginti solidorum ibidem felonice depredatus fuit; quod quidem indictamentum prefati iusticiarij pacis iusticiarijs hic liberarunt venit coram iusticiarijs hic per vicecomitem ductus et allocutus qualiter se velit de felonia predicta acquietare dicit quod ipse in nullo est inde culpabilis et de hoc ponit se de bono et malo super patriam. Ideo fiat inde iurata. Iuratores veniunt qui ad hoc electi triati et iurati dicunt super sacramentum suum quod predictus Robertus in nullo est culpabilis de felonia predicta nec ea occasione vnquam se retraxit. Ideo idem Robertus eat inde quietus etc. *Marg:* Quietus

Robert Mustyll chaplain indicted before Richard Abberbury and fellow justices of the peace for at Burford on 2 March 1392 with various unknown Irishmen at eleven at night breaking into the vicarage of Henry Derlyng perpetual vicar of Burford and feloniously robbing him of tablecloths, towels, and other household goods to the value of 20s.; pled not guilty, was tried, and acquitted.

38. *Marg:* Oxon' William Carlet seruiens Thome Abberbury captus pro eo quod indictatus fuit coram prefatis iusticiarijs pacis de eo quod ipse apud Thame die Iouis proximo post festum apostolorum Simonis et Iude anno regni domini regis nunc Anglie sextodecimo quandam grangiam ipsius Thome Abberbury felonice fregit et asportauit quatuor bussellos fabarum precij decem denariorum de bonis et catallis predicti Thome; venit coram iusticiarijs hic per vicecomitem ductus et allocutus qualiter se velit de felonia predicta acquietare dicit quod ipse in nullo est inde culpabilis et de hoc ponit se de bono et malo super patriam. Ideo fiat inde iurata. Iuratores venit qui ad hoc electi triati et iurati dicunt super sacramentum suum quod predictus Willelmus in nullo est culpabilis de felonia predicta nec ea occasione vnquam se retraxit. Ideo idem Willelmus eat inde quietus etc. *Marg:* Quietus

William Carlet servant of Thomas Abberbury indicted before the aforesaid justices of the peace for on 31 October 1392 feloniously breaking into the grange of the said Thomas at Thame and carrying away four bushels of beans, price 10d.; pled not guilty, was tried, and acquitted.

39. *Marg:* Oxon' Thomas Wheteley et Robertus Nasserton' capti pro eo quod indictati fuerunt coram prefatis iusticiarijs pacis de eo quod ipsi in festo natiuitatis beate Marie anno regni domini regis nunc Anglie quintodecimo apud Chepyngnorton quoddam pendule vnius zone cum quatuor stipatis argentis precij duorum solidorum de bonis Roberti Quenynton' amputauerunt in ecclesiam eiusdem ville et felonice furati fuerunt; veniunt coram iusticiarijs hic per vicecomitem ducti et allocuti qualiter se velint de felonia predicta acquietare dicunt quod ipsi in nullo sunt inde culpabiles et de hoc ponunt se de bono et malo super patriam. Ideo fiat inde iurata. Iuratores veniunt qui ad hoc electi triati et iurati dicunt super sacramentum suum quod predicti Thomas et Robertus Nasserton' in nullo sunt culpabiles de felonia predicta nec ea occasione vnquam se retraxerunt. Ideo ijdem Thomas et Robertus eant inde quieti etc. *Marg:* Quieti

Thomas Wheteley and Robert Nasserton indicted before the aforesaid justices of the peace for on 8 September 1391 in the church at Chipping Norton cutting off and stealing four silver tassels, price 2s., from a belt belonging to Robert Quenynton; pled not guilty, were tried, and acquitted. [*See above Roll C, no. 28.*]

40. *Marg:* Oxon' Iohannes Aleyn filius Iohannis Aleyn de Henle captus pro eo quod indictatus fuit coram prefatis iusticiarijs pacis de eo quod ipse die Dominica proximo post festum sancti Thome apostoli anno regni domini regis nunc Anglie sextodecimo Iohannem Wilcokes de Southweston' apud Wyfold' felonice interfecit; et de eo quod ipse die

anno et loco supradictis Robertum filium Iohannis Shepherd de Monygroue felonice interfecit; venit coram iusticiarijs hic per vicecomitem ductus et allocutus qualiter se velit de felonia predicta acquietare dicit quod ipse in nullo est inde culpabilis et de hoc ponit se de bono et malo super patriam. Ideo fiat inde iurata. Iuratores veniunt qui ad hoc electi triati et iurati dicunt super sacramentum suum quod predictus Iohannes Aleyn culpabilis est de felonia predicta. Catalla ipsius Iohannis nulla. Ideo idem Iohannes suspendeatur etc. *Marg:* Suspendeatur catalla nulla

John Aleyn son of John Aleyn of Henley indicted before the aforesaid justices of the peace for on 22 December 1392 feloniously killing John Wilcokes of South Weston at Wyfold; and in the same place, Robert son of John Shepherd of Maidensgrove; pled not guilty, was tried, convicted, and sentenced to be hanged; no chattels.

41. *Marg:* Oxon' Willelmus Bocher de Rollandryght' captus per suspeccionem secundum statutum Wynton' et iusticiarij pacis de eo inquisiuerunt et nichil malum de eo inueniunt etc. Et super hoc proclamacio pro domino rege facta est quod si aliquis sit qui prosequi voluerit versus predictum Willelmum de aliquibus felonijs veniat et audietur et nullus venit etc. Ideo idem Willelmus deliberatur et inuenit plegios de bono gestu erga dominum regem et populum suum videlicet Nicholaum Chansey Ricardum Marnyon' Iohannem Herdewyk' et Iohannem Vynctit' qui eum manuceperunt etc. *Marg:* deliberatur

William Bocher of Rollright taken on suspicion according to the statute of Winchester, having been found by the justices of the peace to be of good repute, was released.

42. *Marg:* Oxon' Thomas Duddele captus apud Dadyngton' per suspeccionem latrocinij secundum statutum Wynton' et iusticiarij pacis de eo inquisiuerunt et nichil malum de eo inueniunt etc. Et super hoc proclamacio pro domino rege facta est quod si aliquis sit qui prosequi voluerit versus prefatum Thomam de aliquibus felonijs veniat et audietur et nullus venit. Ideo idem Thomas deliberatur etc. *Marg:* deliberatur

Thomas Duddele taken at Deddington on suspicion of larceny according to the statute of Winchester, having been found by the justices of the peace to be of good repute, was released.

43. *Marg:* Oxon' Iohannes Godale plomer captus per suspeccionem secundum statutum Wynton' et iusticiarij pacis de eo inquisiuerunt et nichil malum de eo inueniunt. Et super hoc proclamacio pro domino rege facta est quod si aliquis sit qui prosequi voluerit versus predictum Iohannem veniat et audietur et nullus venit. Ideo idem Iohannes deliberatur etc. *Marg:* deliberatur

John Godale, dealer in lead or in feathers taken on suspicion according to the statute of Winchester, having been found by the justices of the peace to be of good repute, was released.

44. *Marg:* Oxon' Willelmus Eleford Iohannes Wotton' de Thame et Willelmus White capti per suspeccionem latrocinij secundum statutum Wynton' et iusticiarij pacis de eis inquisiuerunt et nichil malum de eis inueniunt. Et super hoc proclamacio pro domino rege facta est quod aliquis sit qui prosequi voluerit versus eos veniat et audietur et nullus venit etc. Ideo ijdem Willelmus Iohannes et Willelmus deliberantur etc. Marg: deliberantur

William Eleford, John Wotton of Thame, and William White taken on suspicion of larceny according to the statute of Winchester, having been found by the justices of the peace to be of good repute, were released.

Dominus rex mandauit dilectis et fidelibus suis Roberto Cherlton' Iohanni Hill' et Henrico Broun breue suum patens in hec verba. Ricardus dei gratia rex Anglie et Francie et dominus Hibernie dilectis et fidelibus suis Roberto Cherlton' Iohanni Hill' et Henrico Broun salutem. Sciatis quod constituimus vos et duos vestrum quorum alterum vestrum vos prefati Roberte et Iohannes vnum esse voluimus iusticiarios nostros ad gaolam nostram castri Oxon' de prisonibus in ea existentibus deliberandam. Et ideo vobis mandamus quod ad certum diem quem vos vel duo vestrum quorum alterum vestrum vos prefati Roberte et Iohannes vnum esse volumus ad hoc prouideritis conueniatis apud Oxon' ad gaolam illam deliberandam facturi inde quod ad iusticiam pertinet secundum legem et consuetudinem regni nostri Anglie saluis nobis amerciamentis et alijs ad nos inde spectantibus. Mandauimus enim vicecomiti nostro Oxon' quod ad certum diem quem vos vel duorum vestrum quorum alterum vestrum vos prefati Roberte et Iohannes vnum esse volumus ei scire facietis omnes prisones eiusdem gaole et eorum attachiamentos coram vobis et duobus vestrum quorum alterum vestrum vos prefati Roberte et Iohannes vnum esse volumus ibidem venire faciat. In cuius rei testimonium has litteras nostras fieri fecimus patentes. Teste me ipso apud Westm' xxvj die Iunij anno regni nostri decimo septimo [26 June 1393].

Deliberacio gaole domini regis castri Oxon' facta ibidem coram Roberto Cherlton' Iohanne Hill' et Henrico Broun iusticiarijs domini regis ad gaolam illam deliberandam assignatis die Martis proximo ante festum sancte Margarete virginis anno regni regis Ricardi secundi post conquestum decimo septimo [15 July 1393].

45. *Marg:* Oxon' Willelmus Campion webbe de Firyngford captus pro eo quod indictatus fuit coram Ricardo Abberbury et socijs suis iusticiarijs domini regis ad pacem in comitatu predicto conseruandam assignatis de eo quod ipse simul cum alijs die Sabati in festo sancte Marie Magdalene[1] anno regni domini regis nunc Anglie sextodecimo felonice furatus fuit apud Fyryngford vnum equm cum cella et freno vnam par caligarum vnum baselardum vnum tapetum cuiusdam lecti et vnam togam ad valenciam quadraginta solidorum de bonis et catallis Rogeri Baret persone ecclesie de Firyngford et Iohannis Baret; quod quidem indictamentum prefati iusticiarij pacis iusticiarijs hic liberarunt venit coram iusticiarijs hic per vicecomitem ductus et allocutus qualiter se velit de felonia predicta acquietare dicit quod ipse in nullo est inde culpabilis et de hoc ponit se de bono et malo super patriam. Ideo fiat inde iurata. Iuratores veniunt qui ad hoc electi triati et iurati dicunt super sacramentum suum quod predictus Willelmus in nullo est culpabilis de felonia predicta nec ea occasione vnquam se retraxit. Ideo idem Willelmus eat inde quietus etc. *Marg:* Quietus

William Campion weaver of Fringford indicted before Richard Abberbury and fellow justices of the peace for with others at Fringford in July 1392 feloniously stealing a horse with a saddle and bridle, one pair of hose, a dagger, a bed cover, and a coat valued at 40s. from Roger Baret parson of Fringford and John Baret; pled not guilty, was tried, and acquitted.

[*m. 9d.*]
46. *Marg:* Oxon' Iohannes Hakkare captus pro eo quod indictatus fuit coram Ricardo de Abberbury et socijs suis iusticiarijs domini regis ad pacem in comitatu predicto conseruandam assignatis de eo quod ipse die Sabati proximo ante festum sancte trinitatis anno regni domini regis nunc Anglie quintodecimo vnum equum Willelmi Cook precij duodecim solidorum apud Sonyngwell' felonice furatus fuit; et de eo quod ipse die Sabati proximo ante festum sancti Iohannis baptiste anno regni domini regis nunc Anglie septimo noctanter vnum multonem Thome Grey precij viginti denariorum apud Sonyngwell' felonice furatus fuit; et de eo quod ipse die Lune proximo ante festum purificacionis beate Marie predicto anno septimo duos multones Willelmi Elyot precij quadraginta denariorum apud Sonyngwell' felonice furatus fuit; et de eo quod ipse die Martis proximo ante festum sancti Martini predicto anno septimo vnum cultrum Ricardi Rogers precij decem et octo denariorum apud Sonyngwell' felonice furatus fuit; et quod est communis latro; quod quidem indictamentum prefati iusticiarij pacis iusticiarijs hic liberarunt venit coram iusticiarijs hic per vicecomitem ductus et allocutus qualiter se

[1]There is an error in the date. In 16 Richard II (1392-3) the feast of St Mary Magdalene, 22 July, was on a Monday, not a Saturday.

velit de felonijs predictis acquietare dicit quod ipse in nullo est inde culpabilis et de hoc ponit se de bono et malo super patriam. Ideo fiat inde iurata. Iuratores veniunt qui ad hoc electi triati et iurati dicunt super sacramentum suum quod predictus Iohannes in nullo est culpabilis de felonijs predictis nec ea occasione vnquam se retraxit. Ideo idem Iohannes eat inde quietus etc. *Marg:* Quietus

John Hakkare indicted before Richard de Abberbury and fellow justices of the peace for at Sunningwell [Berks.] on 8 June 1392 feloniously stealing a horse, price 12s., from William Cook, at night on 20 June 1383 a wether, price 20d., from Thomas Grey, on 1 February 1384 two wethers, price 40d., from William Elyot, and on 10 November 1383 a coulter, price 18d., from Richard Rogers, being a common thief; pled not guilty, was tried, and acquitted.

[*m. 10*]
Dominus rex mandauit dilectis et fidelibus suis Roberto de Cherlton' Laurencio Dru et Iohanni Rede litteras suas patentes in hec verba. Ricardus dei gratia rex Anglie et Francie et dominus Hibernie dilectis et fidelibus suis Roberto de Cherlton' Laurencio Dru et Iohanni Rede salutem. Sciatis quod constituimus vos et duos vestrum iusticiarios nostros ad gaolam nostram castri Oxon' de prisonibus in ea existentibus deliberandam. Et ideo vobis mandamus quod ad certum diem quem vos vel duo vestrum ad hoc prouideritis conueniatis apud Oxon' ad gaolam illam deliberandam facturi inde quod ad iusticiam pertinet sẹcundum legem et consuetudinem regni nostri Anglie saluis nobis amerciamentis et alijs ad nos inde spectantibus. Mandauimus enim vicecomiti nostro Oxon' quod ad certum diem quem vos vel duo vestrum ei scire faciatis omnes prisones eiusdem gaole et eorum attachiamentos coram vobis et duobus vestrum ibidem venire faciat. In cuius rei testimonium has litteras nostras fieri fecimus patentes. Teste me ipso apud Westm' xx die Februarij anno regni nostri decimo septimo [20 February 1394].
Pretextu quarum litterarum preceptum fuit vicecomiti quod venire faceret coram prefatis iusticiarijs vel duobus eorum apud Oxon' die Veneris in festo apostolorum Philipi et Iacobi tunc proximo sequente [1 May 1394] omnes prisones eiusdem gaole vna cum eorum attachiamentis. Et quod de (quolibet)[i] hundredo burgo et villa vnde prisones predicti indictati sunt xxiiij[or] tam millites quam alios liberos et legales homines coram prefatis iusticiarijs vel duobus eorum tunc ibidem venire faceret ad faciendum etc. Et vicecomes fecit inde execucionem prout patet in sequentem.

Deliberacio gaole domini regis castri Oxon' facta ibidem coram prefatis Roberto de Cherlton' et Iohanne Rede die Veneris in festo apostolorum

Philipi et Iacobi anno regni regis Ricardi secundi decimo septimo [1 May 1394].

47. *Marg:* Oxon' appellum Iohannes Pountfrayt procurator ecclesie de Haliwell' iuxta Oxon' venit coram prefatis iusticiarijs in propria persona sua et appellat Robertum Baron' capellanum alias vocatum Sauage Matheum Siluestre Willelmum Bysshop' alias dictum Brunne Iohannem Chaunflour alias vocatum White Adam Barbour alias dictum Gilbertum Englyssh' de Hibernia et Stephanum Richard de robaria et pace domini regis fracta. Et inuenit plegios de prosequendo appellum suum predictum videlicet Iohannem Kyngesmull' et Gilbertum Burton' et vnde idem Iohannes Pountfrayt instanter appellat predictos Robertum Baron' et alios de eo quod ipsi die Mercurij proximo ante festum omnium sanctorum anno regni regis Ricardi secundi decimo septimo ecclesiam sancte crucis de Haliwell' predicta ibidem noctanter felonice fregerunt et ipsum Iohannem Pountfrayt de vno missali precij decem librarum et vno alio missali precij centum solidorum duobus calicibus deauratis precij quatuor marcarum vno processionali precij dimidij marce vno psalterio precij xl d. vno quaterno de quodam missali precij xij d. duobus superpelicijs pro clericis vno coopertorio pro lecto precij xx d. duobus blankette' pro lecto precij xvj d. duobus manutergijs pro altari precij dimidij marce sex quaternis de gramatica cum chartiwario et salutare precij dimidij marce vno coopertorio lineo pro altari et vno manutergio veteri pro altari precij xx d. vno tuello de magno altari cum literis in se tractatis de blodeo filo videlicet nomen datoris precij sex solidorum vno par linthiaminum precij xx d. et alijs bonis et catallis precij centum librarum de bonis ecclesie predicte in custodia sua infra ecclesiam predictam existentis felonice depredati fuerunt; et si predicti Robertus Baron' et alij robariam predictam velint dedicere predictus Iohannes Pountfrait hoc paratus est versus eos probare prout curia etc.
Marg: appellum Venit eciam tunc coram prefatis iusticiarijs Thomas Skynner de Dadyngton' in propria persona sua et appellat predictos Robertum Baron' capellanum et alios de eo quod ipsi nocte diei Veneris proximo ante festum sancte Lucie virginis anno regni domini regis nunc decimo septimo apud Dadyngton' in comitatu predicto post horam medij noctis domum ipsius Thome Skynnere ibidem felonice fregerunt et ipsum Thomam de vna longa iupa furrata cum albo agno Iohannis de Abberbury de Abberbury precij xxvj s. et viij d. vna longa iupa furrata cum albo agno Rogeri Dogepol precij xx s. quatuor longis iupis cum duabus furris de albo agno et vna furrera de calabre Iohannis de Hulton' precij centum solidorum vna furrera nigra Roberti Makkeney precij j marce vna iupa furrata cum albo agno Thome Child de Abberbury precij x s. vna iupa cum nigra furrera Ricardi Preest de Dadyngton' precij x s. vna tunica

furrata Thome Glasyere de Dadyngton' precij iiij s. vna iupa longa furrata Willelmi Brudenell' de Ayno precij j marce vna iupa cum alba furrera Henrici Webbe de Aston' precij ix solidorum vna tunica sengle Agnetis Hayle de Dadyngton' precij v s. magrercorum suorum in custodia sua ad furrandum apud Dadyngton' existenta ac ipsum Thomam Skynnere de furrera de albo agno et nigro et vno reuers de menyuer precij xl s. de bonis et catallis suis proprijs tunc ibidem felonice depredati fuerunt; et si predicti Robertus Baron' et alij feloniam predictam velint dedicere predictus Thomas Skynnere hoc paratus est versus eos probare prout curia etc. Et profert plegios de prosequendo appellum suum predictum videlicet Iohannem Hulton' et Iohannem Abberbury etc.
Et predicti Robertus Baron' et alij veniunt per vicecomitem ducti et allocuti sunt separatim qualiter de premissis sibi tam ad appellum predicti Iohannis Pountfrait quam predicti Thome Skynnere separatim impositis eos velint acquietare qui dicunt quod ipsi in nullo sunt culpabiles de premissis nec aliquo premissorum et inde de bono et malo ponunt se super patriam etc. et tam predictus Iohannes Pountfrayt quam predictus Thomas Skynnere similiter. Ideo fiat inde iurata. Iuratores exacti veniunt qui ex assensu parcium predictarum super premissis omnibus et singulis electi et iurati dicunt super sacramentum suum quod predicti Robertus Baron' Matheus Siluestre Willelmus Bysshop' Iohannes Chaunflour Gilbertus Englyssh' et Stephanus Richard' culpabiles sunt tam de omnibus et singulis superius in appello predicti Iohannis Pountfrayt contentis prout idem Iohannes Pountfrait superius eos appellauit quam de omnibus et singulis superius in appello predicti Thome Skynnere contentis prout idem Thomas Skynnere superius eos appellauit. Et dicunt vlterius quod predicti Robertus Baron' et omnes alij capti fuerunt ad sectam predictorum Iohannis Pountfrait et Thome Skynnere etc. et dicunt quod predicti Robertus Baron' et omnes alij nulla habent bona seu catalla terras nec tenementa etc. Et statim predicti Robertus Baron' Willelmus Bysshop' Iohannes Chaunflour Gilbertus Englyssh' et Stephanus Richard' dicunt separatim quod ipsi clerici sunt et petunt beneficium clericale et super hoc venit [*blank*] decanus Oxon' et rector ecclesie sancti Aldati Oxon' vicem gerens Iohannis episcopi Lincoln' ad quoscumque clericos de quocumque crimine coram quibuscumque iusticiarijs domini regis senescallis seu alijs ministris suis irretitos seu impetitos infra comitatum Oxon' calumpniandos et recipiendos et profert litteras ipsius episcopi promissa testificantes in hec verba. Vniuersis sancte matris ecclesie filijs presentes litteras inspecturis Iohannes permissione diuina Lincoln' episcopus salutem in omni saluatore vniuersitati Christiane notum facimus per presentes quod ad exigendum et recipiendum vice et auctoritate nostris secundum libertatem ecclesiasticam et regni consuetudinem appliatam quoscumque clericos seu alios viros ecclesiasticos pro quocumque crimine seu transgressione

captos et in comitatu Oxon' incarceratos seu incarcerandos a quibuscumque iusticiarijs domini nostri regis senescallis balliuis seu ministris alijs quibuscumque ipsos liberandos habentibus potestatem vt de eis fiat in foro ecclasiastico quod canonice dictauerunt sanctiones dilectis filijs decano Oxon' rectori ecclesie sancti Aldati et vicario ecclesie parochie sancte Marie Magdalene Oxon' coniunctim et diuisim tenore presencium committimus vices nostros cum cuiuslibet cohercionis canonice potestate. In cuius rei testimonium sigillum nostrum presentibus est appensum. Datum in palacio nostro Lincoln' vicesimo die mensis Ianuarij anno domini millesimo ccc nonogesimo tercio et nostre consecracionis tricesimo primo [20 January 1393]. Et petit ipsos tanquam clericos conuictos liberari et tradito eis libro pro prefato ordinario legunt vt clericos et quia predictus Matheus Siluestre nonlegit nec clericus est nec clamat priuelegio clericali etc. Ideo ipse suspendatur. *Marg:* Suspendatur

Et consideratum est quod tam predictus Iohannes Pountfrayt quam predictus Thomas Skynnere rehabeant omnia bona et catalla sua predicta ad quorumcumque manus ea seu eorum aliqua deuenerunt etc. Et quidam testatum est propter iusticiarios hic pro iusticiarijs domini regis ad pacem in comitatu Oxon' conseruandam assignatis quod predicti Robertus Baron' Willelmus Bysshop' Iohannes Chaunflour Gilbertus Englysshe et Stephanus Richard coram eis in sessionibus suis de diuersis felonijs et prodicionibus indictati sunt prefati iusticiarij hic nondum auisant ipsos prefato ordinario ex causa predicta et alijs de causis liberandi set per eosdem iusticiarios remittuntur prisone sub custodia Thome Farendon' vicecomitis saluo custodiendo periculo quod incumbit quousque etc. *Marg:* remittuntur prisone

John Pountfrayt churchwarden of Holywell church near Oxford appealed Robert Baron chaplain alias Savage, Mathew Silvestre, William Bysshop alias Brunne, John Chaunflour alias White, Adam Barbour alias Gilbert Englyssh of Ireland, and Stephan Richard for robbery and breach of the king's peace; pledges, John Kyngesmull and Gilbert Burton. He accused the aforenamed of the following: on the night of 29 October 1393 they feloniously broke into the church of the Holy Cross at Holywell and feloniously robbed him of a missal, price £10, a missal, price 100s., two gold chalices, price 4 marks, a procession book, price ½ mark, a psalter, price 40d., a quire from a missal, price 12d., two surplices, a bed cover, price 20d., two blankets, price 16d., two altar towels, price ½ mark, six quires from a cartulary, price ½ mark, a linen altar cloth and an ancient altar towel, price 20d., a towel for the high altar with the name of the donor in blue beading, price 6s., a pair of sheets, price 20d., and other goods belonging to the church and in his charge, price £100; the accuracy of the above he will prove in court. Thomas Skynner of Deddington appealed

the same six men for feloniously breaking into his house after midnight on 12 December 1393 and feloniously robbing him of a long tunic lined with white lamb's fur property of John de Abberbury of Adderbury, price 26s. 8d., the same, property of Roger Dogepol, price 20s., four long tunics, two lined with lamb's fur and one with squirrel, property of John de Hulton, price 100s., a black fur lining property of Robert Makkeney, price 1 mark, a tunic lined with white lamb's fur property of Thomas Child of Adderbury, price 10s., a tunic lined with black fur property of Richard Preest of Deddington, price 10s., a furred tunic property of Thomas Glasyere of Deddington, price 4s., a long furred tunic property of William Brudenell of Aynho [*Northants.*], *price 1 mark, a tunic lined with white fur property of Henry Webbe of Aston, price 9s., an unlined tunic property ofAgnes Hayle of Deddington, price 5s., in his care to be lined with fur; and of his own goods consisting of black and white lamb's fur for lining and a rever of miniver, price 40s.; the accuracy of the above he will prove in court; pledges for Pountfrayt and Skynner, John Hulton, John Abberbury.*
The six pled not guilty, were tried, and found guilty; no chattels; Baron, Bysshop, Chaunflour, Englyssh, and Richard proved clergy; Silvestre sentenced to be hanged; Pountfrayt and Skinner to receive back their goods; because the five convicted clerks had been indicted before the justices of the peace they were not released to the bishop's ordinary but returned to prison in the custody of the sheriff Thomas Farendon.

[*For further process on the five see below nos. 53, 54. The first entry on m. 10d. records that John Chaunflour, captured at Banbury with stolen goods, was appealed for the thefts by Edward Draper of Tetbury in Gloucestershire. Because the offence was committed outside Oxfordshire, Chaunflour was returned to prison*].

[*m. 10d.*]
48. *Marg:* Oxon' Dauid Walysshman de Thame fysshere et Iohannes David Walysshman capti et ad gaolam predictam commissi pro eo quod ipsi alias indictati fuerunt coram iusticiarijs domini regis ad pacem in comitatu Oxon' conseruandam assignatis de eo quod ipsi die Iouis in vigilia assumpcionis beate Marie anno regni regis Ricardi secundi decimo septimo venerunt apud Suldern' et ibidem tres equos precij xxx s. Iohannis Goldewell' felonice furati fuerunt; et quod sunt communes latrones; et modo coram prefatis iusticiarijs veniunt predicti Dauid et Iohannes Dauid per vicecomitem ducti qui instanter allocuti qualiter de felonijs predictis se velint acquietare dicunt separatim quod ipsi in nullo sunt inde culpabiles et inde de bono et malo ponunt se super patriam. Ideo fiat inde iurata. Iuratores veniunt qui de premissis electi et iurati dicunt super sacramentum suum quod predictus Iohannes Dauid in nullo est culpabilis de felonia predicta sibi imposita nec vnquam ea occasione se retraxit et quod predictus Dauid culpabilis est de felonia predicta et nulla

habet terras nec tenementa bona seu catalla. Ideo consideratum est quod predictus Iohannes Dauid eat inde quietus et quod predictus Dauid suspendatur. *Marg.* Quietus Suspendatur catalla nulla terre nec tenementa

David Walysshman of Thame, fisherman and John David, Welshman, committed to gaol on indictment before the justices of the peace for at Souldern on 14 August 1393 feloniously stealing three horses, price 30s., from John Goldewell, being common thieves, appeared separately and pled not guilty; they were tried and the jury acquitted John David and pronounced David guilty and sentenced him to be hanged; no chattels nor lands.

49. *Marg:* Oxon' Robertus Freman nuper portarius de Newenton' captus et ad gaolam predictam commissus pro eo quod ipse indictatus fuit coram iusticiarijs domini regis ad pacem in comitatu Oxon' conseruandam assignatis de eo quod ipse die Sabati proximo ante festum epiphanie domini anno regni regis Ricardi secundi decimo septimo apud Hethrop' vnum bouem precij xiij s. et iiij d. Ricardi Taillour de Spellesbury noctanter felonice furatus fuit; modo venit coram prefatis iusticiarijs per vicecomitem ductus qui instanter allocutus qualiter de felonia predicta se velit acquietare dicit quod ipse in nullo est inde culpabilis et inde de bono et malo ponit se super patriam. Ideo fiat inde iurata. Iuratores veniunt qui ad hoc electi et iurati dicunt super sacramentum suum quod predictus Robertus culpabilis est de felonia predicta. Ideo ipse suspendatur. Catalla eius nulla terre nec tenementa etc. *Marg:* Suspendatur catalla nulla terras nec tenementa etc. *Marg:* Suspendatur catalla nulla terras nec tenementa etc.

Robert Freman former porter at Newington committed to gaol on indictment before the justices of the peace for at Heythrop at night on 3 January 1394 feloniously stealing an ox, price 13s. 4d.,from Richard Taillour of Spelsbury; pled not guilty, was tried, convicted, and sentenced to be hanged; no chattels nor lands.

50. *Marg:* Oxon' Robertus Bartelot filius Iohannis Bartelot de Lechelade captus et ad gaolam predictam commissus pro eo quod ipse alias indictatus fuit coram iusticiarijs domini regis ad pacem in comitatu Oxon' conseruandam assignatis de eo quod ipse die Mercurij proximo post Dominican in ramis palmarum anno regni regis Ricardi secundi decimo septimo venit apud Carsewell' in parochia de Witteneye noctanter et ibidem in vnam domum Thome Bernard' ignem felonice et proditorie imposuit et ipsam domum cum quadraginta et nonem bidentibus Thome Batyn et Willelmi Batyn precij lx s. in eadem domo existentibus felonice et proditorie combussit; et quod predictus Robertus die et anno supradictis venit noctanter apud Carsewell' predictam et

ibidem felonice furatus fuit ducentas sexagintes et vndecim bidentes Thome Batyn precij xxvj librarum; et quod est communis latro; modo venit coram prefatis iusticiarijs per vicecomitem ductus qui instanter allocutus qualiter de felonijs predictis sibi impositis se velit acquietare dicit quod ipse in nullo est inde culpabilis et inde de bono et malo ponit se super patriam. Ideo fiat inde iurata etc. Iuratores exacti veniunt qui ad veritatem de premissis dicendam electi et iurati dicunt super sacramentum sacramentum suum quod predictus Robertus Bartelot culpabilis est de felonia predicta sibi imposita. Ideo ipse suspendatur. Catalla eius nulla terre nec tenementa etc. *Marg:* Suspendatur catalla nulla terre tenementa

Robert Bartelot son of John Bartelot of Lechlade [*Gloucs.*] *committed to gaol on indictment before the justices of the peace for at night on 15 April 1394 at Caswell in the parish of Witney feloniously and treacherously setting fire to the house of Thomas Bernard and burning it together with forty-nine sheep, price 60s., belonging to Thomas Batyn and William Batyn, and stealing 271 sheep, price £26, from Thomas Batyn, being a common thief; pled not guilty, was tried, convicted, and sentenced to be hanged; no chattels nor lands.*

[*For the pardon, 22 October 1394, of Henry Bonde of Barrington* (*Gloucs.*), *accessory, see C. P. R. 1391-1396, p. 502.*]

Cherlton'

Plus in rotulo huic consuto de eodem

[*m. 11*]

Adhuc de deliberacione castri Oxon' facta ibidem coram Roberto de Cherlton' et Iohanne Rede iusticiarijs etc. prout patet rotulo hinc consuto.

51. *Marg:* Oxon' Iohannes Shareshull' bercarius Oliueri Belyeter de Dadyngton' captus et ad gaolam predictam commissus eo quod ipse indictatus fuit coram iusticiarijs domini regis ad pacem in comitatu Oxon' conseruandam assignatis de eo quod ipse die Dominica proximo ante festum sancti Barnabe apostoli anno regni regis Ricardi secundi post conquestum decimo septimo[1] venit apud Dadyngton' et ibidem xiiij bidentes Thome Draper de Dadyngton' Iohannis Maggen Thome Nostward' et Willelmi Smyth' de Dadyngton' precij xxiij s. et iiij d. in campo de Dadyngton' felonice furatus fuit; modo venit coram prefatis iusticiarijs per vicecomitem ductus qui instanter allocutus qualiter de premissis sibi impositis se velit acquietare dicit quod ipse in nullo est inde culpabilis et inde de bono et malo ponit se super patriam. Ideo fiat inde iurata etc. Iuratores exacti veniunt qui ad veritatem de premissis

[1]The year must be in error as the offence postdates the gaol delivery session.

dicendam electi triati et iurati dicunt super sacramentum suum quod predictus Iohannes Shareshull' in nullo est culpabilis de felonia predicta nec vnquam ea occasione se retraxit. Ideo ipse eat inde quietus etc. *Marg:* Quietus

John Shareshull shepherd of Oliver Belyeter of Deddington committed to gaol on indictment before the justices of the peace for in the field of Deddington on 7 June 1394 feloniously stealing fourteen sheep, price 23s. 4d., from Thomas Draper of Deddington, John Maggen, Thomas Nostward, and William Smyth of Deddington; pled not guilty, was tried, and acquitted.

52. *Marg:* Oxon' Willelmus Skynnere de Sutton' iuxta Langeley Mareys et Iohannes Goul de eadem capti et ad gaolam predictam commissi eo quod ipsi alias indictati fuerunt coram iusticiarijs domini regis de pace in comitatu Oxon' conseruanda assignatis de eo quod ipsi die Iouis proximo ante festum natiuitatis beate Marie anno regni regis Ricardi secundi quartodecimo domum Iohannis Bourman de Dadyngton' apud Dadyngton' noctanter felonice fregerunt et ibidem vnum equum eiusdem Iohannis Bourman precij xl s. felonice furati fuerunt; modo veniunt coram prefatis iusticiarijs per vicecomitem ducti qui instanter allocuti qualiter de premissis sibi impositis se velint acquietare dicunt separatim quod ipsi in nullo sunt inde culpabiles et inde de bono et malo ponunt se super patriam. Ideo fiat inde iurata etc. Iuratores exacti veniunt qui ad veritatem de premissis dicendam electi et iurati dicunt super sacramentum suum quod predicti Willelmus Skynnere et Iohannes Goul in nullo sunt culpabiles de premissis nec vnquam se occasione predicta retraxerunt. Ideo ipsi eant inde quieti etc. Quietus Quietus

William Skynnere and John Goul both of Sutton near Langley Marish [*Bucks.*] *committed to gaol on indictment before the justices of the peace for at night on 1 September 1390 feloniously breaking into the house of John Bourman of Deddington at Deddington and feloniously stealing a horse, price 40s.; pled not guilty, were tried, and acquitted.*

[*m. 12*]
Dominus Rex mandauit dilectis et fidelibus suis Roberto de Cherleton' Iohanni Cassy Iohanni Hill Willelmo Wylicotes et Iohanni Rede litteras suas patentes in hec verba. Ricardus dei gratia rex Anglie et Francie et dominus Hibernie dilectis et fidelibus suis Roberto de Cherlton' Iohanni Cassy Iohanni Hill' Willelmo Wylicotes et Iohanni Rede salutem. Sciatis quod assignauimus vos quatuor tres et duos vestrum quorum aliquem vestrum vos prefati Roberte Iohannes Cassy et Iohannes Hill' vnum esse volumus iusticiarios nostros ad inquirendum per sacramentum proborum et legalium hominum de comitatu Oxon' tam infra libertates quam extra per quos rei veritas melius sciri poterit de omnimodis felonijs et

prodicionibus per quoscumque prisones in gaola nostra castri Oxon' detentos in comitatu predicto perpetrantis et de premissis omnibus et singulis ac alijs articulis et circumstancijs ea omnia et singula qualitercumque concernentibus plenius veritatem et ad premissa omnia et singula audiendis et terminandis secundum legem et consuetudinem regni nostri Anglie. Et ideo vobis mandamus quod ad certos dies et loca quos vos quatuor tres vel duo vestrum quorum aliquem vestrum vos prefati Roberte Iohannes Cassy et Iohannes Hill' vnum esse volumus ad hoc prouideritis inquisiciones super premissis factas et premissa omnia et singula audiatis et terminetis in forma predicta facturi inde quod ad iusticiam pertinet secundum legem et consuetudinem predictas saluis nobis amerciamentis et alijs ad nos inde spectantibus. Mandauimus enim vicecomiti nostro comitatus predicti quod ad certos dies et loca quos vos quatuor tres vel duo vestrum quorum aliquem vestrum vos prefati Roberte Iohannes Cassy et Iohannes Hill' vnum esse volumus ei scire facietis venire faciat coram vobis quatuor tribus et duobus vestrum quorum aliquem vestrum vos prefati Roberte Iohannes Cassy et Iohannes Hill' vnum esse volumus tot et tales probos et legales homines de balliua sua tam infra libertates quam extra per quos rei veritas in premissis melius sciri poterit et inquiri. In cuius rei testimonium has litteras nostras fieri fecimus patentes. Teste Edwardo duce Ebor' custode Anglie apud Westm' quinto die Februarij anno regni nostri decimo octauo [5 February 1395].
Pretextu quarum litterarum preceptum fuit vicecomiti quod venire faceret coram prefatis iusticiarijs quatuor tribus vel duobus eorum quorum etc. apud Oxon' die Veneris proximo ante festum sancti Petri in cathedra tunc proximo sequentem [19 February 1395] de quolibet hundredo burgo et villa vbi etc. xxiiij^{or} tam milites quam alios etc. ad inquirendum etc. Et vicecomes fecerit inde execucionem prout patet in sequente.

Oxon'

53. Indictamenta capta apud Oxon' coram prefatis Iohanne Cassy et Iohanne Rede predicto die Veneris anno supradicto [19 February 1395] per sacramentum Iohannis Yerman Iohannis Comptone Iohannis Archere Roberti atte Groue Iohannis Waryn Ricardi Whytsond Iohannis Lytholf Willelmi atte Mulle Roberti Owayn Iohannis Yonge Willelmi Hocard' et Iohannis Terry qui dicunt super sacramentum suum quod Iohannes Sauage de Hibernia Robertus Baron' capellanus alias dictus Sauage Willelmus Bysshop' alias dictus Broune Iohannes Chaunflour alias dictus White Adam Barbour alias vocatus Thomas Barbour alias dictus Gilbertus Englyssh' Irysshman et Stephanus Richard' die Sabati proximo ante festum sancti Michelis archangeli anno

regni regis Ricardi secundi post conquestum decimo septimo in parochia sancti Egidij in suburbio Oxon' ex eius felonicis imaginacionibus et compassamentis inter eos tunc ibidem habitatis felonice et proditorie vt proditores et felones domini regis contra ligeanciam suam controfecerunt cuneam domini regis et fecerunt falsam monetam de peutre mixtum cum plumbo et alconomye videlicet grotes dimidias grotes denarios obulos et ferlinges et ibidem die et anno predictis et infra villam Oxon' per duas septimanas extunc proximas sequentes falsam monetam predictam felonice et prodiciose apud domos Iohannis Scryueyn Iohannis Daubere et Cristine Potter launder et alijs diuersis hominibus infra villam Oxon' et comitatum predictum vt bonam et legalem monetam exposuerunt warantizauerunt et deliberauerunt in deceptionem populi domini regis etc.

The jurors present before John Cassy and John Rede that John Savage of Ireland, Robert Baron chaplain alias Savage, William Bysshop alias Broune, John Chaunflour alias White, Adam Barbour alias Thomas Barbour alias Gilbert Englyssh Irishman, and Stephen Richard on 27 September 1393 in the parish of St Giles in the suburbs of Oxford feloniously and treasonably made counterfeit money of pewter mixed with lead and alchemy, i.e. groats, half groats, pennies, halfpennies, and farthings, which they passed in Oxford as legal money to John Scryueyn, John Daubere, Christine Potter laundress and others.

[*For process see below no. 54; see also above no. 47*].

54. Item dicunt super sacramentum suum quod Iohannes Sauage de Hibernia Iohannes Chaunflour alias dictus White et Adam Barbour alias dictus Thomas Barbour alias dictus Gilbertus Englyssh' Irysshman qui nuper coram iusticiarijs domini regis ad pacem in comitatu Oxon' conseruandam assignatis de diuersis proditionibus et felonijs indictati fuerunt et per eosdem iusticiarios commissi gaole castri Oxon' et in eadem detenti et nunc coram Iohanne Cassy et Iohanne Rede iusticiarijs ad audiendum et terminandum etc. de eisdem proditione et felonijs per ipsos iuratores indictati circa medium noctis proxime sequentis diem Veneris in festo natiuitatis domini anno regni regis Ricardi secundi decimo octauo felonice fregerunt et burgauerunt gaolam domini regis castri Oxon' et inerunt ad capellam castri que est infra muros et custodiam castri predicti et securi extra gaolam predictam traxerunt Iohannem Sprot Robertum Shepherd Edwardum Astell' et Iohannem Chaunflour pro suspectione felonie in gaola predicta tunc detentos contra voluntatem eorum eos de vita et membris minando quod nisi transire vellent cum eis ad capellam predictam eos interficerent et ipsos ante se fugauerunt ad capellam predictam et sic ipsi pro metu mortis et pro saluacione vite sue vna cum predictis Iohanne Sauage et alijs in capellam predictam inerunt et in eadem fuerunt vsque diem Sabati tunc

proximum sequentem; quo die ijdem Iohannes Sprot Robertus Shepherd et Edwardus Astell' gratis et spontanea voluntate sua absque alicuius cohercione se reddiderunt gaole predicte; predicti quidem Iohannes Sauage et Iohannes Chaunflour nocte eiusdem diei Sabati tunc proximi sequentis voluntare exierunt capellam predictam pro naturali pondere deponendo et pro aisiamentis sibi intraijs et antequem capellam predictam reintrare potuerunt ministri vicecomitis gaole predicte ipsos ceperunt et in gaolam predictam duxerunt; ac postmodum circa mediam noctem diei Lune in festo conuersionis sancti Pauli anno supradicto quidam homines extranei et adhunc ipsis iuratoribus ignoti ex assensu voluntate et conductu predictorum Iohannis Chaunflour alias dicti White et Ade Barbour muros domini regis castri predicti felonice et proditorie fregerunt et capellam predictam intrauerunt et ipsos Iohannem et Adam ceperunt et portauerunt versus dictos muros sic per ipsos fractos ministri quidem vicecomitis vigiles hoc audientes et videntes cum hutesio leuato predictos Iohannem Chaunflour et Adam de predictis felonibus ignotis ceperunt manuforti et ipsos ad gaolam predictam securo duxerunt; et ijdem felones ignoti vltra muros predictos fugierunt et euaserunt; et sic Thomas Barentyn vicecomes comitatus predicti in cuius tempore premissa facta fuerunt habet promptos et paratos coram prefatis iusticiarijs hic ad barram predictos Iohannem Sauage Iohannem Chaunflour alias dictum White Adam Barbour Iohannem Sprot Robertum Shephird Edwardum Astell' et Iohannam Chaunflour ad respondendum domino regi de quibuscumque proditoribus et felonijs super ipsos impositis seu imponendis etc. Et modo coram prefatis iusticarijs hic veniunt predicti Iohannes Sauuage Robertus Baron' capellanus Willelmus Bysshop' alias dictus Broune Iohannes Chaunflour alias dictus White Adam Barbour et Stephanus Richard per custodem gaole predicte ducti et instanter allocuti sunt separatim videlicet predicti Iohannes Sauuage Iohannes Chaunflour alias dictus White et Adam Barbour qualiter de proditione et burgaria predictis ac predicti Robertus Baron' Willelmus Bysshop' alias dictus Broune et Stephanus Richard qualiter de proditione predicta se velint acquietare dicunt separatim quod ipsi in nullo sunt inde culpabiles et inde de bono et malo ponunt se super patriam. Ideo fiat inde iurata etc. Iuratores exacti veniunt qui ad veritatem de premissis dicendam electi et iurati dicunt super sacramentum suum quod predictus Iohannes Sauuage culpabilis est de proditione et burgaria predictis; et quod predicti Iohannes Chaunflour alias dictus White et Adam Barbour in nullo sunt culpabiles de proditione predicta set solomodo de burgaria gaole predicte et nulla habent bona seu catalla terras nec tenementa etc.; et quod predicti Robertus Baron' Willelmus Bysshop' et Stephanus Richard in nullo sunt culpabiles de proditione predicta nec vnquam ea occasione se retraxerunt. Ideo consideratum est quod predictus Iohannes

Sauuage distrahatur et suspendatur. Catalla eius nulla terre nec tenementa. Et quo ad predictos Iohannem Chaunflour alias dictum White Adam Barbour Robertum Baron' Willelmum Bysshop' alias dictum Broune et Stephanum Richard pro eo quod prefati iusticiarij non auisantur ad iudicium de eis in hac parte reddendum ac pro eo quod tam per vicecomitem comitatus predicti et seruientes et ministros eiusdem vicecomitis gaole predicte quam ex relatu quam proborum fidedignorum eisdem iusticiarijs cercificatum est quod ijdem Iohannes Chaunflour et alij coram Roberto de Cherlton' et socijs suis iusticiarijs ad gaolam illam nuper deliberandam assignatis de diuersis felonijs per quandam inquisicionem patrie hic coram eis capte in quam inde de bono et malo se posuerunt conuicti fuerunt et per eosdem iusticiarios pro eo quod ipsi adtunc non auisati fuerunt ad iudicium inde super eos reddendum remissi fuerunt gaole predicte saluo custodiendo. Per quod ex causis predictis et alijs de causis prefatos nunc iusticiarios hic specialiter mouentibus ijdem Iohannes Chaunflour alias dictus White Adam Barbour Robertus Baron' Willelmus Bysshop' alias dictus Broune et Stephanus Richard remittuntur gaole predicte in custodia predicti vicecomitis saluo custodiendo periculo quod incumbet quousque etc. *Marg.* distrahiatur Suspendatur catalla nulla terre nec tenementa remittuntur prisone

The jurors also present that John Savage of Ireland, John Chaunflour alias White, and Adam Barbour alias Thomas Barbour alias Gilbert Englyssh Irishman who had been indicted before the Oxfordshire justices of the peace for various treasons and felonies and imprisoned in Oxford Castle gaol and who are now appearing before John Cassy and John Rede did the following: at night on Friday, Christmas 1394, they feloniously broke and burgled the gaol and went into the chapel of the castle; they released from the gaol John Sprot, Robert Shepherd, Edward Astell, and John Chaunflour, imprisoned on suspicion, and threatened to kill them unless they entered the chapel which they did, remaining there until Saturday when Sprot, Shepherd, and Astell returned to gaol voluntarily; Savage and Chaunflour leaving the chapel to relieve themselves were taken back to gaol by the officials; at midnight on 25 January 1395 men unknown to the jurors with the assent of John Chaunflour alias White and Adam Barbour treacherously broke into the castle and took away Chaunflour alias White and Barbour; the officials raised the hue and cry and Chaunflour and Barbour were returned to gaol; the unknown men escaped.
The sheriff Thomas Barentyn was ready to produce John Savage, John Chaunflour alias White, Adam Barbour, John Sprot, Robert Shepherd, Edward Astell, and John Chaunflour to answer for the treasons and felonies with which they were charged; Savage, Robert Baron chaplain, William Bysshop alias Broune, Chaunflour alias White, Barbour, and

Stephen Richard appeared; Savage, Chaunflour alias White, and Barbour pled not guilty of the treason and the prison break; Baron, Bysshop alias Broune, and Richard of the treason; the jury found Savage guilty of both treason and the prison break; Chaunflour alias White and Barbour not guilty of treason but guilty of the prison break; the three have no chattels or land; the jury found Baron Bysshop, and Richard not guilty of treason, and acquitted them. Savage was sentenced to be drawn and hanged. Chaunflour alias White, Barbour, Baron Bysshop alias Broune, and Richard are returned to goal because they are under indictment for felony.

[*For pardon on 2 May 1395 to Thomas Barentyn for money due the king because of the escape of Savage, Chaunflour alias White, Barbour, Sprot, Shepherd, Astell, and Chaunflour from Oxford Castle gaol on Christmas night 1394 see C.P.R. 1391-1396, p. 565; see also above, nos. 47, 53.*]

[*m. 13*]
Dominus rex mandauit dilectis et fidelibus suis Roberto de Cherlton' Iohanni Hille et Iohanni Rede litteras suas patentes in hec verba. Ricardus dei gratia rex Anglie et Francie et dominus Hibernie dilectis et fidelibus suis Roberto de Cherlton' Iohanni Hille et Iohanni Rede salutem. Sciatis quod constituimus vos et duos vestrum iusticiarios nostros ad gaolam nostram castri Oxon' de prisonibus in ea tam pro proditionibus quam alijs felonijs existentibus deliberandam. Et ideo vobis mandamus quod ad certum diem quem vos vel duo vestrum ad hoc prouideritis conueniatis apud Oxon' ad gaolam illam deliberandam facturi inde quod ad iusticiam pertinet secundum legem et consuetudinem regni nostri Anglie saluis nobis amerciamentis et alijs ad nos inde spectantibus. Mandauimus enim vicecomiti nostro Oxon' quod ad certum diem quem vos vel duo vestrum ei scire faciatis omnes prisones eiusdem gaole et eorum attachiamentos coram vobis et duobus vestrum ibidem venire faciat. In cuius rei testimonium has litteras nostras fieri fecimus patentes. Teste me ipso apud Westm' xxx die Iunij anno regni nostri decimo octauo [30 June 1394].

Deliberacio gaole domini regis castri Oxon' facta ibidem coram Iohanne Hille et Iohanne Rede iusticiarijs domini regis ad gaolam illam deliberandam assignatis die Veneris proximo ante festum sancte Margarete virginis anno regni regis Ricardi secundi post conquestum Anglie decimo octauo [17 July 1394].

55. *Marg:* Oxon' Robertus Grey captus pro eo quod indictatus fuit coram Thoma Paynell' et socijs suis iusticiarijs domini regis ad pacem in comitatu predicto conseruandam assignatis de eo quod ipse die Lune proximo ante festum conuersionis sancti Pauli anno regni domini regis

nunc Anglie sextodecimo apud Haywerebrugge felonice interfecit Robertum Dogge de Henle; et quod est communis latro; quod quidem indictamentum prefati iusticiarij pacis iusticiarijs hic liberarunt venit coram iusticiarijs hic per vicecomitem ductus et allocutus qualiter se velit de felonia predicta acquietare dicit quod ipse in nullo est inde culpabilis et de hoc ponit se de bono et malo super patriam. Ideo fiat inde iurata. Iuratores veniunt qui ad hoc electi triati et iurati dicunt super sacramentum suum quod predictus Robertus Grey in nullo est culpabilis de felonia predicta nec ea occasione vnquam se retraxit. Ideo idem Robertus Grey eat inde quietus etc. *Marg:* Quietus

Robert Grey indicted before Thomas Paynell and fellow justices of the peace for on 20 January 1393 at Haywerebrugge feloniously killing Robert Dogge of Henley, being a common thief, pled not guilty, was tried, and acquitted.

56. *Marg:* Oxon' Thomas atte Hyde de comitatu Herford' captus pro eo quod indictatus fuit coram prefatis iusticiarijs pacis de eo quod ipse in festo sancti Barnabe apostoli anno regni domini regis nunc Anglie sextodecimo in parco de Walyngton' quendam equm dun precij decem solidorum Henrici seruientis Iohannis Knyght' de Walyngton' felonice furatus fuit; quod quidem indictamentum prefati iusticiarij pacis iusticiarijs hic liberarunt venit coram iusticiarijs hic per vicecomitem ductus et allocutus qualiter se velit de felonia predicta acquietare dicit quod ipse in nullo est inde culpabilis et de hoc ponit se de bono et malo super patriam. Ideo fiat inde iurata. Iuratores veniunt qui ad hoc electi triati et iurati dicunt super sacramentum suum quod predictus Thomas in nullo est culpabilis de felonia predicta nec ea occasione vnquam se retraxit. Ideo predictus Thomas eat inde quietus etc. *Marg:* Quietus

Thomas atte Hyde of Hertfordshire indicted before the aforesaid justices of the peace for on 11 June 1393 feloniously stealing a dun horse, price 10s., from Henry servant of John Knyght of Wallington [*Berks.*] *in the park at Wallington; pled not guilty, was tried, and acquitted.*

57. *Marg:* Oxon' Willelmus Palmere de Oxon' irmongere captus pro eo quod indictatus fuit coram Thoma Paynell' et socijs suis iusticiarijs domini regis ad pacem in comitatu predicto conseruandam assignatis de eo quod vbi quidam Thomas Talbot alias dictus Thomas Brode qui fuit in prisona domini regis apud Bocardo in Oxon' pro felonia et felonice fregit predictam prisonam domini regis die Dominica proximo post festum sancti Michelis anno regni domini regis nunc Anglie quartodecimo predictus Willelmus receptauit predictum Thomam in domo sua in festo sancte Fredeswyde virginis anno regni eiusdem domini regis nunc quartodecimo apud Oxon' sciens ipsum felonem esse et euasorem et fractorem predicte prisone et similiter de ecclesia sancti Michelis infra

portam borialem Oxon' euasorem; quod quidem indictamentum tam de principali felonia predicta quam de accessorio eiusdem felonie prefati iusticiarij pacis iusticiarijs hic liberarunt ac eciam vtlagariam in ipsum Thomam Talbot occasione principalis felonie predicte per processum coram eis factum promulgatam ostenderunt et super hoc venit predictus Willelmus per vicecomitem ductus et allocutus qualiter se velit de accessorio felonie predicte acquietare dicit quod ipse in nullo est inde culpabilis et de hoc ponit se de bono et malo super patriam. Ideo fiat inde iurata. Iuratores veniunt qui ad hoc electi triati et iurati dicunt super sacramentum suum quod predictus Willelmus in nullo est culpabilis de accessorio felonie predicte nec ea occasione vnquam se retraxit. Ideo idem Willelmus eat inde quietus etc. *Marg:* Quietus

William Palmere ironmonger of Oxford indicted before Thomas Paynell and fellow justices of the peace for the following: when a certain Thomas Talbot, alias Thomas Brode, imprisoned in the Bocardo for felony, broke prison on 2 October 1390, the said William received him in his house knowing him to be a felon who had broken prison and also from the church of St Michael at the North Gate; the indictments of the principal and of the accessory being before the justices of gaol delivery and also the record of the outlawry of Thomas Talbot, William pled not guilty as an accessory, was tried, and acquitted.

58. *Marg:* Oxon' Willelmus Taillour nuper de Midlyngton' captus pro eo quod indictatus fuit coram prefatis iusticiarijs pacis de eo quod ipse die Sabati proximo ante festum purificacionis beate Marie anno regni domini regis nunc Anglie quartodecimo apud Somerton' nonem solidos et sex denarios in denarijs numeratis de Iohanne Webbe de Burcestre felonice depredauit et furatus fuit; et quod est communis latro; quod quidem indictamentum prefati iusticiarij pacis iusticiarijs hic liberarunt ac eciam vtlagariam in ipsum Willelmum occasione felonie predicte promulgatam per processum coram eis factum eisdem iusticiarijs ostenderunt venit coram iusticiarijs hic per vicecomitem ductus [*entry unfinished*]

William Taillour late of Middleton indicted before the aforesaid justices of the peace for on 28 January 1391 at Somerton feloniously robbing John Webbe of Bicester of 9s. 6d. in pennies, being a common thief, the indictment and the outlawry promulgated on William because of the aforesaid felony were before the justices [*of gaol delivery*]

[*m. 13d.*]
Deliberacio gaole castri domini regis Oxon' facta apud Oxon' coram Roberto Cherlton' et Iohanne Hille iusticiarijs domini regis ad gaolam illam deliberandam assignatis die Lune proximo ante festum sancte

Margarete virginis anno regni regis Ricardi secundi post conquestum decimo nono [19 July 1395].

59. *Marg:* Oxon' Thomas Bungey captus per suspectionem latrocinij secundum statutum Wynton' et nullum habetur de eo indictamentum et iusticiarij pacis de eo inquisiuerunt et nichil mali de eo inueniunt. Et super hoc proclamacio pro domino rege facta est quod si aliquis sit qui versus predictum Thomam de aliquibus felonijs prosequi voluerit veniat et audietur et nullus venit etc. et testatum est hic in curia quod predictus Thomas est bone fame. Ideo idem Thomas deliberetur etc.

Thomas Bungey taken on suspicion of larceny according to the statute of Winchester, having been found by the justices of the peace to be of good repute, to be released.

60. *Marg:* Oxon' Iohannes Stranton' captus per suspectionem latrocinij secundum statutum Wynton' et nullum habetur de eo indictamentum et iusticiarij pacis de eo inquisiuerunt et nichil mali de eo inueniunt. Et super hoc proclamacio pro domino rege facta est quod si aliquis sit qui versus predictum Iohannem prosequi voluerit de aliquibus felonijs veniat et audietur et nullus venit etc. et testatum est hic in curia quod predictus Iohannes est bone fame. Ideo idem Iohannes deliberetur etc.

John Stranton taken on suspicion of larceny according to the statute of Winchester, having been found by the justices of the peace to be of good repute, to be released.

61. *Marg:* Oxon' Iohannes Furneys captus per suspectionem latrocinij secundum statutum Wynton' et nullum habetur de eo indictamentum et iusticiarij pacis de eo inquisiuerunt et nichil mali de eo inueniunt. Et super hoc proclamacio pro domino rege facta est quod si aliquis sit qui versus predictum Iohannem de aliquibus felonijs prosequi voluerit veniat et audietur et nullus venit etc. et testatum est hic in curia quod predictus Iohannes est bone fame. Ideo idem Iohannes deliberetur etc.

John Furneys taken on suspicion of larceny according to the statute of Winchester, having been found by the justices of the peace to be of good repute, to be released.

62. *Marg:* Oxon' Iohannes Styward' de Swynesey captus per suspectionem latrocinij secundum statutum Wynton' et nullum habetur de eo indictamentum et iusticiarij pacis de eo inquisiuerunt et nichil mali de eo inueniunt. Et super hoc proclamacio pro domino rege facta est quod si aliquis sit qui versus predictum Iohannem de aliquibus felonijs prosequi voluerit veniat et audietur et nullus venit etc. et testatum est hic in curia quod predictus Iohannes est bone fame. Ideo idem Iohannes deliberetur etc.

John Styward of Swynesey taken on suspicion of larceny according to the statute of Winchester, having been found by the justices of the peace to be of good repute, to be released.

[*m. 14*]
Rex mandauit dilectis et fidelibus suis Iohanni Hill' Iohanni Woderoue et Henrico Broun litteras suas patentes in hec verba. Ricardus dei gratia rex Anglie et Francie et dominus Hibernie dilectis et fidelibus suis Iohanni Hill Iohanni Woderoue et Henrico Broun salutem. Sciatis quod constituimus vos tres vel duos vestrum iusticiarios nostros ad gaolam nostram castri Oxon' de prisonibus in ea existentibus hac vice deliberandos. Et ideo vobis mandamus quod ad certum diem quem vos vel duo vestrum ad hoc prouideritis conueniatis apud Oxon' ad gaolam illam deliberandam facturi inde quod ad iusticiam pertinet secundum legem et consuetudinem regni nostri Anglie saluis nobis amerciamentis et alijs ad nos inde spectantibus. Mandauimus enim vicecomiti nostro Oxon' quod ad certum diem quem vos vel duo vestrum ei scire facietis omnes prisones eiusdem gaole et eorum attachiamentos coram vobis et duobus vestrum ibidem venire faciat. In cuius rei testimonium has litteras nostras fieri fecimus patentes. Teste me ipso apud Westm' vj die Iulij anno regni nostri vicesimo [6 July 1396].

Deliberacio gaole domini regis castri Oxon' facta ibidem coram Iohanne Woderoue et Henrico Broun iusticiarijs domini regis ad gaolam illam deliberandam assignatis die Veneris proximo ante festum sancte Margarete virginis anno regni regis Ricardi secundi post conquestum Anglie vicesimo [14 July 1396].

63. *Marg:* Oxon' Willelmus Dobbe captus pro eo quod indictatus fuit coram Willelmo Wilicotes et socijs suis iusticiarijs domini regis ad pacem in comitatu predicto conseruandam assignatis de eo quod ipse die Martis in festo apostolorum Petri et Pauli anno regni domini regis nunc Anglie decimo nono incipiente in rectoriam de Hasele noctanter intrauit et ibidem quatuor boues Reymundi persone ecclesie de Hasele precij quatuor marcarum apud Hasele felonice furatus fuit et abduxit; quod quidem indictamentum prefati iusticiarij pacis iusticiarijs hic liberarunt venit coram iusticiarijs hic per vicecomitem ductus et allocutus qualiter se velit de felonia predicta acquietare dicit quod ipse in nullo est inde culpabilis et de hoc ponit se de bono (et malo)[i] super patriam. Ideo fiat inde iurata. Iuratores veniunt qui ad hoc electi triati et iurati dicunt super sacramentum suum quod predictus Willelmus Dobbe in nullo est culpabilis de felonia predicta nec ea occasione vnquam se retraxit. Ideo idem Willelmus eat inde quietus etc. *Marg:* Quietus

William Dobbe indicted before William Wilicotes and fellow justices of the peace for at night on 29 June 1395 entering the rectory at Haseley and feloniously stealing four oxen, price 4 marks, from Reymund the rector; pled not guilty, was tried, and acquitted.

64. *Marg:* Oxon' Thomas Lyngtolne capellanus et Willelmus Purye capti per suspectionem latrocinij secundum statutum Wynton' et nullum habetur de eis indictamentum et iusticiarij pacis de eis inquisiuerunt et nichil mali de eisdem Thoma et Willelmo inueniunt. Et super hoc proclamacio pro domino rege facta est quod si aliquis sit qui versus prefatos Thomam et Willelmum de aliquibus felonijs prosequi voluerit veniat et audietur et nullus venit etc. et testatum est hic in curia quod predicti Thomas et Willelmus sunt bone fame. Ideo ijdem Thomas et Willelmus deliberentur etc. *Marg:* deliberentur

Thomas Lyngtolne chaplain and William Purye taken on suspicion of larceny according to the statute of Winchester, having been found by the justices of the peace to be of good repute, to be released.

65. *Marg:* Oxon' Iohannes Turberuyle et Thomas Heppecok capti per suspectionem latrocinij secundum statutum Wynton' et nullum habetur de eis indictamentum et iusticiarij pacis de eis inquisiuerunt et nichil mali de eisdem Iohanne et Thoma inueniunt. Et super hoc proclamacio pro domino rege facta est quod si aliquis sit qui versus prefatos Iohannem et Thomam de aliquibus felonijs prosequi voluerit veniat et audietur et nullus venit etc. et testatum est hic in curia quod predicti Iohannes et Thomas sunt bone fame. Ideo ijdem Iohannes et Thomas deliberentur etc. *Marg:* deliberentur

John Turbervyle and Thomas Heppecok taken on suspicion of larceny according to the statute of Winchester, having been found by the justices of the peace to be of good repute, to be released.

Dominus rex mandauit dilectis et fidelibus suis Iohanni Hill' et Hugoni Huls litteras suas patentes in hec verba. Ricardus dei gratia rex Anglie et Francie et dominus Hibernie dilectis et fidelibus suis Iohanni Hill et Hugoni Huls salutem. Sciatis quod constituimus vos iusticiarios nostros ad gaolam nostram castri nostri Oxon' de prisonibus in ea existentibus deliberandam. Et ideo vobis mandamus quod ad certum diem quem ad hoc prouideritis conueniatis apud Oxon' ad gaolam illam deliberandam facturi inde quod ad iusticiam pertinet secundum legem et consuetudinem regni nostri Anglie saluis nobis amerciamentis et alijs ad nos inde spectantibus. Mandauimus enim vicecomiti nostro Oxon' quod ad certum diem quem ei scire facietis omnes prisones eiusdem gaole et eorum attachiamentos coram vobis ibidem venire faciat. In cuius rei testimonium has litteras nostras fieri fecimus patentes. Teste me ipso apud Westm' xxviij die Ianuarij anno regni nostro vicesimo [28 January 1397].

Deliberacio gaole domini regis castri Oxon' facta apud Oxon' coram Iohanne Hill' et Hugone Huls iusticiarijs domini regis ad gaolam illam deliberandam assignatis die Lune proximo ante festum sancti Petri in cathedra anno regni regis Ricardi secundi vicesimo [19 February 1397].

66. *Marg:* Oxon' Galfridus Langgeley captus pro eo quod indictatus fuit coram Willelmo Wilicotes et socijs suis iusticiarijs domini regis ad pacem in comitatu predicto conseruandam assignatis de eo quod ipse die Veneris proximo ante festum sancte Margarete virginis anno regni domini regis nunc Anglie decimo nono apud Bereford sancti Michelis vnum equm nigrum precij decem solidorum de Radulfo Neel felonice furatus fuit; quod quidem indictamentum prefati iusticiarij pacis iusticiarijs hic liberarunt venit coram iusticiarijs hic per vicecomitem ductus et allocutus qualiter se velit de felonia predicta acquietare dicit quod ipse in nullo est inde culpabilis et de hoc ponit se de bono et malo super patriam. Ideo fiat inde iurata. Iuratores veniunt qui ad hoc electi triati et iurati dicunt super sacramentum suum quod predictus Galfridus culpabilis est de felonia predicta. Catalla ipsius Galfridi decem solidi vnde Thomas Barentyn nuper vicecomes oneratur. Ideo idem Galfridus suspendatur etc. *Marg:* catalla (x. s.)[e] Suspendatur

Geoffrey Langgeley indicted before William Wilcotes and fellow justices of the peace for on 16 July 1395 having at Barford St Michael feloniously stolen a black horse, price 10s., from Ralph Neel; pled not guilty, was tried, convicted, and sentenced to be hanged; chattels, 10s., in charge to Thomas Barentyn former sheriff.

67. *Marg:* Oxon' Iohannes Cuele captus pro eo quod indictatus fuit coram Willelmo Wilcotes et socijs suis iusticiarijs domini regis ad pacem in comitatu predicto conseruandam assignatis de eo quod ipse die Lune proximo ante festum sancti Michelis archangeli anno regni domini regis nunc Anglie vicesimo apud Litulbaldyndon' quoddam iumentum precij quinque solidorum de quodam Roberto Bradele felonice cepit et abduxit; quod quidem indictamentum prefati iusticiarij pacis iusticiarijs hic liberarunt venit coram iusticiarijs hic per vicecomitem ductus et allocutus qualiter se velit de felonia predicta acquietare dicit quod ipse in nullo est inde culpabilis et de hoc ponit se de bono et malo super patriam. Ideo fiat inde iurata. Iuratores veniunt qui ad hoc electi triati et iurati dicunt super sacramentum suum quod predictus Iohannes in nullo est culpabilis de

felonia predicta nec ea occasione vnquam se retraxit. Ideo idem Iohannes eat inde quietus etc. *Marg:* Quietus

John Cuele indicted before William Wilcotes and fellow justices of the peace for at Little Baldon on 25 September 1396 feloniously taking a draught animal, price 5s., from Robert Bradele; pled not guilty, was tried, and acquitted.

68. *Marg:* Oxon' Thomas Clopton' et Petrus Carswell' capti per suspectionem latrocinij secundum statutum Wynton' et nullum habetur de eis indictamentum et iusticiarij pacis de eis inquisiuerunt et nichil mali de eisdem Thoma et Petro inueniunt. Et super hoc proclamacio pro domino rege facta est quod si aliquis sit qui versus prefatos Thomam et Petrum de aliquibus felonijs prosequi voluerit veniat et audietur et nullus venit etc. et testatum est hic in curia quod predicti Thomas et Petrus sunt bone fame. Ideo ijdem Thomas et Petrus deliberentur etc. *Marg:* deliberentur

Thomas Clopton and Peter Carswell taken on suspicion of larceny according to the statute of Winchester, having been found by the justices of the peace to be of good repute, to be released.

69. *Marg:* Oxon' Willelmus Pury captus per suspectionem latrocinij secundum statutum Wynton' et nullum habetur de eo indictamentum et iusticiarij pacis de eo inquisiuerunt et nichil mali de eodem Willelmo inueniunt. Et super hoc proclamacio pro domino rege facta est quod si aliquis sit qui versus prefatum Willelmum de aliquibus felonijs prosequi voluerit veniat et audietur et nullus venit etc. et testatum est hic in curia quod predictus Willelmus est bone fame. Ideo idem Willelmus deliberatur etc. *Marg:* deliberatur

William Pury taken on suspicion of lareny according to the statute of Winchester, having been found by the justices of the peace to be of good repute, was released.

70. *Marg:* Oxon' Willelmus Colbury captus per suspectionem latrocinij secundum statutum Wynton' et nullum habetur de eo indictamentum et iusticiarij pacis de eo inquisiuerunt et nichil mali de eodem Willelmo inueniunt. Et super hoc proclamacio pro domino rege facta est quod si aliquis sit qui versus prefatum Willelmum de aliquibus felonijs prosequi voluerit veniat et audietur et nullus venit etc. et testatum est hic in curia quod predictus Willelmus est bone fame. Ideo idem Willelmus deliberetur etc. *Marg:* deliberetur

William Colbury taken on suspicion of lareny according to the statute of Winchester, having been found by the justices of the peace to be of good repute, was released.

[*m. 14d.*]
71. Iohannes Tannere de Morton' captus per suspectionem latrocinij secundum statutum Wynton' et nullum habetur de eo indictamentum et iusticiarij pacis de eo inquisiuerunt et nichil mali de eodem Iohanne inueniunt. Et super hoc proclamacio pro domino rege facta est quod si aliquis sit qui versus prefatum Iohannem de aliquibus felonijs prosequi voluerit veniat et audietur et nullus venit etc. et testatum est hic in curia quod predictus Iohannes est bone fame. Ideo idem Iohannes deliberetur etc. *Marg:* deliberatur

John Tannere of Moreton taken on suspicion of larceny according to the statute of Winchester, having been found by the justices of the peace to be of good repute, to be released.

[*m. 15*]
Deliberacio gaole domini regis castri Oxon' facta ibidem coram Iohanne Hulle et socijs suis iusticiarijs domini regis ad pacem in comitatu predicto conseruandem assignatis die Veneris in crastino sancti Valentini anno regni regis Ricardi secundi post conquestum Anglie vicesimo primo [15 February 1398].

72. *Marg:* Oxon' Alicia Bodyn vxor Iohannis Bodyn de Magna Tywe capta pro eo quod indictata fuit coram Willelmo Wilicotes et socijs suis iusticiarijs domini regis ad pacem in comitatu predicto conseruandam assignatis de eo quod ipsa simul cum Thoma Ridere die Dominica proximo ante festum natiuitatis sancti Iohannis baptiste anno regni domini regis nunc Anglie decimo nono apud Magnam Tywe Iohannem Bodyn maritum suum felonice interfecit; venit coram iusticiarijs hic per vicecomitem ad barram ducta et allocuta qualiter se velit de felonia predicta acquietare dicit quod ipsa in nullo est inde culpabilis et de hoc ponit se de bono et malo super patriam. Ideo fiat inde iurata. Iuratores veniunt qui ad hoc electi triati et iurati dicunt super sacramentum suum quod predicta Alicia culpabilis est de felonia predicta. Catalla ipsius Alicie nulla. Ideo eadem Alicia ardeatur etc. *Marg:* catalla nulla Ardeatur

Alice Bodyn wife of John Bodyn of Great Tew indicted before William Wilicotes and fellow justices of the peace for with Thomas Ridere at Great Tew on 18 June 1396 feloniously killing her husband John Bodyn; pled not guilty, was tried, convicted, and sentenced to be burned; no chattels.

[*For the indictment of Thomas Ridere see above Roll B, no. 3*].

73. *Marg:* Oxon' Iohannes Adam captus pro eo quod indictatus fuit coram Willelmo Wilicotes et socijs suis iusticiarijs domini regis ad pacem in comitatu predicto conseruandam assignatis de eo quod ipse die Martis

proximo ante festum decollacionis sancti Iohannis baptiste anno regni domini regis nunc Anglie vicesimo primo apud Richelfeld' Pippard' Iohannem Bokynden' de Chalgraue felonice interfecit et murdrauit; venit coram iusticiarijs hic per vicecomitem ad barram ductus et allocutus qualiter se velit de felonia et murdro predictis acquietare dicit quod ipse in nullo est inde culpabilis et de hoc ponit se de bono et malo super patriam. Ideo fiat inde iurata. Iuratores veniunt qui ad hoc electi triati et iurati dicunt super sacramentum suum quod predictus Iohannes Adam culpabilis est de felonia et murdro predictis. Catalla ipsius Iohannis nulla. Ideo idem Iohannes suspendeatur etc. *Marg:* catalla nulla Suspendeatur

John Adam indicted before William Wilicotes and fellow justices of the peace for at Rotherfield Peppard on 28 August 1397 feloniously killing and murdering John Bokynden of Chalgrove; pled not guilty, was tried, convicted, and sentenced to be hanged; no chattels.

[*For indictment see above Roll B, no. 1*].

74. *Marg:* Oxon' Willelmus Heryng' captus pro eo quod indictatus fuit coram prefatis iusticiarijs ad pacem de eo quod ipse die Veneris proximo post festum natiuitatis beate Marie anno regni domini regis nunc Anglie vicesimo primo duos porcos precij duorum solidorum et sex denariorum de bonis et catallis Ricardi Tywe magistri hospitalis extra portam orientalem Oxon' et Iohannis Hay apud Hedyngton' hironus felonice furatus fuit; et quod est communis latro; venit coram iusticiarijs hic per vicecomitem ductus et allocutus qualiter se velit de felonia predicta acquietare dicit quod ipse in nullo est inde culpabilis et de hoc ponit se de bono et malo super patriam. Ideo fiat inde iurata. Iuratores veniunt qui ad hoc electi triati et iurati dicunt super sacramentum suum quod predictus Willelmus in nullo est culpabilis de felonia predicta nec ea occasione vnquam se retraxit. Ideo idem Willelmus eat inde quietus etc. *Marg:* Quietus

William Heryng indicted before the aforesaid justices of the peace for on 14 September 1397 feloniously stealing two pigs, price 2s. 6d., from Richard Tywe master of [*St John's*] *hospital outside the East Gate of Oxford and John Hay at Headington 'hirn' [i.e. bend or corner], being a common thief; pled not guilty, was tried, and acquitted.*

75. *Marg:* Oxon' Iohannes Carlet captus pro eo quod indictatus fuit coram Willelmo Wilicotes et socijs suis iusticiarijs domini regis ad pacem in comitatu predicto conseruandam assignatis de eo quod ipse die Martis proximo ante festum natiuitatis beate Marie anno regni domini regis nunc Anglie vicesimo primo apud Filkynge quendam bouem precij decem solidorum de bonis et catallis Willelmi Taillour felonice furatus fuit; venit

coram iusticiarijs hic per vicecomitem ductus et allocutus qualiter se velit de felonia predicta acquietare dicit quod ipse in nullo est inde culpabilis et de hoc ponit se de bono et malo super patriam. Ideo fiat inde iurata. Iuratores veniunt qui ad hoc electi triati et iurati dicunt super sacramentum suum quod predictus Iohannes in nullo est culpabilis de felonia predicta nec ea occasione vnquam se retraxit. Ideo idem Iohannes eat inde quietus etc. *Marg:* Quietus

John Carlet indicted before William Wilicotes and fellow justices of the peace for at Filkins on 4 September 1397 feloniously stealing an ox, price 10s., from William Taillour; pled not guilty, was tried, and acquitted. [*For indictment see above, Roll B, no. 20*].

75. *Marg:* Oxon' Iohannes Fletcher captus pro eo quod indictatus fuit coram prefatis iusticiarijs domini regis ad pacem etc. de eo quod ipse die Dominica proximo post festum sancte Marie Magdalene anno regni domini regis nunc Anglie decimo nono apud Wodestoke Thomam Burgeys de Wodestoke felonice interfecit; venit coram iusticiarijs hic per vicecomitem ad barram ductus et allocutus qualiter se velit de felonia predicta acquietare dicit quod ipse in nullo est inde culpabilis et de hoc ponit se de bono et malo super patriam. Ideo fiat inde iurata. Iuratores veniunt qui ad hoc electi triati et iurati dicunt super sacramentum suum quod predictus Iohannes in nullo est culpabilis de felonia predicta nec ea occasione vnquam se retraxit. Ideo idem Iohannes eat inde quietus etc. *Marg:* Quietus

John Fletcher indicted before the aforesaid justices of the peace for on 25 July 1395 at Woodstock feloniously killing Thomas Burgeys of Woodstock; pled not guilty, was tried, and acquitted.

APPENDIX TO ROLL C

COMMISSIONS AND SESSIONS, DELIVERY OF OXFORD CASTLE GAOL, 1389-1398

These lists are compiled from commissions and sessions recorded on JUST. 3/180 and printed above, supplemented by information in Public Record Office, Calendar of the General and Special Assize and General Gaol Delivery Commissions on the dorse of the Patent Rolls, Richard II (1377-1399), 1966, kindly shown me by Mr. C. A. F. Meekings who prepared the list. All sessions were held in Oxford.

	Commissions		Sessions	
	Date	*Justices*	*Date*	*Justices*
1389	24 April[1]	Robert Cherlton John Hill	30 April	Robert Cherlton John Hill
1390			18 February[2]	John Hill and associate justices of the peace
	12 February[3]	Robert Cherlton John Hill Henry Brown	15 July	Robert Cherlton John Hill
1391			20 February	Robert Cherlton John Hill
			17 July	Robert Cherlton John Hill
1392	26 January[4]	Robert Cherlton John Hill Henry Brown	19 February	Robert Cherlton John Hill
	16 July[5]	Robert Cherlton John Hill Lawrence Dru John Rede Richard Overton		
1393			14 April[6]	Robert Cherlton and associate justices of the peace

[1] See also P.R.O. Calendar, p. 32, no. 416.

[2] Presumably held under the peace commission of 10 November 1389.

[3] P.R.O. Calendar, p. 35, no. 455.

[4] *Ibid.*, p. 40, no. 512.

[5] *Ibid.*, p. 41, no. 530.

[6] Held under the peace commission of 24 December 1390.

	Commissions		Sessions	
	Date	*Justices*	*Date*	*Justices*
	26 June[7]	Robert Cherlton John Hill Henry Brown	15 July	Robert Cherlton John Hill Henry Brown
1394	8 January[8]	Robert Cherlton John Hill Henry Brown		
	20 February[9]	Robert Cherlton Lawrence Dru John Rede	1 May	Robert Cherlton John Rede
	30 June[10]	Robert Cherlton John Hill John Rede		
	10 July[11]	Robert Cherlton John Hill Henry Brown	17 July	John Hill John Rede
1395			19 July	Robert Cherlton John Hill
1396	6 July[12]	John Hill John Woderove Henry Brown	14 July	John Woderove Henry Brown
1397	28 January[13]	John Hill Hugh Huls	19 February	John Hill Hugh Huls
1398	28 January[14]	John Hill Hugh Huls	15 February[15]	John Hill and associate justices of the peace

The special commission of 5 February 1395, issued to Robert Cherlton, John Cassy, John Hill, William Wilicotes, John Rede, held a session on 19 February 1395, Cassy and Rede sitting.[16]

[7] See also P.R.O. Calendar, p. 44, no. 561.

[8] *Ibid.*, p. 45, no. 574.

[9] See also *ibid.*, p. 45, no. 576.

[10] See also *ibid.*, p. 46, no. 584.

[11] *Ibid.*, p. 46, no. 587.

[12] In *ibid.*, p. 53, no. 657 the year is given as 1397. For 1396 see Patent Roll 346, m. 21d. and above p. 148.

[13] See also P.R.O. Calendar, p. 52, no. 648.

[14] *Ibid.*, p. 56, no. 690.

[15] Held under the peace commission of 12 November 1397.

[16] See also *C.P.R.* 1391-1396, p. 588.

INDEX OF PERSONS AND PLACES

The numbers in brackets following the page numbers refer to cases. Place-names have been indexed under their modern form with a cross-reference from the form found in the text. The names of hundreds have been added to place-names in Oxfordshire, and the names of counties, both before and after 1974, to others. Unidentified place-names are italicised. Justice of the peace is represented by J.P., son by s., wife by w., and daughter by d.; bishop by bp., and clerk (in Orders) by cl.

INDEX OF SUBJECTS